Cooperation, Technology, and Japanese Development

Cooperation, Technology, and Japanese Development

Indigenous Knowledge, the Power of Networks, and the State

Donna L. Doane

Routledge
Taylor & Francis Group
New York London

Transitions: Asia and Asian America

First published 1999 by Westview Press

Published 2019 by Routledge
52 Vanderbilt Avenue, New York, NY 10017
2 Park Square, Milton Park, Abingdon, Oxon OX14 4RN

First issued in hardback 2019

Routledge is an imprint of the Taylor & Francis Group, an informa business

Copyright © 1998 Taylor & Francis

A CIP catalog record for this book is available from the Library of Congress

ISBN 13: 978-0-367-31521-4 (hbk)
ISBN 13: 978-0-8133-3737-1 (pbk)

Contents

Preface

In developing countries as well as advanced industrial countries, the issue of cooperative technological ties has been recognized in recent years as an important means to broaden the technological capabilities of enterprises and counter the limitations of atomistic and individualistic organizations. Cooperative technological ties can be encouraged on a number of different levels: e.g., ties can be fostered among micro-enterprises, NGOs, and other organizations in contexts that are very far from the "technological frontier," or they can be used by private and public enterprises that are close to or at the frontier. The goal in either case is to move beyond the limitations of the existing knowledge and experiences embodied in individual, relatively isolated organizations.

This study is an outgrowth of an inquiry into questions of technological advance that first began in the late 1970s and early 1980s in the form of empirical dissertation research. At that time Japan was beginning to be recognized as a world class producer of altogether new and original— i.e., frontier—technologies. It was a time when many were still debating whether Japanese researchers and technicians were "capable" of carrying out original and creative technological innovations, as opposed to simply being "good at the application of others' ideas."

At that time, the VLSI project and its breakthroughs began to dramatically alter perceptions of Japan's technological strengths. In this context, I decided to examine the ways in which firms in Japan were able to pool their knowledge and resources to first "catch up" technologically, and then undertake frontier forms of innovation: this case study material is presented throughout the present study, but particularly in the middle chapters (Chapters 3-5).

Unfortunately but predictably, after the VLSI and other technological breakthroughs in Japan, the siren was sounded that other advanced industrial countries were likely to lose the technology "wars" in industry after industry to "the Japanese." Many of the ensuing discussions and debates about industrial and technology policies, and many of the political commentaries about the "Japanese System"—particularly as reflected in media pronouncements during trade negotiations—were exaggerated and inflammatory, and incited bitter feelings on both sides of the Pacific.

Put off by this climate, I did not want to participate in these debates, and turned to other concerns. Over time, however, I began to examine both more historical and comparative aspects of these issues, and decided to place the case studies in a broader comparative framework. My work in India and Thailand also underscored for me the importance of the promotion of cooperative technological ties *across the economy*, both to help develop and integrate the local ("indigenous") knowledge and technology base (including, in some cases, "technology blending"), and to support a wide spectrum of local organizations and enterprises (both the "less" and the "more" technologically advanced of these). The need for local solutions to deal with local problems—i.e., in a way that is in tune with the specific conditions of the local social, economic and ecological setting—has become particularly acute in recent years.

In addition, the vulnerability and boom/bust patterns associated with countries that have not emphasized the development and integration of the *local* technology and knowledge base, and instead have had to rely excessively on imported capital and technologies, have for me reinforced the need for a relatively stable, egalitarian, and well-integrated economic and technological environment that serves local needs more effectively. Cooperative ties that create technological "networks" across the economy can be promoted equally within "market socialist," "cooperative capitalist," and other forms of late developing economies, as will be illustrated through examples cited in Chapter 6 below.

We will begin this discussion with a detailed study of the evolution and recent forms of cooperative technological ties in Japan. This work will on one level complement other studies that have been made of industrial policy, the government-industry relationship, and enterprise behavior in Japan. Studies to date dealing with cooperative R&D in Japan have tended to focus primarily on *government-sponsored large-scale projects involving cooperation between competitors* (i.e., one specific type of intra-industry cooperation), as these have been the projects of particular interest to the advanced industrial countries (no doubt this interest was fueled—in the U.S. at least—by the fact that many private enterprises as well as policy makers have been interested in a loosening of antitrust laws and increased government financial support). I have included references to these studies, particularly in the discussion sections of Chapters 3 and 4 below—i.e., the chapters presenting case studies that illustrate *intra-industry* cooperative ties.

One set of issues that has been of particular interest to advanced industrial countries in recent years is tied to debates concerning the structure and behavior of Japanese business and industrial groups ("keiretsu" has become a familiar term through these debates). The case study chapter dealing with *inter-industry* cooperative technological ties during the period in question (Chapter 5) is particularly relevant to these issues, and may be of interest to those concerned with the "keiretsu" debates.

It is important to keep in mind that the primary focus of the present study is the *range* and *evolution* of cooperative technological ties in Japan up through the early 1980s, and particularly during the postwar catch up and early frontier periods of technological advance (roughly, the 1960s through the early 1980s). Thus, it provides a discussion of the historical context, along with empirical research that may help illuminate both the keiretsu (group) and government-industry sets of issues that have been of particular concern to the advanced industrial countries.

My main concern, however, has been to explore the use of cooperative ties for technological advance during the period of technological catch up, specifically within a *late development context*. These issues have direct relevance to the aspirations of many developing countries, whether "socialist," "capitalist," or somewhere in between. For better and for worse, technological advance, the development of indigenous technological strengths, and relative technological self-reliance (i.e., learning from, but not being continually dependent on imported ideas and technologies) are goals of a large number of developing countries today. Many in these countries are, in fact, trying to learn from the development experiences of Japan and the East Asian NICs as an alternative to the early industrializing examples, without necessarily trying to head in the same direction. Many of the late developers have institutional characteristics that are similar to those present in Japan during the earlier stages of its industrial development, such as "dualistic" (or "multistructured") industrial structures, enterprise groupings, and certain aspects of the government-industry relationship that have interesting parallels to conditions in prewar and early postwar Japan. Thus, Japan's experience—illustrating both the possibilities for and potential problems associated with different forms of cooperative technological ties—is particularly relevant to the development experiences of many of these countries. It is argued that cooperative technological ties in this context can be used, under the right circumstances, for socially beneficial purposes with widespread applications, and not simply to give individual enterprises a "competitive edge," even though they certainly can do this as well.

This study is organized in the following way. Chapter 1 is concerned primarily with an examination of the historical background of technological cooperation in Japan. It examines in particular Japan's position as an "early" late developer—i.e., a country attempting to catch up to the international technological standard later than the early developers, but before current-day developing countries (including, for our purposes, the "NICs," "next NICs," and "least industrialized countries"). It discusses the rise of inter-enterprise forms of cooperation for purposes of adopting and transforming imported technologies as part of the firms' attempts to advance technologically. These include ties between modern sector firms (e.g., zaibatsu and their affiliates); ties between relatively large modern firms and small semi-traditional firms (whether independents, subcontractors, or other types of affiliates); and ties involving both public and private sector organizations (including public enterprises, government agencies, public research institutions, and private enterprises, in various combinations). It also discusses government policies and other influences that have affected the emergence and transformation of these inter-enterprise ties.

These ties are seen as aiding in the diffusion and adaptation of imported technologies, as well as in the more ambitious attempts in recent decades to transform the new technologies in altogether original ways. It is argued that networks of firms and other organizations, working together in different capacities across the economy, aided in the accumulation of small innovations that helped establish over time a flexible, responsive and well-integrated technological base and allowed the "breakthrough" projects of recent years. Thus, in this chapter we lay out the origins and variety of cooperative technological ties found in prewar and early postwar Japan, and lay the basis for possible comparisons with technological efforts in other late developing countries that aspire to meet their own needs, and ultimately become more technologically self-reliant.

Chapter 2 provides more detail regarding the background of innovation in the early postwar period in Japan, dividing it into the "catch up" phase and then the "frontier" phase that required new, highly original forms of innovation. It also discusses general changes in firm structure and behavior that were undertaken in Japanese firms as they attempted to do increasingly original forms of innovation. This chapter thus begins to illustrate how cooperative ties can increase dramatically the organizational and technological flexibility of individual organizations and enterprises.

The chapter then focuses specifically on the rise of the computer and telecommunications industry in postwar Japan, and on the "Big Six" manufacturing firms in the industry. This is a combined industry, involving a number of quite distinct fields of knowledge that can be pooled to generate a wide range of new products and technologies, and thus is amenable to cooperative technological ties. (The same would be true for any complex industry—e.g., autos, aircraft—or for any innovative process that requires or can benefit from the combining of many different types of skills and knowledge.)

In Chapters 3-5 case studies based on my earlier dissertation research are presented as a means to explore the *range* and *dynamics* of cooperative relationships for technological innovation during the late catch up/early frontier stage of innovation in this industry in Japan—again, roughly the 1960s through the 1980s. We begin with a discussion of *intra-industry applied* research projects in Chapter 3, move on to *intra-industry* cooperative projects of a relatively *basic* nature in Chapter 4, and then focus on *inter-industry* cooperative projects in Chapter 5.

It is important to keep in mind that the main focus of these chapters is *not* the frontier projects of the 1980s and 1990s, but rather the longer period of technological catch up, and in particular the later catch up phase through the transition to frontier innovation. The main purpose of these middle chapters is to illustrate some of the *many* types of cooperative technological ties that have developed over time in Japan to facilitate technological advance. (In fact, those already familiar with some of the intra-industry cases discussed in Chapters 3 and/or 4 may want to skip directly to the discussion in Chapters 5 and 6.)

It should be kept firmly in mind throughout that although the large-scale intra-industry frontier projects have attracted the most international attention, it is the smaller-scale and inter-industry cooperative technological efforts (examples of which are given in Chapter 5) that have been far more frequent and widespread in Japan. Moreover, as noted above, from the point of view of technological advance in a latecomer context, the accumulation of small innovations can be judged to be equally or even more important than the singular, although more dramatic, projects (the small and large projects are complementary, but the large may not even be possible without the small). On a related but distinct note, it is also argued here that in the Japanese case, cooperative ties of many different types throughout the economy and across many different types of enterprises and organizations—public and private—have helped overcome the marked technological and industrial dualisms that tend to be characteristic of a late development context.

For these reasons, we emphasize the range and dynamics of cooperative technological ties of *all* types that have been used in Japan, rather than focus exclusively on the very narrow range of intra-industry projects that have been of interest to advanced industrial countries in recent years. We will find that the vast majority of cooperative projects have involved individual firms and one or more firms or organizations with which they have a formal or informal, but ongoing, relationship (as affiliates, subcontractors, or independents), with no direct government assistance in this (although certainly, government policies encouraging or allowing inter-enterprise cooperation did assist indirectly in the formation of cooperative technological ties, and are becoming increasingly important, particularly with respect to "social infrastructural" as well as other projects). Again, both the larger, more ambitious projects and the far more numerous and diverse small-scale projects together constitute the totality of cooperative research efforts in Japan, and it is this *totality*— rather than one segment alone—that is seen as contributing to the technological dynamism of private and public enterprises during these years.

In Chapter 6 we turn to an explicit consideration of the possible implications of this study for late developing economies. Additional examples of cooperative technological ties and attempts at encouraging such ties are drawn from both "NICs" (e.g., the Republic of Korea and Taiwan) and "next NICs" (e.g., the People's Republic of China and India), and current debates, possibilities, and potential problems associated with cooperative ventures are discussed.

In this chapter we focus once again on the issues of industrial dualism, the existence of family-based inter-enterprise groupings, and the role of public sector institutions in terms of how they affect the possibilities for the emergence of cooperative technological ties in different parts of the developing world today. This study helps to illustrate the limitations to purely laissez-faire policies and individualistic or atomistic behavior in the process of technological change in a late development context.

Moreover, with respect to developing countries in particular, we find that cooperative ties can be extended not only to public and private enterprises and organizations, but also increasingly to "third sector" organizations (NGOs and other non-profit sector institutions) and the small-scale "peoples' sector." The small-scale and microenterprises are critically important in a large part of the developing world, and as the examples below illustrate, cooperative technological ties may be a very important element in their viability. A much more careful analysis of cooperation involving micro- and small-scale organizations and enterprises is critical, particularly since the tendency at the present time is to assume that technologically advancing enterprises and organizations in the "leading" segments of the economy will automatically help pull up all other segments in due course of time. In fact, if small-scale organizations rather than large are given public support and are encouraged to use cooperative ties to extend their access to knowledge, experience, and other resources, a far more balanced industrial structure may be possible, without the technologically "backward" organizations necessarily being marginalized or eliminated in the changing economy.

There are certainly significant hurdles to be overcome in order to establish either cooperative ties among "modern" sector firms or across very different segments of a developing economy. However, serious efforts to establish these types of technological ties are likely to be rewarded, as will be discussed and illustrated below, and particularly in the last chapter of this book.

Donna L. Doane

Acknowledgments

This study has been made possible through the efforts of a large number of individuals who contributed their time, knowledge, friendship, and guidance. I would like to express my thanks to the following individuals and research institutions:

For guidance and help during and after my years as a graduate student at Yale University, I am particularly grateful to Professors David P. Levine, Hugh Patrick, Merton J. Peck, Richard R. Nelson, and William N. Parker. This study has roamed very far from my original concerns, but it is beginning to point back toward the earlier questions. This has made me aware once again of how important their guidance has been, and continues to be, on a personal as well as an intellectual level.

Regarding the initial research phase of this study in Tokyo, I most gratefully acknowledge the assistance of a large number of very helpful and talented staff members associated with many of the public and private enterprises mentioned in this study, as well as MITI officials, research institute staff members, and others who volunteered their time and effort in a way that made this study possible. At the time of these interviews, many chose to act as representatives of their organizations rather than be acknowledged individually; however, with their permission, I hope to acknowledge their individual contributions in the future. During my stay at Hitotsubashi University, which was made possible by a JUSEC Fulbright Doctoral Dissertation Fellowship, I benefited greatly from the help of Professors Ken-ichi Imai, Juro Teranishi, Noriyuki Hirai, and Yoshihiro Takasuga. In addition, I am very grateful to the library staff at Hitotsubashi's Keizai Kenkyujo, the Hitotsubashi Aikido Club, and the Hirai, Higashi, Yanagihara and Tagawa families; their help and generosity in so many different dimensions transcended the boundaries of this research. Finally, I would like to thank Akira Goto and Sachiko Higashi, without whose friendship and assistance (with interviews, questionnaires, and endless other areas of concern) this study would not have been possible. If there is any merit to this study, it is their input that made it so.

At UC Berkeley I was helped by Professors Irv Scheiner, Thomas C. Smith, and Albert Fishlow, as well as Eugenie Bruck. This was a hectic, but very useful period, and I am very grateful to each of them for their guidance. I am also grateful to the Center for Japanese Studies at UC Berkeley for the postdoctoral fellowship that made this period of rethinking possible.

In India, I benefited greatly from the help of Professors P.N. Dhar, N.S. Siddharthan, S.N. Mishra, and later Bishwanath Goldar and others at the Institute of Economic Growth; Krishna Bharadwaj for talks during that last period at JNU; and Poochi Dhar, Malika Jalan, and Renana Jhabvala, for their insights and inspiration. In addition, Professor S.K. Goyal and the staff at the Institute for Studies in Industrial Development (as well as the library staff at the IIPA and especially the IIC) were very helpful to me in the second phase of this study, and I gratefully acknowledge their input and assistance.

In the final phase of this study, Mark Selden and Carol Jones gave very useful suggestions as the chapters fell into place, and Henning Pape-Santos' extensive help (even up to the last minute) made the final version possible. The comments of the *Social Concept* summer conference participants were very helpful for one part of the project, as were the suggestions and assistance of several other colleagues.

I would also like to thank Ibipo Johnston-Anumonwo, the Seely-Humphries family, the Syeds, and the Doanes for their ongoing support on so many fronts. Above all, I would like to express my deepest gratitude to, and moreover, dedicate this book to my parents. They saw it through and gave their unceasing support, even when it was not clear to them what all the commotion was about. In this way, they made the greatest contribution of all. (And they are not responsible for any of the mistakes!)

Finally, I would like to thank Professors Eleanor Hadley and F.M. Scherer. They, and several of the other individuals noted above (including those mentioned first), offered help and suggestions selflessly and freely. I learned both from their knowledge and their humanity. To all of them, my deepest thanks.

D. L. D.

1

The Background of Inter-Enterprise Cooperative Ties in Japan

Introduction: Late Development and Cooperative Ties in Japan

In this study it will be argued that the wide range of cooperative ventures, as well as in-house activities, that began in the prewar and wartime eras and developed further in the postwar period contributed to a rapid learning process and helped enterprises in Japan advance technologically in a surprisingly effective way. It will also be argued that both ties between private firms, and the ties between firms and public sector organizations (public enterprises, government agencies, research institutions, and others) that have been important for purposes of technological catch up and frontier innovation, have tended in Japan to be based on relatively long-term commitments and, in an important sense, on the extension of ties of mutual trust and support to affiliated enterprises and organizations in both the public and private sectors. This study will focus on how these ties have emerged, how they have been transformed under changing economic conditions, and how we might begin to explain these and other important related economic features that appear to be so different in nature from their counterparts in other advanced industrial countries. This study therefore provides some of the background to recent proposals and debates in advanced industrial countries regarding the establishment of Japanese-style keiretsu, "R&D consortia" (of both a national and, increasingly, international nature), MITI-like organizations, and other cooperative institutions. Even more so, it directly addresses the current debates in many developing countries regarding industrial and technology policies and the promotion of institutions and practices similar to those found in Japan and in some of the Asian newly industrialized countries that are seen as contributing to a broadening of the local knowledge and technology base.

This study will consider a set of factors that appear to help explain the development of cooperative institutions in Japan. Rather than regard the development of particular types of institutions and practices as being purely culturally or functionally based, this study will attempt to examine certain aspects of the historical conditions that favored the development of cooperative ties such as those found in the Japanese case of technological advance.

We will focus in particular on three elements that appear to have aided in the development of cooperative technological ties in Japan. The first is the *relatively mild form of industrial dualism and a surmountable technology gap* that allowed the development of informal but ongoing ties between relatively large-scale "modern" firms and relatively small-scale "semi-traditional" units or enterprises in Japan. These ties initially took a very hierarchical and exploitative form, but as the semi-traditional enterprises advanced technologically and in other ways, the relationship became more egalitarian over time and set the basis for a wide range of cooperative technological ties among firms across the economy.[1]

The second element explored below involves the *industrial houses and other group formations* in prewar and postwar Japan. It will be argued that these institutional structures fostered cooperative technological ties among modern sector firms (of various sizes) that even more explicitly allowed firms to learn to cooperate with one another in ongoing, long-term technological relationships. These more formal ties within the modern sector were also often hierarchical, but they were somewhat less exploitative than the relationship between the modern large and small semi-traditional enterprises of the prewar period. These group ties also became somewhat looser, more fluid and egalitarian over time, particularly in recent decades. Zaibatsu and, later, keiretsu group ties in particular have been recognized as setting important precedents for the recent cooperative research projects near and then at the technological frontier.

The third element to be examined is the *role of the public sector*: specifically, the ways in which government initiatives and institutions (including public enterprises and government agencies) have helped promote a wide range of inter-enterprise cooperative technological ties in Japan. In this chapter we will note the extent to which government policies contributed to both the formation of cooperative ties among the modern and semi-traditional firms as well as among the more formally tied "group"-based enterprises in the modern sector. In the following chapters we will examine in more detail the ways in which specific public enterprises and government agencies have helped foster and influence the evolution of cooperative technological ties over time, and in recent years have acted as "central coordinators" for the larger cooperative projects that first approached and then began to move beyond the technological frontiers.

All three elements are associated with late development. In fact, the presence within contemporary developing countries of (1) a "dualistic" (or "multistructured," as will be discussed below) industrial structure; (2) various forms of cooperative ties among industrial house members, among enterprises in wider kinship-based networks, and across private and public enterprises and organizations; and (3) a relatively important public sector and close government-industry relationship, make comparisons between Japan's institutional evolution and that of the more industrially advanced developing countries particularly interesting.

In the discussion that follows, we will argue that all three of these elements helped foster a wide range of cooperative technological ties over time in Japan. Specifically, we find that cooperative ties developed in the prewar years, and were further extended and developed in the postwar years, not only among enterprises in the well-defined group formations, but often across firms that had no such formal ties. In this way, *both* the "group" type of cooperative technological ties among modern sector firms and the "modern–semi-traditional" type of tie-ups (as well as other types of cooperative ties) can be seen as contributing to the development of a strong and well-integrated technological base over time, as a wide variety of enterprises were linked technologically in a way that helped to diffuse, transform, and ultimately substantially upgrade imported technologies, paving the way toward frontier innovation. All of these cooperative ties—fostered through both private and public sector initiatives generated in a late development context—can be seen as contributing significantly to the dynamism and technological strength of Japanese firms *across the economy*, both in the prewar and particularly in the postwar period, and as contributing to the development of a flexible and responsive technological base that preserved indigenous adaptations and innovations while incorporating international knowledge and expertise into that base ("technology blending" within an initially dualistic, and later an advanced industrial context).

Cooperative Technological Ties Involving Large "Modern" and Small "Semi-Traditional" Enterprises: Industrial Dualism and Late Development

It may be helpful in this context to examine briefly the form that industrial dualism took in the Japanese case earlier in the century. As will be discussed in Chapter 6, in contrast with the *least* industrialized countries of the contemporary world—in which ties between the relatively large-scale modern sector and the small-scale semi-traditional industrial sector are practically non-existent—in Japan there were strong ties between the two sectors from early on. These ties were certainly exploitative, sometimes extremely so, but at the same time, cooperative technological ties gradually developed in a way that (1) helped pull up the technological abilities of the small-scale sector, and (2) contributed to the transformation of ties between large firms and smaller affiliates away from relatively hierarchical, short-term relationships toward relatively *egalitarian, long-term ties,* particularly in the postwar period.

As a result of these developments, by the late catch up and early frontier period (roughly, from the 1960s through the early 1980s in Japan) true joint research became possible involving both large and small technologically progressive enterprises, with different knowledge and skills provided by each and with ideas and technological solutions flowing in both directions. This appears to be important for the development of a flexible and responsive local knowledge base. Moreover, in Japan's case as a result of these developments, it was not simply that the semi-traditional occupations and small-scale enterprises or units died out and an entirely separate modern small-scale sector emerged as an offshoot of the large; rather, in Japan's case, *the semi-traditional production units were also to a large extent able to transform themselves and modernize in association with the modern sector.* Cooperative technological ties appear to have played an important role in this process.

The Hungarian economist Eva Ehrlich has explored the historical relationship between the two sectors in her study entitled *Japan: A Case of Catching Up.* She sees economic and, more specifically, industrial dualism (as opposed to the Lewis type of pre-capitalist agricultural/capitalist industrial concept of dualism) as being common to all late developers. This is due to the fact that the latecomers' attempts to pursue economic growth and transformation are defined in large part by a context created by the early industrializers, which profoundly influences latecomers' attempts at technological advance. Specifically, Ehrlich is concerned with the effects of latecomers' attempts to overcome the technology gap, which leads her to focus on dualism (again, economic, and then more specifically, industrial dualism) in late developing economies:

> The introduction of these up-to-date techniques (technology) into a backward social and economic environment will necessarily result in a kind of duality: advanced techniques with corresponding institutional and organizational frameworks and a better trained labour force on the one hand, and traditional techniques on the other. Therefore, the transplant of techniques and technology from outside dissolves the uniformity rooted in the underdevelopment (backwardness) of the economy and brings about differences and inequalities. This is economic dualism.[2]

Ehrlich's main question, then, has to do with the dualism that she sees as necessarily accompanying attempts at development, in a world economy already populated by firms with advanced techniques and their own supportive institutional environment. Specifically, Ehrlich asks: will this dualism act to aid or hold back economic growth and transformation in late developers?

Ehrlich ultimately concludes that in Japan's case the dualism created in the economy appears to have aided its growth and transformation, but that this need not be the case in all country contexts. She notes, as have many others, the considerable development and transformation that had already taken place in Japan by the eve of attempts at catching up through the importation of foreign technologies and institutions (economic, educational, political and other). Therefore, she notes that although economic dualism in her sense can be seen in Japan throughout the last century in "almost every 'partial element' (labour, capital, production organization, etc.)," the dualism found in that country has been by no means of the extreme nature found in regions that had not had that prior degree of transformation. This allowed, in Ehrlich's view, the emergence of not only the coexistence, but also a "symbiosis" between the modern large-scale sector and the "traditional" sector (or "semi-traditional" as used in the present study), the latter of which included "not only agriculture, but also the cottage industries found so often in Japan within the agricultural framework, the urban handicraft industry, and finally, the mass small-scale mini-plants often arising within the family and developing from it."[3]

Ehrlich contrasts the Japanese case with the well-known model of LDC development that starts with a country's heavy emphasis on participation in world trade "relying on its already developed natural endowments and traditional products and requiring usually only a low level of production culture," and then later incorporates a strategy of import substitution industrialization that makes it even more dependent on the economy of developed countries, with the result that "the process of industrialization will be beset by difficulties and contradictory elements, and its dynamism will therefore lose impetus." (Ehrlich would no doubt say the same of current policies based on the rapid "opening up" of the economy.) Regarding the relationship between the two sectors, Ehrlich quotes Hungarian economists whose studies show "what terrible shackles are involved for economic growth in the developing countries...in the build-up of a modern economy which is separated and isolated from the traditional one. The former has to spread inside a completely alien and restricting medium. Furthermore, traditional sectors will be ruined, deformed and dissolved by the new one which may pauperize considerable strata of the population and evoke other serious conflicts."[4]

In Japan's case, she argues, the (semi-) "traditional" sector became tied to the "modern" sector, and itself became progressively more sophisticated technologically and organizationally. She discusses how the relationship between the two sectors changed over time (with somewhat different relationships in the 1870s-World War I, interwar, and post-World War II periods), with the economy moving from an early orientation toward barely processed agricultural goods and goods from the extractive industries, to agricultural and industrial products "adjusted to specific Japanese conditions and requiring relatively sophisticated working methods." These goods were produced both for the domestic market and, increasingly, for export. The two sectors are seen as providing labor, ideas, attitudes to production, production techniques, and markets for each other and, although the relationship was not at all times and in all ways "symbiotic," it provided resources for further growth and transformation in both sectors (e.g., through the rapid spread of outwork for large-scale industry, and the proliferation of ever-changing workshops and village and urban mini-plants, that maintained direct production relations with the large-scale plants). She argues that in recent decades in Japan (after 1970—which, it might be noted, marked the end of the catch up phase in many industries) "traditional and modern elements have fused more and more and a process has started whereby large-scale industry does not simply integrate traditional elements, but, as a matter of course, includes and amalgamates them."[5]

Ehrlich's view of Japan's rapid postwar economic development experience thus builds on an analysis of a good deal of *prior transformation* in the direction of a commodity-generating economy and society that allowed for rapid growth through the absorption, spread, and further modification of imported technology throughout the economy. In fact, a great deal has been written about both Japan's economic dualism and the prior development that appears to have been critical for the country's capacity to absorb new technologies. Ehrlich's contribution has been to put many of these arguments together in the context of the analysis of latecomers that are either helped or hindered by their economic dualism as they attempt to catch up technologically, and carry out the profound transformations that are required as they do so.

Ehrlich not only begins to explore the *interrelated* conditions that allowed Japan to take advantage of the "beneficial possibilities of the country" available at this point in historical time, but also stresses the specific ways in which older institutions, behaviors and ideologies were used in order to meet the new requirements of economic development. Specifically, her narrative leads us to consider that these "symbiotic" relationships across large numbers of technologically advancing enterprises in both sectors may constitute one of the most important aspects of

the interrelated conditions that fostered an economy in Japan characterized by an accumulation of small (and increasingly ambitious) innovations involving a mobilization of indigenous (as well as external) ideas
and resources. These symbiotic relationships may also help account for
patterns of "cooperation and competition" among indigenous firms
oriented toward technological advance, rather than the pattern of
indigenous firms acting either as stagnant oligopolies or as "junior partners" to foreign firms, dependent largely on a succession of imported
technologies, as often occurs in developing countries lacking complex
and comprehensive technological ties among indigenous firms.

It is important for our purposes to note that Ehrlich has not only
recognized that industrial dualism is a strong tendency in late developing countries, but has also persuasively made the case in her study that,
in spite of the historical exploitation (in terms of wage differentials,
working conditions, and other factors) of the small-scale, relatively
"traditional" sector by the large-scale sector and middlemen—which has
been the subject of numerous studies in the past—there was also in a
very important sense a strong "symbiotic" relationship that developed
between the two sectors over time in Japan. This allowed both sectors to
be "pulled up" and transformed, contributing to the far more egalitarian
relationship that developed between them over time. Moreover, we
would argue that *this symbiotic relationship allowed for technological diffusion and technological affiliations across broad sectors of the economy*, aiding
significantly in the development of Japan's diverse, flexible and creative
technological base. It did this by facilitating the proliferation and technological advance of small firms and units in the economy as well as large,
together with the formation of a wide range of formal and informal ties
between the two sectors.

As Koji Taira noted, much of prewar Japan was made up of what
might now be called "unorganized sector" units and enterprises: "Large-
scale operations...did increase in number. But prewar Japan was a country of small craftsmen and shopkeepers surrounded by masses of even
more minute enterprises of roadside stands for sake, tobacco, noodles,
candies, and what not, and millions of urban and rural households
burning the midnight oil under putting-out arrangements..."[6] However,
this was an unorganized sector with a difference: over time, much of this
sector—including both the consumer and producer goods segments—
became "organized," with ongoing ties not only to merchants, but also in
some cases to large-scale firms and factories, banks, trading companies,
and other institutions associated with the modern sector.[7] Through association with these modern private sector institutions, and through public
sector involvement (in its promotion of subcontracting, the merging of
small with large enterprises, and the redirection of production efforts of

the small-scale as well as large-scale sector during the war years, as will be discussed below), the formerly "atomistic" small-scale and micro-enterprises were able to transform and upgrade their skills, products, and services.[8]

Thus, the direct and indirect ties between the small units/firms and larger establishments (enterprises, trading companies, banks and others) resulted in new skills and greater flexibility for both sectors. Moreover, since the political-economic background of prewar and, even more so, postwar Japan provided public investment in health, education, market protection, and other aspects of a stable legal and economic environment, the small establishments were by and large able to transform themselves as conditions required. As Ehrlich puts it, "Thus, in consequence of the weight and diversity of the small establishments, the very mobile, jack-of-all-trades, labour force remained and was recreated en masse, suscep-tible to and capable of acquiring new methods."[9]

This stands in sharp contrast to contemporary developing countries in which most of the very small units are not entrepreneurial in character, but rather are concerned with survival. Particularly in countries favoring laissez-faire policies with little protection or support for these units, and particularly where only minimal educational, health, and other services are available to the labor force in this segment of the industrial structure, the ability of these very small units to successful adapt to a rapidly changing economy (which provides opportunities, but may also threaten their particular livelihoods) remains limited.

Thus, it appears that the circumstances of the semi-traditional (and soon to become "modern") small-scale sector in early twentieth century Japan were substantially different from those characterizing much of the unorganized sector in contemporary developing countries, whose ties to the private sector are tenuous at best. This is a significant point with regard to the possibility for cooperative technological ties across the economy, and it will be taken up in more detail in Chapter 6.

Prewar ties between small units and larger enterprises in Japan were often made either directly through sales/service and subcontracting relationships or indirectly through brokers or merchants (and trading companies, in the case of export items) who linked the units up with larger distributors and enterprises.[10] Subcontracting was encouraged at first through government initiatives in the armaments industry, and later in other industries over which the public sector had influence. Up through the 1940s brokers and other intermediaries were active in estab-lishing subcontractor relationships, but over time brokers tended to be replaced by direct linkages between larger firms and subcontractors, or through the absorption of smaller firms into the larger enterprises.

Subcontracting in prewar and early postwar Japan displayed many of the characteristics found in developing countries today. For example, in the auto parts industry the small size of the market, and the fact that domestic auto manufacturers did not have the capital to undertake mass production of all parts, drove the manufacturers to rely on imports for key parts, but to depend on smaller local plants for simpler parts; this pattern persisted in spite of the low quality of metal, and the backwardness of the mechanical engineering field in Japan at the time, together with the continued use of low precision machine tools. Even in the immediate postwar period, the technical level of subcontractors continued to be low, and given the small market, they could not specialize but rather typically had to produce not only auto parts, but also other parts and accessories for textile and sewing machines, utensils, and office appliances.[11] Moreover, their power vis-à-vis parent companies remained very low, and as often occurs in today's developing countries, payments to them were often delayed far beyond the agreed upon date.

Exploitation is a word commonly used to describe the early relationship between the small-scale and large-scale sectors, particularly in the case of subcontracting (and even more so when brokers served as intermediaries). With the coming of the permanent employment system, large firms often found it economical to subcontract work out just to take advantage of the wage differentials associated with the small family workshops, and very low wages and very poor working conditions were often the norm in this latter sector.

The significance of the Japanese case is again that the small-scale sector was able to transform itself over time, based on its own efforts and in association with the large-scale sector. Its technological "backwardness" did not result in its being eliminated in favor of foreign subsidiaries or imported goods (nor was it transformed into a means by which goods were imported), and there was *economic space* to tolerate the "inefficiencies" associated with the sector. Under protective policies, and based on the education, motivation and initiative of individuals in the small-scale sector—together with cooperative technological ties and other favorable conditions—the technological capabilities of the small-scale sector rose sharply over time. As a consequence, wage differentials became much less important (particularly after the 1960s) and the technological interdependence between the two sectors increased.[12] Smaller affiliates and subcontractors as well as independents increasingly supplied the larger firms with goods the latter firms could not make themselves—in other words, a technological division of labor came into being. This laid the basis for the rise of relatively egalitarian long-term ties between large and small firms (all "modern" sector now), and *created the possibility of technological cooperation*—and not just diffusion—including joint R&D of many different types (involving both intra- and inter-industry R&D).

Many studies indicate the significance of these ongoing technological ties between firms in the large and small sectors in the postwar period. Although the empirical study of Chapters 2-5 below focuses for the most part on the large firm sector, the *Keiretsu no Kenkyu* volumes that served as one of the starting points for this study indicate a large number of joint research projects that involve relatively small firms, either in association with larger enterprises or with other small firms. Watanabe also cites a survey that shows the extent of joint research between subcontractors affiliated with a large firm and their parent company.[13] Watanabe argues, "As industrialization advances and as the technological standard of the small sector rises, small firms become an increasingly important source of new technologies."[14] Nishiguchi (1994) also finds that in the face of shortened lead times and product cycles, cooperation between large firms and smaller affiliates and subcontractors aids greatly in quality improvement and cost reduction. Moreover, as Odagiri and Goto (1993) point out, "Improvements in the product or production process by the supplier or subcontractor will be noted and rewarded by the parent company and, if possible, will be utilized in other firms in the group. In many occasions, cooperative R&D will be carried out between the parent and the supplier(s)."[15]

Additional evidence comes from Clark, who notes the importance of small subcontractors and affiliates in providing ideas to their parent companies.[16] This is echoed in the opinion of Ken-ichi Imai, a leading specialist on Japan's industrial economy, that the small-scale firms located in such areas as Ota-ku in Tokyo have contributed a great deal to the innovative efforts of the larger firms.[17]

Watanabe points out that in recent decades the larger purchasers of products and ideas from small firms (the latter of which may be subcontractors, independents, or "group" affiliates) are important sources for both technological cooperation (joint research) and technological assistance because the relationship between the customer (sometimes, but not always a "parent company") and the small firm is a *long-term* one. In other words, the large firm is the small firm's "regular customer," and they have established a relationship of interdependence and trust over a long period of time. Small firms in more formal hierarchical relationships with large firms (e.g., as "sub-subcontractors" low in the keiretsu hierarchy, or as "affiliates" relatively high in the hierarchy) have strong incentives to improve their own technological capabilities and rise up in the hierarchy of, for example, Nissan or Hitachi-affiliated firms.[18] Moreover, a number of subcontractors associated with a particular large firm can even engage in technological cooperation to try to raise their level of technological capabilities: this was one strategy pursued in the 1980s and 1990s in the face of the slowdown and restructuring of the Japanese economy.[19] The well-publicized technological accomplishments resulting from these joint (together with individual) research efforts is to continue to improve their product and process technologies, often to an extent that has surprised international competitors.

In this way, many subcontractors have been able to move into a position of participating in a relatively egalitarian cooperative relationship with larger firms based on a technological division of labor. Both sides thus contribute important inputs into their pooled technological knowledge base.

Again, this is certainly not the case in all industries: in some industries, exploitative conditions remain. Particularly for women and "non-Japanese," working conditions and wages remain low and job security is often non-existent. Moreover, once larger companies learn how small firms produce a certain desired input, they often try to copy the process themselves, rather than enter into long-term relationships, forcing the small company into other product areas or out of business. Thus, although in some industries conditions have improved tremendously, in other industries, conditions are not so rosy.[20]

Under certain conditions, then, relatively cooperative technological ties can develop between the "large" and "small" firms sectors in late developing economies. The technological upgrading of the small firm sector is clearly the key to this process; otherwise, the sector is likely to remain simply a source of cheap, highly exploitable labor (to the extent that it remains at all). The role of cooperative technological ties in this process will be taken up again in Chapter 6 as we explore the possibilities and problems associated with the promotion of such ties in different developing country contexts.

Technological Cooperation Involving the Industrial House (Zaibatsu And Keiretsu) Groupings

We have discussed the importance of inter-enterprise ties as one factor that helped to narrow the potential problems posed by industrial dualism, which is a feature common to most late developing countries. Another characteristic of late development in many parts of the world is the family-based business group or enterprise network. This sometimes takes the specific form of "industrial houses," which in the Japanese case can be seen in the *zaibatsu* groupings of the prewar period. As will be discussed in Chapter 6, the zaibatsu have similarities to the present-day industrial houses of Argentina, Brazil, India, Pakistan, the Philippines,

South Korea, Taiwan, Thailand, and many other contemporary developing countries.

Japan's main "older" zaibatsu arose from merchant capital origins—specifically, from families involved in money-lending, trading, and other activities, and from mining activities.[21] After the Meiji Restoration of 1868 they provided financial services to the government, and during the 1880s they obtained factories, mines, and other enterprises set up and sold off by the Meiji government. Each industrial house tended to specialize in a certain cluster of related industries, but invested in a number of industries unrelated to this cluster as well.[22]

This pattern of investment seems to occur for several reasons. First, in an "underdeveloped" context, there may be a need to invest simultaneously in several related industries in order to eliminate supply, marketing and other bottlenecks; in contrast to this, a producer in an earlier and more gradually developing economy could find a wide range of domestic firms and industries already in existence that could be drawn upon for these purposes. Second, in an "underdeveloped" context, the domestic market for each industry is relatively shallow, causing firms (including industrial houses) to look to other industries as well as potential areas for investment.

The industrial house form had a number of other advantages. For example, on the financial side, the zaibatsu maintained their own banks and other financial ties that were crucial to their growth, particularly prior to the 1930s, given that capital markets were not well-developed.[23] On the commercial side, the zaibatsu trading companies, with their international connections, played a critical role in supplying raw materials, new foreign technologies, and other services to zaibatsu members, and in marketing their products (particularly to overseas markets), all of which were functions that firms could not carry out easily by themselves at this time. On the all-important political side, the zaibatsu were able as powerful economic units to exert considerable political pressure on successive governments.

The prewar and war years were critically important for the transformation of the zaibatsu and the rise of economic institutions and practices that would come to characterize the Japanese economy in the postwar period. Interfirm cooperation and the government-industry relationship are two such areas of economic activities that underwent major changes during these years, and set the basis for postwar practices.

With respect to interfirm cooperation, there was an expansion of cooperation among group members supplying one another with raw materials and other inputs as the firms expanded and diversified their activities during the boom brought on by the First World War, and in subsequent years. However, the most significant changes with respect to cooperation among group members (and even between groups in the later war years) occurred as the Japanese economy was forcibly reorganized by the government for military purposes in the late 1930s and early 1940s. For example, under the reorganization small firms were eliminated and/or absorbed into larger, often zaibatsu firms, and large numbers of firms that suffered financial setbacks and came to rely on zaibatsu funds—particularly during years of recession or depression—were also merged into the zaibatsu. In addition, foreign investments in and funds for Japanese firms were curtailed. This often resulted in the firms becoming fully "Japanized" and pulled into the zaibatsu circuit (this was the case with NEC, for example, as will be discussed in Chapter 2). Among other benefits to the zaibatsu, these developments widened the scope for cooperation among group members, and new supplier relationships developed during these years. Outside of the zaibatsu circuits, as noted above, similar processes resulted in relatively small firms and factories being subordinated to and absorbed by larger firms in the same or related industries, building up large firm-small firm supplier and subcontracting networks.

The prewar and war years also set important precedents with respect to the government-industry relationship. With the rise of political parties in the early twentieth century, the zaibatsu found these political organizations to be useful vehicles to bring about laws favorable to their growth. (For example, the 1927 Seiyukai party government was called the "Mitsui Cabinet" by the rival Minseito party, which itself was backed by the Mitsubishi zaibatsu.[24]) A strong public response, both from the right and the left, in the 1920s to the close connection between the zaibatsu and successive governments appears to have been a critical factor contributing to the political climate of the times, which was marked by assassinations and intense social tensions. The public response was particularly intense after a long series of scandals involving bribery, favoritism, and other forms of corruption, as well as evidence of zaibatsu support for the often brutal repression of labor.[25] This in turn contributed to conditions conducive to the takeover of the government by the military.

As Japan moved toward war, the zaibatsu leadership made the changeover to war industries in the 1930s and kept on good terms with the government and bureaucracy. The zaibatsu leadership may have regretted the curtailment of trade due to the war effort, and might have worried about the government's support for "new zaibatsu" (Nissan and others) that were established to help in this effort, but at the same time, the zaibatsu families were thought to be supportive of the idea of a strong government committed to expansion overseas and favorable to their interests.[26]

The zaibatsu support for the wartime government and the government's need for zaibatsu expertise appears to have led to a situation in which the business elite helped to direct the wartime economy, with highly placed zaibatsu officials working together to help with the reorganization of the economy in the 1930s and 1940s (the most famous of these may have been Seihin Ikeda, Mitsui's *obanto*, or top manager, who acted concurrently as Finance Minister and Minister of Commerce and Industry in the late 1930s). This, too, has been seen by some as setting a precedent for postwar economic practices.

Many other institutions took on something closer to that postwar form during this period. For example, it is said that the Ministry of Commerce and Industry's experience with wartime controls laid the basis for MITI's relationship with firms and the practices the latter undertook in the postwar period. In fact, the "guidance" of firms by the bureaucracy (which was actually a two-way street) was the rule rather than the exception in the wartime economy, as well as in many postwar industries. Similarly, the relationship between banks (and other "authorized financial institutions") and firms is said to have been solidified during this period, as was the system of subcontracting, the atmosphere of cartelization, practices with respect to labor, and other important economic features. This is not to say that these institutions and practices had no equivalent before the war years; however, we need to keep in mind the importance of wartime economic conditions in evolving forms close to those that came to predominate in the postwar economy.

With respect to cooperative technological ties, it should be noted that during the war years firms were asked to work closely with the laboratories of public corporations and other government agencies on needed technologies, and sometimes with each other as well. Particularly when needed technologies could no longer be imported, these efforts toward national self-reliance were cited by persons interviewed as laying a strong precedent for postwar cooperative research efforts.

During these years, then, the groups expanded greatly, moved into the heavy and chemical industries (where they no longer faced international competition, and had the war effort as a ready market), gained expertise in a wide range of new technologies and industries, and gained a great deal of experience in both the practices of cooperation between group firms and cooperation with government agencies and public corporations.[27] Moreover, it is interesting to note that not only was the zaibatsu leadership made to work together during the war, but it is said that by the late 1930s the direct or indirect ties of marriage between the leading zaibatsu families was also commonplace, presumably helping to ensure an atmosphere of cordiality and accommodation among the leading zaibatsu.[28]

The Early Postwar Years:
The Business Groups, Industrial Groups,
and Technological Cooperation

By the end of the war the zaibatsu's predominance over the economy was striking, as indicated by all available statistics. Because of this, the policy of "zaibatsu dissolution" was initiated, but this was only partly carried out before the policy was reversed in 1949. The zaibatsu were now reorganized in the new form known as *kigyo shudan*, or more loosely, as "horizontal *keiretsu*" ("intermarket" or "business" groups), which came to be characterized by such practices as intercorporate shareholding, interlocking directorates, and coordination through group trading companies, group banks, "President's clubs," and other regular group meetings on a wide range of levels.[29]

This reorganization or re-formation into business groups occurred despite the fact that holding companies were outlawed and the former zaibatsu members were made into legally independent firms. Business group members found group coordination and cooperation to be important in the postwar period for primarily financial, sales, information and technological reasons, among other advantages that the group form offers. In fact, in addition to the former zaibatsu-type business groups, other groups have formed as well around important non-zaibatsu banks, for similar reasons.

The six major business groups of the postwar period thus came to include four zaibatsu successor groups and two bank-centered groups. The former are the Mitsubishi, Mitsui, Sumitomo, and Fuyo (or Fuji, formerly Yasuda) groups, and the latter are the Dai-ichi Kangin Bank (DKB) and Sanwa (Bank) groups. These six groups accounted for 22.9% of the assets of all incorporated firms in Japan in the mid-1970s, i.e., toward the end of the technological catch up period. (These figures are based on presidents' club members only; if affiliates in which 25% or more stock is owned by these companies are included, the total would rise to 28.2%, according to the Fair Trade Commission.[30])

In the early postwar period several business group members in related fields would typically pool their financial and technical resources in order to set up a firm in a new industry on the basis of imported technology. Peck and Tamura cite as an illustrative case the entrance of firms into the new low-density high-pressure process polyethylene industry between 1955 and 1970. The first entrants were firms established by three major business groups (Sumitomo, Mitsubishi and Mitsui), and later firms established by smaller business groups (e.g., Showa) and individual companies; these all used different sources of foreign technology in order to enter the new industry.[31] Similarly, Ozawa describes how groups established firms in other branches of the emerging postwar petrochemical industry; these include the Mitsui, Furukawa (which is part of the Dai-ichi Kangyo Bank) and Showa groups, in addition to the Mitsubishi and Sumitomo firms cited in the polyethylene case.[32]

The nuclear power industry is often cited as a good example of "group" development of an industry in the early postwar period. The costs of setting up production were very high, and the nuclear industry was a very controversial one in post-Hiroshima and Nagasaki Japan. The Japanese government set up a nuclear research institute as a "special corporation" with equal investment by the government and private industry, and worked with the major groups to set up group atomic power projects. In the Mitsui case, forty-two companies joined together, centering on Toshiba (a Mitsui affiliate), with Mitsui Bussan (Trading Company) in a coordinating role, to create the Nippon Atomic Industry Group (NAIG).[33]

The case of the aluminum industry also gives us a good idea as to how these group projects have been devised, coordinated, and carried through. It may be useful to quote an interview with an Executive Vice-President of Mitsui Aluminum Company regarding this case, from the point of view of the Mitsui group (the following references all refer to Mitsui companies, e.g., Mitsui Real Estate Development):

The way in which new companies are formed by the group reveals Mitsui's characteristic mode of operation. There is no brain trust handing down decisions from on high. Ideas usually originate from opportunities recognized or needs felt by executives of individual companies, who in frequent social contacts with colleagues in other Mitsui firms exchange their ideas. If a proposal appeals to fellow members of one of the executives' clubs, a committee will be set up to examine the possible contributions from or benefits to various companies of the group and to evolve a plan accordingly. In the case of the Mitsui Aluminum Company, established in 1969, the idea was based upon three considerations: Mitsui was weak in light metals, which were of increasing importance in the economy; huge new deposits of bauxite had become available from Australia; and the coal business was in the doldrums. Why not use surplus coal, then, to generate electric power for making aluminum?

Schematically, such a project is worked out somewhat as follows, using aluminum as an example. A committee decides where the power and ore can be brought together for reduction: this turns out to be Omuta, site of the Miike coal mines, which has good port facilities owned by Mitsui. A development plan is drawn up by Real Estate, land is reclaimed adjacent to the harbor by Construction, and meanwhile, Bussan is rounding up suitable technology and equipment through its foreign branches. In Australia a new company—Mitsui Alumina—is set up by Trading and other interested members, together with local partners, to mine bauxite and process it nearby to reduce the cost of shipping, aboard Mitsui O.S.K. Lines' special carriers. The alumina and aluminum plants and docks are built and equipped through combined efforts of Consultants, Shipbuilding & Engineering, Construction, Sanki Engineering, Toshiba, and Miike Machinery. Metallurgical experience is furnished by Mining & Smelting, while Mining supplied coal, carbon for electrodes, and housing for employees. Bank has coordinated the financing, assisted by Trust & Banking, Mutual Life, and Taisho Marine and Fire. Before the mill is completed, Bussan works out marketing plans, the toughest job because in Japan aluminum is already in oversupply due to imports and stiff competition from other groups. However, there is one stable, built-in market: the Mitsui Group itself. Having a big aluminum producer within the group offers certain advantages that help to compensate for losses anticipated by the new company during its first few years of operation. Also, much of the money spent by Aluminum accrues as income to other member companies, who in turn cooperate to make it profitable.[34]

In these and a great many other cases, it appears that the complementary technical and financial resources of affiliated firms (i.e., group members) in related industries often allowed a rapid and effective entry into new fields opening up.[35] The groups' influence on MITI no doubt had a significant role in speeding up this process, given MITI's control over entry in the early years; however, this influence in itself was presumably not enough to guarantee successful entry.

Although it is not clear what proportion of new industries had entrants established by business groups in this way, Miyazaki argued that the groups did try to establish a new member firm in each new industry that was considered to be important; this is the basis for his famous "one set theory."[36] These industries tended to be characterized by costly ventures that required a combining of resources from different fields, as in the cases of "space technologies," ocean development, and nuclear power (as discussed above), rather than being natural outgrowths of well-established industries (e.g., consumer durables industries). In addition, new coordinating mechanisms were developed to try to pool the expertise of group members into new project areas.[37]

"Independent" firms as well (i.e., those without ties, or with only weak ties, to former zaibatsu or bank-centered keiretsu) entered into new industries in the postwar period. Many of these independent firms formed their own groupings of affiliated firms that cooperate with each other in a variety of ways, leading to the distinction between "business groups" and "industrial groups." (Again, business groups are made up of firms in different industries, while industrial groups are typically composed of a large firm and its affiliates in the same or closely related industries.) These ties are not mutually exclusive; for example, Toshiba and its affiliates make up the "Toshiba Group," but they are also part of the larger "Mitsui Group," a business group. In addition, as will be discussed below, new informal groupings and ongoing affiliations emerged in response to technological and other requirements for competition in the late catch up and early frontier period.

The groups we have been discussing are often highly controversial due to their political clout and checkered histories. The point here is simply to note the degree to which they—and other enterprises and organizations in Japan—recognized over time the important benefits of ongoing technological ties and other forms of cooperative behavior: collective efforts of organizations working together in an atmosphere of mutual support can often achieve far more than can the isolated, individual organization, particularly when ideas and resources need to be pooled. In Japan's case, the use of cooperative technological ties thus appears to be an important element that contributed to the ability of these "non-Western" (late industrializing) enterprises and organizations to progress technologically and not simply remain dependent on ideas and technologies developed in the "West" (i.e., the early industrializing countries).

Over time, then, extensive interfirm and inter-organizational cooperation became an important characteristic of firm behavior in Japan. Over the past decades, firms have not only cooperated with foreign affiliates for purposes of technology transfer or other forms of cooperation, but moreover have cooperated with extensive chains of subcontractors and suppliers, with domestic affiliates (firms in their own industrial or business group, or through long-term affiliations of a less formal nature), and even with their own competitors in order to transform and upgrade imported technologies and integrate in local ideas and techniques. Firms in the same industry have been able to cooperate, for example, in adapting and improving on imported technology in order to derive technologies that were both more appropriate to the Japanese market and potentially competitive internationally.

Thus, a wide range of precedents were set for the diverse and complementary cooperative technological undertakings of the late catch up/early frontier period—i.e., not just for the well-known cases of cooperation sponsored by MITI, but rather for the entire range of efforts, large and small. It will be argued that these multiple and often overlapping research efforts have helped create a strong and well-integrated technological base, aiding in the country's rapid technological catch up, and contributed strongly to the country's ability to undertake altogether original forms of innovation once the frontier was reached.

The Role of the Public Sector

We have noted above the ways in which the public sector supported and promoted the cooperative ventures of the prewar and postwar groups in Japan. Gerschenkron and others have written extensively about the relatively large role that the public sector tends to play in a late development context. Needless to say, a specific administration's ties to influential family-based groupings would be expected to be particularly close if it is financially or otherwise dependent on those business or industrial groupings, as is often the case in contemporary developing countries; this may have important implications for public policies with respect to the modern large firm sector, and toward the groups in particular. In a number of developing countries we have ample evidence of public policies favoring influential groups and their foreign partners, often to the detriment of the less technologically "advanced" small-scale sector, as will be discussed below.

In Japan's case, from the nineteenth century on the government has continually favored the large-scale sector, but it has also directly or indirectly helped to maintain the modernizing semi-traditional small-scale sector by pursuing such policies as establishing quality control mechanisms for exports produced by small-scale units from the late nineteenth century on. As noted above, the government also directly initiated linkages between modern and semi-traditional firms by promoting subcontracting, beginning with military arsenals in the 1920s, and expanding the range of subcontracting practices greatly with the wartime reorganization of industry. During these years, small firms were often tied to or merged with larger firms, technology sharing among firms was encouraged, and production was often redirected to meet wartime needs.[38] In this way small firms were often exposed to a greater variety of technologies and production methods, even though the small firm sector suffered as well from these coercive methods. (It can also be argued that the level of technological expertise to which the small firm sector was exposed during these years was not high enough to significantly improve their abilities; certainly, the record of technological advance during these years was very uneven.[39])

In the postwar period, the government continued to give large firms preferential access to capital, imported technologies, and other crucial supplies.[40] Among other consequences, this increased the small firms' need to affiliate with large firms in order to obtain these key resources. Still, the government eventually passed laws prohibiting the worst of the prewar exploitative practices, and scholars in developing countries sometimes note the legal protection accorded to the sector in Japan at the present time.

Thus, we can see that the historical relationship between the two sectors involved very strong elements of coercion and exploitation, government favoritism of the large-scale sector, and short-term opportunistic behavior. However, there also emerged over time the conditions that facilitated not only technological diffusion, but also technological cooperation between the two sectors. The promotion of cooperative research involving the larger public and private enterprises, as well as government labs and other research institutions, may have directly benefited the larger enterprises, but to the extent that the broader technology and knowledge base was extended through cooperative technological ties to the small-scale sector (which was advancing in its own right), the effect was to form a technological "grid" or network across the entire economy, and counter the tendency toward widely uneven forms of technological and industrial development.[41]

The achievements of such cooperative efforts between the small-scale and large-scale sectors may not be as dramatic as the well-publicized national projects, but they may be equally or more significant for the economy as a whole. The earlier technological, production and marketing ties facilitated changes in interfirm relationships and contributed to the firms' growing ability to transform products and processes, both through individual and cooperative efforts. In the prewar period these efforts were relatively small-scale, but as Ehrlich puts it, economic transformation is the outcome, or the "sum of tiny, but in effect massive, modifications affecting each other. Accordingly, it is impossible to describe, characterize and numerically trace this process in its entirety" (p. 106). In Japan, this accumulation of know-how via small innovations in both the prewar and postwar periods was accomplished through firms working with other firms and organizations throughout the economy, and not just individual technological "islands" in association with international suppliers of ideas and technologies. This process, in its entirety, laid the basis for rapid technological catch up and then frontier forms of innovation.

Before we move on it may be useful to note that many aspects of the government-industry ties discussed here have been extremely controversial both in the prewar and postwar periods, and as many economists and historians in Japan remind us, much of the economic transformation of Japan was carried out under very harsh circumstances, both to those in Japan and abroad. For example, Tsuru makes the following argument regarding Japan's development experience:

> Japan's economy became...geared to the high rate of growth which could succeed only on the basis of successive gambles of an imperialist character. It will be impossible to narrate the story of Japan's economic development

in the modern period without relating it to the successive and successful wars she fought. It meant that the spearhead of her economic development was, on the one hand, the armament and allied industries always gener-ously supported by the state, and on the other, export industries which prospered on the strength of 'cheap labor' at home and thanks to the extension of spheres of influence abroad as a result of imperialist conquest. The economy could be highly dynamic so long as Japan fought and won wars."[42]

With this in mind, one could argue that in the Japanese case it appears that many of the policies and institutions promoting cooperative techno-logical ties among group members and involving other private and public sector enterprises and organizations were set in place during peri-ods of military and economic aggression (e.g., during the reorganization of the economy during the war years that promoted linkages among domestic firms). The implication of this would be that cooperative tech-nological ties are promoted most effectively when a clear economic, political, or military "enemy" is in view.

Although there is some truth to this, we will argue below that cooper-ative technological ties need not be promoted by public policies only in times of political, military or economic conflict. As will be detailed in the following chapters, more socially useful applications of cooperative research and cooperative technological ties can certainly be promoted by public policy initiatives, and in fact are likely to be promoted, under the right circumstances.

Further Discussion

In this chapter we began to explore three of the important elements that allowed the development of a wide variety of cooperative technolog-ical ties in the late catch up and early frontier period in Japan. These ties rested on the relatively long-term relationships that have developed over time between enterprises (and organizations), including both firms of roughly equal status, and those in very different positions.

The important point here is that (1) the relatively mild degree of industrial dualism, together with (2) the group formations that emerged out of merchant capital (and other) origins and (3) the active role played by public sector organizations, in the context of a latecomer economy, are three of the many factors that facilitated the development of a wide range of ties among firms across the economy in the Japanese case. This allowed increasingly intimate and sophisticated types of cooperative research to develop as firms attempted to advance technologically, and stands in sharp contrast to the atomistic/ individualistic behavior characteristic of the early developers on the one hand, and on the other the pattern of isolated large enterprises, largely dependent on foreign suppliers of technology, that one tends to find in the least industrialized parts of the developing world. It will be argued below that the Japanese case is most relevant to other relatively "early" and "middle" late developers (i.e., the NICs and next NICs), but that the relevance will vary according to the circumstances of each individual country. This will be taken up again in Chapter 6 below.

It should be clear from this historical survey that in Japan's case there were often strong elements of coercion and exploitation in the formation of cooperative ties among enterprises and organizations, particularly during times of military and economic expansion. The more useful lesson to be learned may be that the promotion of cooperative technological ties across the economy can help prevent the marginalizing of a wide range of enterprises and organizations, and can help establish a flexible, well-integrated and responsive knowledge base that is capable of putting indigenous ideas and resources to new uses and producing very innovative solutions to new problems in a changing economy and society. In a developing country context, the use of indigenous resources and approaches may counter the tendency to import "solutions" from advanced industrial countries that are inappropriate or even harmful when placed in a less industrialized context.

In the following chapter, we will begin our empirical study of the computer and telecommunications industry with a brief consideration of the background of innovation in the postwar period in Japan, noting some of the conditions that favored the rapid technological catch up of Japanese enterprises in this period. We will then focus on the rise of the computer and telecommunications industry and the ways in which cooperative ties changed as enterprises in Japan advanced to the late catch up and early frontier stage of innovation, coming finally to be seen not simply as imitators, but as serious innovators as well—a fact that came as a surprise to many, who in a post-colonial global context did not expect this type of challenge to come from a non-"Western" country.

Notes

1. Both the concepts "modern" and "traditional" (and "semi-traditional") are plagued by ambiguity. Particularly in late developing countries, neither sector is stagnant nor pristine, and they are constantly evolving through interaction with one another.

Nonetheless, these concepts serve the purpose of indicating differences in the nature of technologies and modes of organization, motivations to some degree, and certainly access to markets, capital, information, new technologies, and other resources. In the terminology employed in studies of small enterprises in prewar Japan, the "modern" large-scale sector was often counterposed to the more "traditional" small-scale sector because of the type of industrialization undertaken at that time, resulting in differentials in firm size and other attributes. In contemporary developing countries, the "modern" sector (involving a wide range of firm sizes) is referred to by some as the "organized" sector and is counterposed to the "unorganized" sector (involving often, but not exclusively, very small-scale units). Here again, the key distinction has to do with the nature of technologies and modes of organization, motivations, and access to markets and resources; however, the ways in which the terms "organized" and "unorganized" are used vary widely. For present purposes, we will continue to use the terms "modern" and "semi-traditional," with "semi" being used to indicate that some degree of transformation is taking place, as opposed to the more strictly "traditional" sector that does not adapt to economic and social changes and tends to die out as its environment is transformed.

2. Ehrlich (1984), pp. 223-224. Regarding the ideal of industrial dualism as applied to late developing economies, see, for example, the early study by Seymour Broadbridge, *Industrial Dualism in Japan* (1966), and references cited in that study. For more general concepts of dualism in theories of late development, see, for example, Hewlett et al. (1982). For more on Ehrlich's ideas and other works that deal with industrial dualism and late development, see Doane (1993). Regarding the idea of industrial dualism as applied to the very different context of advanced industrial economies (with very different implications), a standard reference is Averitt (1968); one drawback of this study, however, is the failure to distinguish between small technologically advanced firms capable of expanding rapidly—i.e., potentially "large" firms (with optimal size depending on the industry and other considerations)—and small firms that have no such prospects, and have difficulty gaining access to capital, markets, new technologies, or other resources.

3. Ehrlich, p. 227.

4. Ibid., p. 225-226.

5. Ibid., p. 230.

6. Taira (1970), p. 4.

7. As Lockwood noted, "Through a series of laws enacted between 1884 and 1902 the authorities encouraged the formation of local chambers of commerce and guilds of industrialists and merchants for cooperative action. These trade associations were given legal status and tax immunities in order that they might engage in joint investigation, representation, and services like inspection. Although formed in large numbers, it should be added that such limited self-regulation as they achieved did not materially alter the atomistic structure of small-scale business, even in the export trade. This was modified only subsequently *as a network of financial and marketing relationships developed through merchant-employers and wholesale traders linked the small producers, on the one hand, with big banks, export-import firms, and factories, on the other*" (Lockwood, 1954, pp. 561-562; emphasis added).

8. In Japan, the semi-traditional units faced little domestic competition at first,

since the modern sector concentrated initially on manufacturing producer goods and infrastructure. Nakamura (1966) discusses an initial symbiotic relationship between a *modern sector* that uses cheap labor (and supplies) developed through "traditional" industrial activities, and a *"traditional" sector* that benefited from the cheap imports and the market created by modern sector activities. However, Nakamura notes that after the 1920s modern firms (and their more "modern" small affiliates and subcontractors) began competing directly with the "traditional" units, forcing them to change further (e.g., become affiliates, change their product, or change their production methods), or else go out of business, putting further pressure on the semi-traditional enterprises to modernize. On a somewhat different point, Yamanaka and Kobayashi (1957) discuss the emergence of a symbiotic relationship between a "traditional" sector whose goods often earned the foreign exchange necessary for imports of modern equipment and technologies—and therefore helped to keep the country economically independent as much as possible—and a modern sector that supplied new production methods for "traditional" products. The important point is that in Japan the relationship between the two sectors was complex and ever-changing and involved important symbiotic elements, rather than the one simply marginalizing or contributing to the destruction of the other.

9. Ehrlich, p. 90.

10. As an example, an interesting study of the electric lamp industry by Teijiro Uyeda and Tosuke Inokuchi written in 1936 describes a multi-tiered system with Tokyo Electric Company at the top, the "standard" electric lamp companies in the middle (these are the larger-scale "home-made" manufacturers), and the "town" manufacturers (small-scale home-based factories and workshops) at the bottom. The authors discuss how the demand for electric lamps was initially met by imports from Germany and how over time the imports were replaced by the projects of local companies, large and small. The study then focuses on the changing direct and indirect ties between the small and large companies, and between the small and merchant middlemen and exporters (cf. Uyeda and Inokichi, 1936).

11. Cf. Yamanaka and Kobayashi (1957), p. 84, for examples.

12. The importance of wage differentials depends on the industry—e.g., they continue to be more significant in certain segments of the electronics industry, and less important in the auto industry. Cf., for example, Nishiguchi (1994). Nishiguchi describes the 1950s (particularly the late 1950s) through the mid-1960s as the "golden age of dualism" in Japan, after which time the high growth rates, shortages of skilled labor, and an increase in the technological division of labor between larger companies and their smaller affiliates and subcontractors in many industries reduced the wage and other differentials sharply.

13. Cf. Watanabe (1983). Watanabe found from his survey that "parent firms are the most frequent sources of technical guidance, *co-operation in joint research,* and supply of know-how for these enterprises, despite the fact that the survey included both subcontractors and non-subcontractors" (p. 46, emphasis added). Unfortunately, the survey was carried out in 1975, and does not document in detail the content of the joint research projects.

14. Ibid., p. 10.

15. Odagiri and Goto (1993), p. 107.

16. Regarding the findings of Clark (1988) that lead times in automobile projects are one-third faster in Japan than in the U.S. or Europe, and that these shorter times are largely attributable to the high reliance by Japanese firms on outside (affiliated) suppliers, Gerlach (1992b, p. 26) writes, "Clark shows that Japanese suppliers are far more involved in basic component engineering. Whereas about 70% of outside purchases in Japan are of supplier-proprietary parts or black-box parts (i.e., suppliers carry out the detailed engineering in response to the assembler's functional specifications), this figure is only 19% in the U.S. and 46% in Europe. He concludes as follows: `Although supplier management has been in transition in the U.S. companies, the projects in our sample were heavily influenced by the traditional system in which suppliers produced parts under short-term, arm's-length contracts and had little role in design and engineering. In the Japanese system, in contrast, suppliers are an integral part of the development process: they are involved early, assume significant responsibility, and communicate extensively and directly with product and process engineers.'"

Another interesting study of ties among subcontractors discusses both "vertical" and "lateral" exchanges of information—e.g., lateral exchanges among the seventy-seven secondary subcontractors in the case of Toritsu-Kogyo, and vertical exchanges (direct and indirect), making subcontractors a much more immediate participant in new project development undertakings than would be true of unaffiliated (outside) vendors. Cf. Imai, Nonaka and Takeuchi (1985).

17. Personal communication. When one focuses on the more ambitious large-scale projects, it is easy to overlook the contribution of smaller innovative efforts and the general know-how that can be provided by the small-scale sector, including subcontractors, affiliates, and independent small firms.

18. Fruin (1992) details how the R&D contributions of smaller affiliates help them in their efforts to rise in the group hierarchy.

19. Other strategies include cost-cutting, or following parent companies overseas. Regarding all of these strategies, including technological cooperation, cf. "Breaking With Tradition," *Financial Times*, September 13, 1994.

20. Cf., for example, interviews in Miyashita and Russell (1994) for fascinating accounts of problems faced by subcontractors in Japan as a counter to the picture commonly given in management studies. The latter typically emphasize the benefits of subcontracting from the perspective of the "parent" or larger firm, and tend to deemphasize the problems associated with it (e.g., the sudden reversals and dilemmas faced by the subcontractors in times of economic difficulties).

21. For example, Sumitomo's source of wealth for two centuries was copper: the Sumitomo zaibatsu originated in the form of a copper crafting shop in Kyoto in 1590, and in 1691 the "firm" purchased the Besshi mine in Shikoku. Finally, in 1895 Sumitomo Bank was established, and diversification into industrial activities began. Mitsui's origins were more in moneylending and banking. The "political merchants" included the Mitsui, Yasuda, Okura, Fujita, and Mitsubishi

enterprises, and the mining-centered houses included Sumitomo and Furukawa, with Asano as a third category of zaibatsu (non-mining, non-"political merchant"—cf. Morikawa, 1992, Chapter 1).

22. By the turn of the century, most of the zaibatsu were involved in finance, shipping, insurance, warehousing, and some manufacturing, and by the 1930s they diversified decisively into heavy and chemical industries as well. They had a clear-cut vertical structure, with the zaibatsu families at the top, followed by the holding company (*honsha*), which held stock in member companies. This was followed by the main subsidiaries, and then by the rest of the affiliated companies.

These industrial houses were dominant in many of their fields of activity, particularly in the late nineteenth and early twentieth centuries, and were actively involved in extending their range of influence—both through direct investment and by other means—during most of these years. For example, even though the non-zaibatsu sector initiated the profitable and historically important raw silk and cotton export industries, the industrial houses were eventually able to extend their influence over this sector as well through their handling of the financial and trading aspects of these industries. For an interesting discussion of the rise and development of the zaibatsu, see Shibagaki (1966, 1973, 1984).

23. On this point, cf., for example, Morikawa (1992).

24. Cf. Mitsui and Co. (undated), p. 30.

25. Cf., for example, Mitsui and Co. (undated), pp. 28-32, and other zaibatsu histories, regarding some of these incidents and the public reaction to them. The relationship between the zaibatsu and political leaders, the frequent scandals involving various forms of corruption, and the "authorized" repression of labor in Japan's prewar period (and, to some extent, the postwar period) have striking parallels with conditions and incidents in many current-day developing countries; these parallels are certainly worthy of further exploration.

26. The zaibatsu-military relationship, and the zaibatsu's attitude toward war (as opposed to colonial expansion), have been heavily debated over the years. Morikawa argues that "the zaibatsu-military relationship was at best an uneasy one, and zaibatsu support of Japanese military expansion was more a matter of necessity than choice" (Morikawa, p. 228). Nonetheless, in the face of anti-zaibatsu activities and assassinations in the 1930s, the zaibatsu *tenko* (conversion) and cooperation with the military and wartime government—out of choice or necessity—resulted in major changes in the economy and industrial structure.

27. For example, several of the zaibatsu set up cooperative councils (kyoryoku-kai) in the late 1930s and 1940s to coordinate expanding group activities. On this point, cf. Okumura (1983), among other sources.

28. Lockwood (1954, p. 563) cites the U.S. Department of State document, *Report of the Mission on Japanese Combines* (Part I, Washington, D.C., 1946, p. 16), regarding these intermarriages.

29. For more on the dissolution and change to the keiretsu form, cf. Hadley (1970), Yamamura (1964), Rotwein (1976), and Toyo Keizai (1980), among others.

30. Cf. Goto (1982), pp. 54-55.

31. Cf. Peck and Tamura (1976), particularly pp. 553-557.

32. Cf. Ozawa (1980).

33. Later, in 1967, the Japan Nuclear Fuel Company was also set up, this time crossing group boundaries to include one foreign and two domestic firms in the same industry: Toshiba, Hitachi, and General Electric. Cf. Roberts (1973), pp. 482-483. Roberts also details additional group ventures related to the field of nuclear energy.

34. From Roberts' interview with Kawaguchi Iwao, Executive Vice-President, Mitsui Aluminum Company; ibid., p. 483.

35. There are many other forms that intra-group cooperation takes besides cooperative research. For example, Fruin (1992) notes, "Cooperation might consist of the sharing of resources, such as warehouses and wharves, an agreed-upon allocation of raw or intermediate materials, such as differential shares to the output of a petroleum refinery, or consecutive and alternative uses of the same resource, such as scheduled access to a wind-tunnel testing site, to a three-quarter million dollar electron microscope, or to seaside recreational facilities" (p. 187).

36. This theory was first put forward in one of the articles later incorporated into Miyazaki (1966). On Miyazaki's and other related theories, see also Kiyonari and Nakamura (1977).

37. Gerlach (1992a) discusses the establishment of new coordinating institutions in the business and industrial groups in the 1980s. For example, he discusses how "Mitsubishi formed the Mitsubishi C&C Kenkyu-kai in 1981, a study team bringing together forty Mitsubishi companies to develop technologies related to high-level data transmission that will link firms through electronic firm banking, producer-sales agent data exchanges, and other forms of interfirm communication. Mitsui followed in 1982 with the Mitsui Joho Shisutemu Kyogi-kai, with thirty-nine Mitsui companies participating in projects in value-added networks and other telecommunications-related technological fields. In 1983 ten more firms were added, including several large firms that maintain close connections with the Mitsui group but do not participate in its council—Sony, Ito, Yokado, and Tokyo Broadcasting System" (p. 154).

38. For example, during the war with China many small-scale firms (e.g., the tiny metal toy units that had been producing for export markets out of urban working class neighborhoods) were converted to military production (cf. Yamanaka and Kobayashi, 1957). After 1945 many of these returned to their previous activities, and although their quality was initially very low (contributing to the 1950s "made in Japan" stereotype of inferior goods), they were able to become more proficient over time, often with help from trading companies or larger firms.

39. As the son of a small manufacturing unit described, "In 1943 the government passed another law, ordering even more corporate integration, and they basically scrapped all the small factories. They combined all the little firms into bigger units to help fight the war. My father's factory was merged with a bigger factory down the road, one with about a hundred workers. The new plant was designated as a supplier to the Mitsubishi zaibatsu, and it had to make parts for weapons.

A lot of companies like that sprang up, not really small, but not big enough to be important. They were all just subcontractors in the arms business. But a lot of those companies were made up of little firms that weren't really good manufacturers to begin with. They weren't competent to produce some of the things they were asked to turn out, so a lot of the weapons were defective. When I look back on those days and the kind of manufacturing people were doing, it's no wonder we lost the war." (Quoted in Miyashita and Russell, 1994, pp. 154-5.)

40. Pacific Basin Reports (1972) presents evidence and observations made by a number of observers who argue that government policy-making in Japan in the early postwar period continued to be very much directed by top industrial and financial leaders, who used such industry associations as Keidanren (Federation of Economic Organizations) and Sanken (Industrial Problems Study Council) to put pressure on both the Liberal Democratic Party (LDP) and on the bureaucracy. A different point of view is that of Chalmers Johnson, who sees the bureaucracy as meeting its own needs rather than primarily responding to the needs of "clients" (such as the industrial-financial leadership, or *zaikai*). However, even Johnson acknowledges the importance of corporate contributions to the LDP (the ruling party for much of the postwar period) and the growing importance of politicians (as opposed to the bureaucracy alone) in government policy-making. In this regard, Johnson notes that Hitachi, Toshiba, Mitsubishi Electric, and Matsushita were the fourth, fifth, seventh and eighth largest political donors in the country in the mid-1980s (cf. Johnson, 1986, p. 77). The policy-making process may be "messier" than is commonly perceived outside of Japan, but the ultimate compromises between contending ministries, politicians, and large corporate interests certainly give evidence of the substantial influence of the latter.

41. In Japan, according to Kodama (1991), there was a concerted and conscious effort to create such a "grid" via such efforts as the promotion of government-sponsored research associations in the postwar period. Kodama notes, "In the United States, pre-competitive research is usually carried out at a university under the sponsorship of several private corporations. This represents a chronological concept of technological innovation, in which research begins at the scientific state and progresses through the application and development stages. In Japan, however, pre-competitive research achieved through research associations is better represented by *plotting industrial linkages on a graph of coordinates, in which the goal is to create an engineering infrastructure* as the basis for competition" (Kodama, 1991, p. 3, emphasis added).

Another interesting interpretation of these post-1961 research associations (RAs) is given in Wakasugi and Goto (1985). They see the RAs as a transitional phenomenon (i.e., of the late catch up/early frontier period), and argue that "their role has been declining as more and more collaborative research activities are now carried out by research institutions funded jointly by companies or under intercompany technology agreements" (from Odagiri and Goto, 1993, p. 88).

No matter what the future holds for government-supported research associations in Japan, the idea of the public sector trying to create a technological "grid" across enterprises and industries is an interesting one for late developing countries, as such an integrated network across the economy can help to counter tendencies toward uneven development and industrial dualism within the economy and broaden the available pool of experience and expertise from which ideas can be drawn.

42. Shigeto Tsuru, quoted in Saith (1987), p. 248.

2

The Use of Inter-Enterprise
Ties in the Development of the
Computer and Telecommunications
Industry in Japan

This chapter is intended to provide specific details about the context in which cooperative technological ties were strengthened, and then directed toward increasingly ambitious forms of innovation in the late catch up/early frontier period in Japan (i.e., in most industries, extending from the 1960s into the early 1980s). It draws on interviews and unpublished as well as published data.

The chapter begins with an overview of changing conditions of competition in the postwar period in Japan, and the general changes in firm behavior designed to meet the new challenges. It then focuses on the rise of the computer and telecommunications industry in postwar Japan, and details some of the changes in structure and behavior that occurred in the leading firms (private and public) in this emerging industry in response to the new technological requirements.

Finally, and of most importance, the chapter details the ways in which cooperative behavior changed as firms attempted to master and develop increasingly advanced technologies in this emerging industry. Contrasts are drawn between forms of cooperative behavior in the early stages of technological advance (up through the 1950s) and the new patterns that emerged in the late catch up/early frontier period. A discussion section then relates the findings to the experiences of other latecomer countries.

Characteristics of the Early Postwar "Catch Up" Period

The domestic context of the early postwar period in Japan can be characterized by the combination of extensive potential resources for economic development as a legacy of the prewar period, and a general desire after the war to use these resources to achieve economic reconstruction, and then growth and stability, as a reaction to the destruction and insecurity of the preceding years. The prewar legacy derived from both the commercial and military efforts of that period, and included a relatively educated populace, a history of close government-industry and inter-enterprise ties, publicly and privately funded universities, government laboratories and scientific institutions, and a relatively high level of technological development. Moreover, the legacy included a long history of innovation on the part of relatively strong, technologically progressive domestic firms based on the modification of imported technology.[1] (In this regard, we should note that in order to import and modify technology successfully, firms often need almost as much technological and other skills as is necessary to develop the technology itself.)

During the early postwar period, wage levels and incomes were low, and demand consisted primarily of demand for producer goods and relatively low-priced, simple and standardized consumer goods. The industrial structure came to reflect this state of domestic demand, as firms responded within protected markets with a wide range of producer goods and low-priced, simple and standardized products.

In this context, domestic firms turned to export markets as well. Given the type of commodities produced and the low wage levels that existed in Japan, the export strategy of domestic firms initially emphasized price competition in the labor-intensive end of the industrial spectrum. This resulted in the 1950s "made in Japan" stereotype of inexpensive, but relatively low quality products (with its parallels in many developing countries today).

The international context of the postwar period contributed to the growth of firms due to its openness with respect to access to markets and technology. The increasing openness of markets (particularly that of the U.S.) and the high growth rates in many economies allowed Japanese firms to expect not only a growing domestic market, but growing international markets as well. U.S. economic assistance after World War II and U.S. military procurement during the Korean War also contributed to this process by providing additional markets and foreign exchange. Moreover, of crucial importance was the fact that technology was transferred and the protection of markets in Japan was accepted by its trading partners, although not without resistance. (Contrasts can thus be made with contemporary developing countries that face no such "benefits" in the post-Cold War era, and instead face very different conditions in terms of access to technologies, resources and markets, as well as new types of competition, as will be discussed in Chapter 6.)

Government industrial policy contributed to the growth of firms in the catch up phase not only through the protection of domestic markets, but also through the subsidization of water and electricity prices and other infrastructural investments, and a strategy of promoting "key" industries, including heavy and petrochemical industries. It did this through various forms of financial and legal support (e.g., loosening antitrust regulations).[2]

The designation of "key industries" during the late catch up/early frontier period was based to a large extent on Japanese perceptions of how the more advanced industrial economies developed. As the Japanese economy developed and wages and incomes rose, demands changed in a relatively predictable way to include a wide range of new industries, confirming these expectations. Firms in Japan thus not only had technical "blueprints" for basic and supporting industries that could be imported and established in Japan, they also had a relatively clear conception of patterns of change in consumer and producer demand as the economy moved toward a higher income level. In other words, given the prior degree of industrial development and the legacy of relatively strong domestic firms, industrial expansion was able to take place, new jobs were created, a strong domestic market grew, and expectations regarding changes in consumer and producer demand were indeed met; this in turn allowed further plans for the future to be drawn and carried out.

In this way, technology was imported and adapted to the Japanese context in a fairly smooth way, and firms diversified and mastered progressively more difficult types of skills (with respect to technology, production, and marketing) throughout the late catch up period as the economy as a whole grew, and the industrial structure "shifted up" technologically through a rapid succession of new industries.[3] The prewar legacy and government policies in response to industrial needs and political pressures thus provided the domestic conditions, and the international context provided the additional markets and technologies necessary to allow this rapid expansion and succession of new industries to take place as the Japanese economy developed.[4]

Given this rapid succession of industries faced by firms in Japan, both private and public enterprises attempted to become *organizationally* and *technologically* flexible in order to respond quickly to new opportunities and move out of fields that were becoming outmoded. Through their efforts to gain this type of flexibility, the firms evolved many of the characteristics of firm organization and behavior that would be put to use once they had caught up technologically, allowing them to enter quickly into fields that are new to the world, and not just new to firms in Japan; these characteristics will be discussed in more detail below.

In addition to new opportunities and the "outmoding" process, other

conditions also forced firms to gain the flexibility to be able to continually change their fields. For example, as wages and incomes rose, firms in
Japan found it increasingly difficult to compete on the basis of price in
the labor-intensive and low technology range of industries (this as well
has obvious parallels in the recent experiences of many developing
countries—e.g., some of the Asian NICs).

These problems were compounded by (1) the growing resistance on
the part of more industrially advanced countries to the inflow of
Japanese goods, (2) international pressures for the opening up of
Japanese markets, and (3) increasing competition from developing countries. This resulted in a movement overseas of some parts of these industries (e.g., textiles, electronic components), and then a wide range of
industries. It also resulted in a further push toward the higher technology and high value added end of the industrial spectrum as firms
attempted and found that they were able to compete with foreign firms
in this range of products as well.

Japanese firms thus continued to catch up technologically in successive industries, and attempted to move away from a reliance on price
competition alone and instead compete on the basis of quality and
design as well as price in more capital-intensive and technologically
advanced industries. This movement was facilitated by the continuing
growth of the domestic market and the emergence of domestic demand
for new producer and consumer goods, including increasingly technologically sophisticated products.

The Turning Point: Innovation in Frontier Industries

Once firms in Japan had caught up technologically in frontier
industries, however, they found that their conditions of competition had
changed dramatically. At this point there were no longer "blueprints" for
development in the sense of new industries that could easily be entered
on the basis of imported technology. Moreover, these firms now posed a
threat to dominant firms in technologically advanced industries. As a
result, in recent years the new technology Japanese firms attempted to
purchase was often not made available to them unless they had equally
valuable new technology to sell in return.

Faced with these new conditions, firms in Japan were confronted with
the need to do increasingly original innovation, helping to create
altogether new products and industries, rather than simply rationalize
production or improve product design in relatively small ways.[5] In some
industries, they could no longer increase their market shares very much
by engaging in price competition or simple product differentiation alone.

In other industries, firms in Japan were still able to expand through price competition and/or product differentiation where sufficient international differences in design or in production technologies due to different patterns of investment and other practices still exist. However, even here the competitive advantage of these firms has been steadily eroded as firms from other countries (both newly industrialized as well as advanced industrial) became capable of achieving similar designs, methods to ensure uniform quality, and other cost-cutting techniques.

Japanese firms thus found themselves faced with the problems common to all large modern firms that are at the technological frontiers of their respective industries in a "developed" economy. Moreover, although the timing of this juncture differed according to the industry, for many industries it occurred during the mid-1970s. Faced with a worldwide recession, they could not rely solely on the strategy of finding new markets abroad. In response to these new requirements, the structure and behavior of firms in Japan changed over time, as did government industrial policies.

Although a complete discussion of changes in government policies will not be possible here, it should be noted that the earlier policy of "picking winners," or concentrating government support on a limited number of specific industries, no longer appears to be possible when firms have moved up to the technological frontier in frontier industries (i.e., in a "developed" economy) and need to carry out original innovation. During the earlier catch up phase, when firms competed on the basis of price (and later price, quality and design) using relatively well-known technology and adaptive research, government protection of domestic markets and a concentration on particular industries and projects was called for as domestic firms mastered this technology and economic institutions developed. As long as the markets, technology, and products demanded were well known, a focused effort on the part of both government and firms was likely to yield results, given the resources available to these firms (which initially included low wage rates, a relatively educated labor force, and the ability to modify existing commodities and technologies).

However, once the markets, technology and products are less easily identified, a more *generalized* effort on the part of large firms and a more generalized government support for research projects over the entire range of new industries, as well as government support for scientific and educational institutions and the provision of an assured market (e.g., through procurement), begin to emerge at this level of development. Just as firms find that they must experiment with a wide range of new ideas, the government comes to see its role as creating favorable conditions for investment and promoting investment and innovation in a very wide range of industries, some of which will prove to be successful and others of which will not. Moreover, at this point it is felt that both firm efforts and government support for research can no longer be on the applied and developmental side alone. In Japan, these changes ushered in the early frontier research efforts and policies of the 1970s and 1980s.

We should also note that with the maturing of the Japanese economy in this sense, U.S. and European pressures have increasingly been mounted to bring procurement and antitrust policies and other aspects of Japan's legal and political framework in line with those of other advanced industrial nations. Moreover, the Japanese public's demands for social welfare-oriented programs, rather than simply economic growth above all, have resulted in pressures to change the political and legal behavior that had favored rapid economic growth in the earlier period. Finally, and perhaps the most important of all new developments, we find that the overall slowdown in both domestic and international growth rates has put additional pressure on firms to find new ways to continue to grow.

Throughout the catch up period and into the frontier stage of innovation, then, we find that firms in Japan—in the same manner as firms everywhere—have carried over from an earlier context certain institutions and types of learned behavior that they were familiar and comfortable with, as long as those institutions and practices appeared to be effective in the new context. They also appear to have abandoned other types of institutions and practices that were found to hinder their attempts to grow and develop. In this way, enterprises in Japan were able to adapt to and in turn influence their changing context.

General Changes in Firm Structure and Behavior to Facilitate Innovation in New Fields

The process of the evolution of firms to meet the needs of an advanced industrial economy has been particularly dramatic in the Japanese case. As discussed above, the domestic industrial structure changed very rapidly in the postwar period in Japan, and firms found it necessary to learn to invest and innovate in new fields and move out of product areas that were quickly becoming outmoded. For this they had to develop a high degree of flexibility, including flexibility with respect to plant and equipment, labor, and technology.

The need to move quickly into new fields during the catch up phase of industrial development was facilitated by information provided by affiliates, customers and government agencies, among other external and internal sources of information. Flexibility with respect to plant and equipment was facilitated by subcontracting, and building in as much flexibility into "fixed" structures as possible.[6]

The "permanent employment" system posed a potential barrier to the rapid movement into new or out of "older" industries and product lines; skilled labor from other companies could not be easily hired, or permanent employees fired. However, as long as the tasks to be carried out were well-known and relatively simple, and new jobs within the company or its affiliates could be found for "permanent" employees displaced from a field being cut back or automated, as was generally true during this period, the relocating and retraining of employees for new tasks was not a major barrier to this movement. Textiles, autos, steel and shipbuilding were some of the industries that faced the need to relocate or retrain labor during this period.

The fact that labor was defined in terms of firms rather than skills can even be said to have aided this process of moving into new industries. This identification of employees with particular firms is reflected in the organization of labor into company, rather than craft or industrial, unions. These unions generally have been receptive to technological change and shifts in the job structure as long as employees were retrained, relocated or compensated adequately. (This pattern also dovetails with the practice of training employees within the firm in Japan, as opposed to the more common U.S. pattern of expecting employees to train or retrain themselves, or risk losing their jobs.)

Moreover, the practice of at least "permanent" employees staying with one company until retirement in Japan aided the firm's efforts to become more innovative in new fields and achieve technological flexibility in a highly significant way. Malerba observed that the conservatism and "bureaucratic" nature of large European companies appears to arise from the fact that managers are associated with, and therefore have a vested interest in, particular product lines and technologies; new personnel having a knowledge of new products and technologies may be brought in if major changes are to be undertaken by the firm, and therefore the present management is very resistant to innovation unless the changes are absolutely necessary.[7] In Japanese companies, however, managers and executives, and even non-managerial employees, aggressively sought out new ideas during this period as their success was associated with the success of the entire enterprise, rather than being connected with particular product lines or technologies. This difference is one important factor in explaining the extent to which large Japanese firms were able to move quickly into new fields, and avoid the problems of bureaucracy and corporate conservatism that theorists have assumed must emerge as an organization grows large.[8]

During the late catch up/early frontier period, the problem of achieving technological flexibility was addressed by internal transformation, as well as to some extent by interfirm and government-industry efforts, as detailed in the following chapters. As the technology became increasingly difficult and required more expertise and new knowledge, both organization and behavior with respect to the research effort were required to change.

For example, as firms in Japan diversified into promising new fields, the organization of research and development inevitably became more complex as the number of research divisions representing different subfields in the company grew. The rise of the central research institute, which focuses its efforts on relatively basic research and plans and coordinates the more applied research done in the different divisions, was also a natural outgrowth of this process. In some ways, this was the research equivalent of the rise of the central planning unit on the managerial side as the firms diversified over time. It allowed new areas of knowledge to be incorporated quickly into the research structure and allowed different research divisions to cooperate on new technology in a highly flexible way.[9]

Interviews carried out by the author indicated a number of other changes in firm behavior as well. (These interviews began with responses to Questionnaire 1 in the Appendix—i.e., the "Questionnaire on Innovation and Organizational Change.") For example, as the need to do original innovation in new fields became increasingly clear, firms found it critically important to build up a strong technical staff and research structure that could cover all of the important fields and scientific disciplines necessary for the whole range of basic, applied and developmental research involved in this effort (the timing of this expansion depended upon the industry, but in many the expansion began in the latter half of the 1960s). Far greater expenditures on research and new product development became necessary, and eventually the need to hire technical staff with particular skills encouraged the hiring of more technical employees with postgraduate training and encouraged greater mobility among technical personnel. This is still very small compared to the mobility of technical personnel in other advanced industrial countries, and is not statistically significant yet in Japan; however, this phenomenon is an important enough trend to command widespread attention in Japan in recent years.

Interviews further indicated that ties with university scientists and engineers have remained largely informal: contractual work continued to be arranged on the basis of contacts, rather than through more formal channels. However, firms have begun to search for ways to formalize and systematize this process by attempting to conduct ongoing research with foreign or domestic universities and research institutions that are more oriented toward commercial applications, as this form of cooperation for basic research became more important over time. (MIT was cited as a prime candidate for such ventures at the time of the interviews; UC Berkeley was also mentioned.) Ties with government research laboratories in Japan have also remained important to firms in frontier industries, although the relative volume of research sponsored by these labs has declined with the expansion of research carried on within the firms themselves. (The research done in cooperation with the laboratories has generally complemented, rather than substituted for or duplicated, research done within the firms, as will be explained below.) As the need for "pure" scientific research increases in Japan—as opposed to the more commercially oriented "basic" research needed by enterprises in the early frontier period—the importance of government research laboratories and university research is also likely to increase.

Finally, with the need to do highly original innovation, particularly in new fields, interfirm cooperative research emerged as an even more important means of facilitating innovation than was true in the past. In the early postwar years formal group ties, along with less formal groupings, often formed the basis of cooperation that allowed *new industries* to be quickly established; this involved primarily cooperation between firms in different industries. Cooperation between competitors was also important as a means to *import, adapt, and improve upon imported technology* during these early postwar years (the steel and shipbuilding industries were prime examples of this type of cooperation).

At a somewhat later stage, firms also worked with their affiliates in different industries to move out of *declining industries*. For example, when the textile industry was on the decline in Japan due to increased domestic costs of production and competition from low-wage countries abroad, Japanese textile-based firms not only worked with affiliates in order to move their plants overseas, but also worked with affiliates in other industries in order to enter into such new fields as optical fibers, certain subfields of the chemical industry, and even cosmetics.

Finally, during the late catch up/early frontier stage, with the need to undertake far more technologically difficult, costly and risky projects in new fields, cooperative technological ties—both between firms in different industries (and not necessarily group members) and between firms in the same industry (i.e., competitors)—have taken on new forms and significance for the generation of new products and industries. Of these new forms, cooperation for frontier innovation attracted the most attention and was the most controversial of all because it posed the greatest challenge to previously dominant enterprises in advanced industrial countries.

The use of inter-enterprise cooperation for technological catch up and then early forms of innovation can be illustrated through an examination of the combined computer and telecommunications industry in Japan. Again, our primary concern will be with the period extending roughly from the 1960s through the 1980s, as enterprises sought out new responses to the entirely new set of challenges they came to face in this period as they approached the technological frontier.

The Emergence of the Combined
Computer and Telecommunications Industry in Japan

The computer and telecommunications industry is an outgrowth of the merging of two previously distinct fields. For present purposes, it can be considered to be one, rather than two or three separate industries (including semiconductors, computers and telecommunications equipment) because of the increasing difficulty in separating these products and technologies, and because the major firms in this industry in Japan cover all of these fields and compete against each other on the basis of the sum of these diversified skills (although the relative emphases and particular product lines differ from firm to firm). Their different ranges of research projects and uses of interfirm cooperation reflect their different strengths and interests.

The "Big Six" manufacturers in this industry at the time were Fujitsu, Hitachi, Mitsubishi Electric, NEC, Oki Electric Industry, and Toshiba. They entered this new combined industry from two main concentrations: telecommunications equipment in the cases of Fujitsu, NEC, and Oki Electric Industry, and general electrical goods and machinery (both light and heavy) in the cases of Hitachi, Mitsubishi Electric and Toshiba. Many other firms have entered segments of this industry from a wide variety of industries, ranging from pen and camera manufacturing (e.g., Pentel and Canon, respectively, both of which moved into office automation equipment) to textile manufacturing (e.g., Mitsubishi Rayon, which moved into optical fibers). They did this for a wide variety of reasons, including competition from developing countries, stagnant demand, and the perception of new investment opportunities. However, these firms tended to compete only in restricted segments, while the "core" of the combined industry was dominated by the large and highly diversified firms.

It should be kept in mind that although these firms have dominated the computer and telecommunications industry in Japan, their size (in terms of either sales or assets) was in the late catch up period consistently much smaller than the U.S.-based firms that dominated the world market at that time. For example, NEC's sales in the 1980s were one-fourth to one-third of ITT's, one-sixth of IBM's, and one-seventh of AT&T's sales.

Fujitsu and Hitachi were somewhat larger and more diversified, but even if their affiliates in the industry are included, they had less than one-half of ITT's sales and less than one-third of IBM's during this time period. (Of course, the inclusion of affiliates outside of the industry would change this picture considerably.)

The manner of entrance into the industry can be illustrated by examining the cases of NEC and Toshiba, keeping in mind that the pattern differs somewhat for each case.[10] NEC, like Fujitsu and Oki Electric, began in the telecommunications industry, selling largely to the Ministry of Communications.

Like Fujitsu, NEC was established as a joint venture between a Japanese company and a foreign corporation (Western Electric and Nichiden Shokai, a trading company, in NEC's case, and Siemens and Furukawa Electric in Fujitsu's case). During the 1920s, NEC received financial support from the Sumitomo zaibatsu bank, and during the 1930s was made into a fully "Japanese" private company and was renamed Sumitomo Communications Industrial Company in 1937. (Many independent companies became zaibatsu affiliates by having to borrow heavily from zaibatsu banks when they found themselves in financial trouble, particularly during recessions.) During the Second World War the company engaged in the joint development of telephone equipment with researchers from the Ministry of Communications. This continued on after the war in the form of cooperation with Nippon Telegraph and Telephone researchers, particularly regarding large-scale telecommunications systems.

After the war, NEC's name was changed back to its original form ("Nippon Denki Kabushiki Kaisha," or "Nippon Electric Company," now known as NEC), but it remained affiliated with the Sumitomo business group. It also further developed its own "industrial group" consisting of 142 subsidiaries, and numerous other affiliates, by the end of the catch up period. These connections helped NEC to respond to the relative stagnation of demand for telephone equipment after the war by branching out into new non-government markets to become a "general telecommunications and electronics manufacturer." From 1955 to 1965, NEC added equipment, systems, parts and material for primarily telecommunications and industrial applications. As part of the postwar "boom" in radios and household electrical appliances, NEC also ventured into consumer goods production, but decided to leave this up to its subsidiary—Shin Nippon Denki—and focus instead on the other markets that were thought to have more potential. (According to persons interviewed, NEC was later to regret this decision because of its growing need for experience and expertise in consumer-oriented fields as well.)

Because of its focus on goods for industrial rather than consumer use, NEC entered into transistor production relatively late (transistors were used initially for consumer goods in Japan), but it eventually began to use transistors and then integrated circuits for industrial use. By 1958 NEC had developed its first computer, cooperating with Honeywell. It also moved into microwave and satellite communications, cooperating in the latter with Hughes.

Between 1965 and 1975 the computer industry came to be recognized as an important field and began to receive substantial government support. This was a period of rapid growth for electronics as a whole, and the growth in NEC's sales revenues helped it to diversify further into new fields. Finally, by the late 1970s NEC's focus had shifted to the incorporation and development of new technologies as a response to the near-completion of the catch up process, the liberalization of trade, and scientific and technological developments in the rapidly emerging combined industry of computers and telecommunications. NEC continued to diversify and vertically integrate, and focused its research on projects ranging from devices through individual pieces of equipment to complex systems. In addition to establishing a centralized planning division and a central research institute within a general decentralized research structure, sales divisions were reorganized into one section so that products could be unified as part of the unification of the computer and telecommunications fields and the other new fields emerging from the new combined industry.[11]

Toshiba's experience was in many ways similar to that of NEC, but, like Mitsubishi Electric and Hitachi, it moved into the new industry from a position as a "general electrical goods manufacturer." (It also makes telecommunications equipment, but has not specialized as much in that branch of the industry.) It will therefore be used to illustrate the second pattern of entrance into this industry.

Toshiba began as a manufacturer of telegraph equipment in 1875. It received financial support from Mitsui Bank in 1893 and has been affiliated with the Mitsui business group ever since, even though the ties are not as strong as "core" Mitsui members. It also developed its own industrial group, consisting of thirty-seven subsidiaries and sixty affiliates by the end of the catch up period. The sharp rise in military demand during the various wars (Russo-Japanese War, World War I and World War II) helped the company to expand and move from a concentration on light to heavy electrical machinery, and Toshiba modified and expanded its affiliations accordingly.

In the early postwar years, the rising demand for consumer goods (fans, mixers, and other household electrical appliances) and the demand for heavy electrical machinery during the Korean War years, particularly from the steel and electric power industries, helped Toshiba to expand. The 1955-1960 period of rapid growth allowed the company to continue to diversify in both of these directions.

In response to a relative slowdown in the growth rate of demand after 1961, Toshiba decided to concentrate more on new product development and raising the quality of its products. Toshiba strengthened its ties with Ishikawajima Harima Heavy Industries and other firms with different specializations "under pressure from technological innovation, greater competition and internationalization."[12] From 1965-1975 the company moved more forcefully into such new fields as computers, calculators, and integrated circuits (in the same way as transistors, the latter were first used in consumer products), as well as into nuclear power, housing, and "space development."

By the 1970s Toshiba, like NEC and most of the other Big Six companies, had developed broad-based technology as a "general electronics manufacturer," a term that includes the fields of computers and telecommunications, home electrical appliances, heavy electrical machinery, and industrial-use electronics. Like the others, it also came to emphasize frontier technology, new product development, and systems-type products. It decided to withdraw from unprofitable fields, and established its "East Wind Association" to "raise the mutual consciousness of group development" in view of the need for more Toshiba group (and Mitsui group) coordination.[13]

Each of the "Big Six" companies had its own technological and product emphases. Fujitsu specialized more on computer equipment, Oki Electric was relatively small and focused more on telecommunications equipment, Hitachi maintained a very highly diversified structure, and Mitsubishi Electric emphasized electronic industrial machinery along with home electronics and heavy electrical machinery.

No matter what its relative strengths, each of these companies (with the exception of Oki Electric) has attempted to "cover" the key fields of electronics; this includes the increasingly central and rapidly expanding computer and telecommunications industry, as well as various industrial and consumer goods industries related to this core. They did this in order to maintain a constant stream of new products through a mixture of their own efforts, purchasing agreements, cooperation with Nippon Telegraph and Telephone (formerly Public) Corporation and other government laboratories, and cooperation with other private firms, both within their industrial and business groups and outside of these groups. Their efforts to develop new products and technologies were further aided by ready loans from group and other banks, together with government grants and subsidies, government and public corporation procurement, credit allocation, and special tax benefits. (Business group and industrial group affiliations as of the late catch up and early frontier period can be found in most studies of keiretsu ties—including, for example, *Industrial Groupings in Japan*.[14] It is important to keep in mind that in most listings of group ties, only the largest affiliates are shown, and the complete lists of keiretsu ties are far longer.)

To end this profile of the major firms in the Japanese computer and telecommunications industry during the late catch up and early frontier period, we must note the important role of the Nippon Telegraph and Telephone Corporation in this industry (this formerly "public corporation" was "privatized" on April 1, 1985).[15] NTT was established in 1952 as an outgrowth of the old Ministry of Communications. One part of the Ministry's research laboratory was split off in 1948 to become the Electro-Technical Laboratory of MITI, and the other part became NTT's laboratory after 1952.

As a public corporation, NTT held a legal monopoly on telecommunications networks in Japan. Like AT&T, it designed its own equipment, but had no manufacturing facilities. Its resources for research have been recognized for decades as being very strong. In 1980 it had over 2,200 research staff in its four laboratories and operated on a budget of over 75 billion yen (approximately $333 million). This was still small relative to Bell Labs which had a $1.6 billion budget in 1981 and had 22,500 people on its payrolls at the time, nearly half of them researchers, but it stood in sharp contrast to the 566 research staff and nine billion yen budget of MITI's ETL, or the 500-1000 researchers and (up to) 30-40 billion yen budget of most of the large private companies at that time.

Until recent years, NTT worked primarily with NEC, Hitachi, Oki Electric and Fujitsu (some say in that order) and their subsidiaries, along with Furukawa Electric, Fujikura Cable Works, Iwasaki Communications, Dainichi-Nippon Cables, and Showa Electric Wire and Cable companies. These have been known as the "NTT Family" or "Denden Group," even though NTT had nearly 300 suppliers in all. As a response to domestic and international pressures, bidding for NTT contracts was opened up, but it appears that the closest cooperative work continued to be done between NTT and its main suppliers of the past, particularly the "big four" of the NTT Family together with Toshiba, which became an important supplier in 1983. The importance of NTT's technological resources for private firms will be discussed in detail below. (The advanced state of NTT's technology has also been recognized by foreign government agencies and private firms, including IBM and Bell Labs, which negotiated cross-licensing agreements and mutual exchanges of information with NTT in recent years.)

Changing Forms of Inter-Enterprise Cooperation
in the Computer and Telecommunications Industry

An important feature of the process of innovation in the computer and telecommunications industry, in the same manner as other industries in Japan, has been its use of interfirm cooperation as a way to speed up and make possible the development of frontier products and technology. As indicated above, Japanese firms have used cooperation between private firms, as well as cooperation between universities or government agencies and private firms, to develop new products and enter into new industries.

The form and nature of this type of cooperation for innovation changed as Japanese industries moved from the catch up to the original innovation stage. In the catch up stage, when technology was imported and/or modified, cooperation was a relatively simple process, as technicians and managers of different firms had to meet only as often as was required to make sure that the specifications in the imported or modified technology were feasible. In these cases firms might be brought together by a government agency or a central coordinator, such as a leader in a business group. This was the type of cooperative behavior that predominated in the prewar and early postwar periods, often resulting in creative adaptations or improvements upon the technologies, but not of the strikingly ambitious type that would follow in the frontier period.

The advantages of this type of cooperation were clear. Besides requiring large capital outlays which could be met more easily through cooperation, the new industries often had no immediate technological predecessors in the Japanese economy. Under these circumstances, a wide range of companies with different backgrounds and technological skills could set up the new industry faster than could a single company from a related but significantly different field.

In contrast, innovation *near* or *at* the technological frontier involves different problems, and cooperation between firms becomes a much more difficult and significant issue. In a general sense, cooperation at the frontier is not simply a means of planning, developing and fitting together parts of a system. With frontier research, firms also have to decide jointly on the very goals to be met and the best means to achieve those goals, as will be explained in more detail below.

Another important difference between cooperation in the earlier catch up versus the late catch up/early frontier stage was a locational change in cooperative research. In Japan's early postwar years the locus of efforts to develop *advanced* technologies appears to have been primarily, though not exclusively, centered in universities and in government labs, as firms tended to be more concerned with products and technologies that could easily be commercialized, and worked only secondarily on advanced technologies. ("Routine" cooperative efforts took place mostly within the confines of individual cooperating firms.) Japanese firms were still in the catch up stage in most industries at this time, and markets for existing products were expanding rapidly, requiring most of their attention.

Cooperation to develop advanced technologies under these circumstances took place between *individual* firms and university and government labs. For example, one of the first major computer projects in Japan combined the resources of the University of Tokyo and Tokyo Shibaura Co., Ltd. (Toshiba) for the development of the vacuum tube-based Todai Automatic Computer (TAC), begun in 1951 and completed in 1959. Similarly, the development of relay-type mechanical computers was carried out initially by government-industry cooperation in the form of a joint effort of the Electro-Technical Laboratory (ETL, of MITI) and Fujitsu, Ltd. that resulted in the ETL Mark-I and ETL Mark-II computers (completed in 1951 and 1955, respectively). Other projects of the 1950s subsequently following this cooperative pattern include such joint efforts as those between Kyoto University and Toshiba (for the Kyoto University-Toshiba pilot computer), Tohoku University and NEC (for the SENAC computer), ETL and NEC (for the NEAC), and Nippon Telegraph and Telephone Public Corporation (NTT) and Fujitsu (for the Musashino-1 computer). These projects were able to combine the universities' and government labs' skills in relatively basic research with the firms' skills in "basic" and relatively "applied" research and development.

(We should note that the distinction between relatively "basic" and relatively "applied" types of research has been particularly difficult in this field as most of the research until recently was oriented toward specific goals. For present purposes, we will make this distinction based upon the amount of new knowledge required and the proximity to commercialization. "Basic" or "fundamental" research here thus indicates research dealing with more "scientific" principles which is nonetheless directed toward a general commercial goal; this is the definition of basic research that was commonly employed by the firms during this time period, in contrast to the NSF definition, which was generally referred to as "pure" research by Japanese firms. Basic research in this sense meant that which is not expected to show results for at least four to five years, whereas applied research was expected to show results within two years, according to persons interviewed. In addition, the term "frontier applied research" is used here to indicate path-breaking research of a more application-oriented nature. Projects involving both basic and applied research are characterized below by the *predominant* type of research, and both need to be differentiated from "pure" research.)

Over time, the locus of research shifted away from either individual or cooperative efforts centered in university or government laboratories, and increasingly toward private corporations as the latter begin to contribute a growing proportion of the country's basic (in the sense discussed above) as well as applied research. University and government labs continued to play a highly significant role in the innovation process, as did cooperation between these organizations and individual private firms. This has been true particularly when "basic" research has been the focus of attention.

However, there is no doubt that the *relative* contribution of private as well as public enterprises in highly original—and not yet relatively routine—innovation increased notably from the 1960s on. It is at this stage—when firms take on greater research responsibilities for the development of fundamentally new products and technologies—that cooperation between different and even competing firms, rather than simple cooperation between individual firms and university or government labs, can emerge as an important force for innovation on the technological frontier, as it has in the Japanese case.[16]

This change in the locus of innovation appears to be attributable to two related developments. First, the elaboration of the firm structure and expansion of internal research facilities during the postwar period were important developments in Japan, as noted above. Second, the emergence of important new industries in the world economy during the postwar period, together with the possibility of Japanese firms participating in their development, contributed to the shift of research in these fields away from university and government labs and toward the firms themselves. As an industry develops, i.e., as the market for those goods becomes known and the technology moves away from early efforts toward a form closer to commercialization, firms generally begin to take on a larger role in this process.

This clearly happened in the case of computer technology. In view of the growing demand for data processing and with the introduction of the transistorized computer in 1958 heralding the second generation of computers, the industry moved from an early experimental stage toward a more clearly-defined if still rapidly evolving stage of research and development, and firms took on a larger role in the research effort. The shift in the locus of research activity in the more general computer and telecommunications industry undoubtedly reflected both of these processes, i.e., the expansion of the firms' internal research facilities, and their interest in the new technologies and product areas (their interest being in part a reflection of the stage of development of the new industry as well as their growing ability to compete in high technology fields).

In line with these changes, government funds for research moved somewhat away from a concentration on funding universities and government research laboratories toward increased support for research carried out in private as well as public enterprises. In 1975, government support for a wide variety of research activities of the private sector—including the development of industrial technology—accounted for 40.9% of the government science and technology budget; by 1980 the figure had risen to 47.8%, and it continued to rise steadily, given that each of the ministries and other government agencies came to view increasingly basic forms of research as critical to the future of the Japanese economy.

As part of the new emphasis on support for research carried out in private firms, the government also increased dramatically its support for cooperative research involving several private firms. According to one estimate, less than 10% of "conditional loans" or "subsidies" (which require repayment only if profits are made) went toward cooperative research in 1955, whereas by 1963 this had risen to 41%, and by 1983 a new policy dictated that these funds should go only toward cooperative research.[17] By the 1980s, then, government-supported cooperative research was firmly established, supplementing the more widespread but less well-publicized forms of cooperative research that involved little or no government financing.

As another indication of government interest in promoting cooperative as well as individual research, the efforts of various ministries to fund relatively basic research in the telecommunications industry led in 1985 to the creation of the Key Technological Research Promotion Center (Kiban Gijutsu Kenkyu Sokushin Senta). This center was established as a joint public-private sector venture that would, among other functions, help finance risky projects and create joint research projects involving two or more companies.[18]

The late 1980s and early 1990s saw a number of more "advanced" frontier cooperative projects, some of which have been detailed in recent studies (several such studies will be noted in Chapters 3-5). These projects have led to debates regarding how much actual cooperative research was carried out, and whether these highly complex and expensive research projects could or could not have been carried by individual firms acting separately or together without government financing—i.e., whether public funds were put to good use in these cases. Part of the controversy surrounding these projects stems from the fact that at this "later" frontier stage government support can no longer be justified as necessary for a generalized catch up effort, adding to the entire technological and knowledge base available for local use, but rather will tend instead to aid *individual* already-advanced enterprises (which may already be shedding their "local" identities) in their efforts to take the lead in international markets.

Leaving aside for now the highly controversial issues of whether public funds were well spent and whether the government should be funding this research at all (we will return to these concerns in Chapter 6), we can say that cooperative research in a wide variety of forms (*with or without government funding*) in fact became an increasingly important factor in the development of late catch up and early frontier technologies in Japan. This appears to be true not only for the computer and telecommunications industry, but also for the other major new industries, to judge from the examples collected in the *Keiretsu no Kenkyu* volumes and other sources. Firms continued to work with personnel in university and government labs, and as we will see were often brought together under the auspices of government-initiated projects, but by the late catch up/early frontier period it was the firms themselves rather than universities or government labs that did the bulk of the necessary research and initiated cooperative projects for the development of new technologies, often utilizing group ties (in *inter-industry* forms of research), or working through government agencies and public enterprises (particularly for *intra-industry* forms of research involving direct competitors).

It is important to keep in mind that most of the basic and applied research was done within individual firms, and most of the cooperative research efforts consisted of cooperation between only two firms.[19] However, the most costly, risky and ambitious projects came to involve cooperation among several firms (particularly the larger, more dominant firms in their respective industries), and in some ways these were the most important in terms of future orientation and the amount of new knowledge generated, for reasons to be discussed below.

It is this type of interfirm cooperation for late catch up and early frontier innovation that will be the concern of the following three chapters. They will focus on the ways in which cooperation between independent firms, both within the same industry and across different industries, and involving both public and private enterprises, has been used in Japan for purposes of rapid technological catch up and then original technological innovation, through an examination of the computer and telecommunications industry and related industries as an illustrative example. They will not be concerned with cases in which firms as suppliers simply received specifications for products to be made and sold to other firms, as this involved very little cooperative research (this also applies to "co-producers" that simply divided up a product line or stages of product development between themselves). These chapters are also not concerned with inter-enterprise cooperation—whether between domestic firms or between domestic and foreign firms—for the establishment of new industries based on well-known technology. They are not concerned with cases of inter-enterprise cooperation that aided firms in declining or "stagnant" industries to move into other established industries, thus involving little original innovation. Finally, these chapters do not deal in any detail with cooperation between individual firms and public corporations, universities or government labs, even though this is an interesting topic in itself.

The significance of interfirm cooperation for late catch up and early frontier innovation lies in its potential as a means by which firms attempt to exercise more control over the process of innovation, particularly in new fields, by bringing together researchers with the required knowledge and experiences under favorable conditions. Moreover, to the extent that *domestic* enterprises (both private and public) in late developing economies engage in cooperative activities with one another, this may aid in the development of the country's *relative* technological "self-reliance" and allow new technologies to be developed that help to meet local needs in a way that cannot be met through the continual importation of technologies and ideas designed for entirely different social and economic conditions.[20]

Further Discussion

In this chapter we have briefly traced the ways in which firms in Japan changed from being producers of relatively low-wage, low-quality commodities toward—out of desire and necessity (given changes in the national and international economies)—a focus on the development of new, high quality products and technologies. Parallels with other countries (e.g., many of the Asian NICs and, in some significant ways, to the next NICs) can be drawn, as these economies attempt to overcome the last hurdles to their transition from developing country status into that of advanced industrial economies. Judging from the Japanese case, as well as that of the early developers, these economies should ultimately find themselves "caught up" or at least in most sectors highly advanced technologically, with their economies settling into lower growth rates, higher wage levels, increased public demands, and other economic social and political attributes associated with "mature" economies.

For some countries, potential barriers to this transition might include those resulting from international pressures to open markets prematurely (in contrast with the Japanese case, for example); the possibility of continued technological dependence without sufficient local innovative capability; and potential restrictions on access to markets and advanced technologies: these and other issues will be taken up in more detail in Chapter 6. Nonetheless, for those capable of building up local (national) innovative strengths, their enterprises—both public and private—are likely to face the need to master successive new technologies and move up rapidly through the different rungs on the industrial and technological "ladder." They will also need to develop their own creative solutions to meet local technological needs. For this purpose, the enterprises will have to build in some of the features discussed here, particularly those institutional characteristics designed to create maximum flexibility in order to allow them to come up with creative solutions to new problems.

In this process, the ability to engage in cooperative technological efforts can be an important attribute. This includes, in the early stages of technological advance, simple forms of cooperation involving two or more enterprises, or cooperation involving an enterprise and a university or government laboratory, supplementing initial international transfers of technology and then expanded in-house research efforts.

Judging from the Japanese case, cooperative research for advanced technologies during the late catch up/early frontier stage may then tend to shift out of the realm of university and government laboratories (although their contribution remains important and is likely to grow as more "pure" research is desired). In other words, as an economy moves into the late catch up/early frontier stage, cooperative research may move increasingly into the research facilities of private and public enterprises, which become more sophisticated and extensive in response to the perceived need to master and develop new products and technologies.

The variety of cooperative research projects becomes particularly striking during the late catch up/early frontier period: the predominant small-scale efforts involving cooperation between individual enterprises, or an enterprise and research institution, can be complemented by both large- and small-scale efforts involving a number of enterprises in a "group" project or procurement context, as well as large-scale efforts involving coordination by a government organization, among other forms of cooperation. This wide range of efforts, complementing firms' in-house research activities, can give each enterprise a broad spectrum of experiences and capabilities, and the multiple and often overlapping research efforts tend to result in a "grid" or increasingly complex network of technologically interlinked enterprises that can conduct research and developmental activities separately or together, as the new challenges demand. As a result of the accumulation of these experiences, participating enterprises find that they have built up over time a wide range of direct and indirect relationships with other enterprises (public and private, including affiliates, subcontractors, independents, and even direct competitors in some cases), from which information and expertise can be drawn if conditions favor further cooperative efforts.

It is not always easy to establish such ongoing relationships involving mutual trust, as the following chapter will demonstrate. However, in at least some of the late developing countries, the potential is there for the development of well-integrated technological networks involving local public and private enterprises and a wide range of research institutions. These networks could, under the right conditions, be put to very socially beneficial uses (e.g., rather than simply helping already powerful individual enterprises gain a "competitive edge" in international markets), and come up with creative innovations that meet local needs, avoiding both "technological dependence" and the disruptive effects of importing technologies and practices developed within and for an entirely different social and economic context.

The following three chapters will present specific accounts of cases of cooperative research in the late catch up/early frontier period in Japan. Discussion sections, and the final chapter, will continue to relate these findings explicitly to issues of late development and technological advance.

Notes

1. Cf. Nakamura (1981), and other general sources regarding these points. For a statistical overview of innovation in the early postwar decades, cf. Uno (1984), and the Science and Technology Agency's annual Kagaku Gijutsu Hakusho and Kagaku Gijutsu Yoran ("White Paper on Science and Technology" and "Indicators of Science and Technology," respectively).

2. For more on changing government industrial policies in the late catch up/early frontier period (again, roughly the 1960s through the early 1980s) cf., among other sources, Dore (1983), Gresser (1980), Magaziner and Hout (1980), MITI (1981), OECD (1972), OECD (1978), Patrick (1986), Patrick and Rohlen (1987), Peck (1983), Peck and Goto (1981), Saxonhouse (1981), U.S. General Accounting Office (1982a, 1982b), and Wheeler, Janow and Pepper (1982). For counter-arguments to the idea that Japan's industrial policies (including science and technology policies) have been nearly "perfect" during this period, cf. Komiya, Okuno and Suzumura (1988), and the articles in this volume by Goto and Wakasugi ("Technology Policy") and Imai ("Industrial Policy and Technological Innovation") in particular.

More recent accounts of industrial policy in Japan indicate a somewhat more distant relationship between government agencies and private enterprises once the catch up period was over (i.e., when there were no longer relatively straightforward "blueprints" to follow, and private enterprises wanted greater autonomy in the globalized economy); these changes will be discussed in more detail below.

3. We should note that the idea of "catch up," as used here, implies not only the movement up to the international standard in particular technologies, but also the transformation and widening of the economy up through the different levels of the industrial structure and structure of demand, as incomes grow and needs—for both producer and consumer goods—change. In this sense, the "catch up" period implies a great deal of room for growth in the economy, as well as the existence of rough "blueprints" for industrial and technological transformation based on the experiences of other countries. (In this way, the U.S. can be said to have "caught up" to the example set by the U.K. in the late 19th and early 20th centuries, but we cannot say that the U.S. would now need to go through a new catch up phase even if the country were to fall behind others in certain *specific* technologies: the economy has already been fundamentally "widened" and "transformed.")

4. Theorists concerned with Kondratieff waves would note the favorable expansionary phase of the early postwar period as new technologies emerged and markets expanded. Others would point to the market conditions created by the Cold War era (with its successive wars and other "requirements"), while still others would point to the product life cycle characteristics of this era, as contributing to conditions that helped Japanese enterprises catch up technologically and enter into new international markets. (Related to this last point, "riding the product life cycle" has been used to describe the process of transforming or improving upon ideas and technologies—e.g., adopting new product ideas developed elsewhere, and then altering a product line to meet new needs—before competitors, and in this case even the original innovators, think of doing so. This type of rapid and flexible response to the perception of new uses and needs was said to give Japanese manufacturers—including their innovative smaller affiliates and subcontractors—an edge in a wide range of industries during this period.)

5. The concept of "originality" here centers on the amount of new knowledge that is necessary for the new product or industry. An effort that involves a great deal of basic and applied as well as developmental research can be considered to be highly original; however, the simple extension of existing technology must be considered to be less original because there is less new knowledge created in this effort.

In the development of integrated circuits, for example, the movement toward large scale integration was considered to be a relatively simple extension of existing technology for Japanese firms, whereas the movement from large scale integration to very large scale integration is thought to have required a good deal of new knowledge, both of a relatively basic and applied nature. The development of more advanced computers has required far more basic as well as applied and developmental research, and thus has been expected to produce far more new knowledge than in previous efforts; these therefore involve attempts to carry out highly "original" forms of innovation. (This is clearly a more difficult and unpredictable process, as we have seen in the fifth generation computer case and other examples from recent decades.)

6. For example, Japanese auto companies pioneered the building of plants that

can be easily put up or taken down, and then developed a production process that reduces change-over time, allowing a different model to be assembled in a matter of minutes.

7. Malerba (1983), and personal communication.

8. Firms in Japan have for some time been facing the problem of a slowdown in the rate of advancement of managerial employees as the firms' growth rates slow. Entering employees may not be able to advance as fast or as far as in previous decades, producing employee dissatisfaction. Subcontractors and other non-"permanent" employees are also placed in a far worse position in a period of economic slowdown. Nonetheless, this may not necessarily result in resistance to new technologies; in fact, the opposite may be true if the new technology is seen as a way to secure new employment opportunities, and all may have incentives to work together in this process.

9. Research was centralized in one laboratory throughout the early part of this century in most firms, given that a relatively small amount of research was being undertaken at that time. However, as more fields were added to the company's range of expertise, each field typically came to have its own research division.

At NEC, for example, research was initially centralized, but by 1949 had been decentralized and divided up according to field (telegraph, wireless equipment, transmission equipment, and vacuum tubes). With the postwar movement into a wide range of new fields, the increasing volume of research, and the adding on of technical divisions for each field, research eventually had to be reorganized in order to coordinate all of these activities. Gradually, a central research organization came into being (it existed formally by 1965 at NEC) to conduct the bulk of relatively basic and applied research in its own laboratories, and coordinate the more applied and developmental research being done in each division. In 1980 the company's centralized research division was subdivided into one division carrying out "basic technology" research, and another handling research on "production technology and productivity." For details on these changes, cf., for example, NEC (1972, 1980) as well as other company histories.

10. The following information regarding NEC and Toshiba is drawn from interviews, the *Nihon no Kigyo* series (Kato and Noda, eds., 1980a and b), and company histories dealing with the decades of change through the 1980s.

11. Kato and Noda (1980a), pp. 8-47.

12. Kato and Noda (1980b), p. 32.

13. Ibid., p. 37. This summary is taken from pp. 8-39.

14. Dodwell Marketing Consultants publishes this data periodically, as do many other business-oriented publishers.

15. As Johnson notes, "English-speaking observers like to refer to this development as 'privatization' even though, in fact, all shares of the new NTT are under the control of the government and only a portion of them are being sold to the public (none to foreigners) over a five-year period." Cf. Johnson (1986, p. 5; he also cites *The Economist* (London), December 21, 1985, pp. 71-74, on "privatization").

16. As noted above, "pure" scientific research was less of a concern to the enterprises and government agencies during the late catch up/early frontier

period, but the relative underfunding of this type of research has been an issue of late, and the funding for institutions pursuing this type of research is likely to increase in the future.

17. Cf. Samuels (1987), pp. 35-36.

18. Cf. Johnson (1986) regarding the details of this center's activities, and the political tussles between MITI, the Ministry of Posts and Telecommunications (MPT), and the Ministry of Finance, that led to its creation.

19. It has been estimated that in the 1980s two-thirds of all research projects was conducted by firms alone, half of the remaining one-third was interfirm research, and that the rest involved collaboration between firms and national labs, universities, and other research institutes. From Rokuhara (1985), p. 32; quoted in Samuels (1987), p. 54. (It is further estimated that four-fifths of all cooperative research is *inter-industry* in nature, as will be discussed in the following chapters.) Moreover, it was estimated that over 90% of all cooperative research involved only two firms and was done without government help (ibid., p. 39). However, judging from the cases of cooperative research cited in the *Keiretsu no Kenkyu* volumes, cooperative projects have grown over time not only in number, but also in size, involving greater amounts of funding and a greater number of participants than was true in earlier decades. This has been particularly true in industries that have been attempting to do frontier types of innovation.

20. For an example of the starkly disruptive effects and social costs of imported technologies, see, among other sources, Mir and Doane (1995). These costs are often seen in economies that have not yet effectively confronted the need for the development of a more locally-oriented technology and knowledge base due to the heavy emphasis on the importation of international ideas and technologies, without the systematic local transformation and adaptation of these technologies.

3

Cooperation Between Firms in the Same Industry: Case Studies Involving Applied Research

Introduction to the Case Studies

In order to analyze the changing forms of interfirm cooperation and the role it has played in innovation in the computer and telecommunications industry, we will examine several of the major cooperative innovative efforts of the late catch up and early frontier period in Japan in this and the following chapters. The more applied research efforts of the 1960s and 1970s, both successful and relatively unsuccessful, will be compared to the relatively basic research projects that emerged in the 1970s and 1980s.

At first, several projects involving cooperation between firms in the *same* industry—i.e., competitors ("intra-industry research")—will be analyzed, beginning with the *applied* research efforts of the 1960s through the 1980s, and then the later relatively *basic* intra-industry research projects (in Chapters 3 and 4, respectively). This will be followed by an analysis of cases of cooperation between firms in *different* industries ("inter-industry research," in Chapter 5).

Examples of the first type ("intra-industry" research) include the more applied DIPS computer project involving three firms, organized by the Nippon Telegraph and Telephone Corporation (formerly Public Corporation), and the relatively basic VLSI project, involving five firms and two joint ventures, which was sponsored by MITI. Examples of "inter-industry" research include several projects sponsored by business and industrial groups, and projects involving firms representing different groups. (Examples include research in such fields as optoelectronics, linear motor cars, biomass, and others.) The reasons for cooperation, and the relative successes and failures of these different types of projects, are analyzed in detail in these chapters. Finally, comparisons are made between the different types of cooperation, and generalizations are drawn.

It should again be noted that the projects detailed in Chapters 3 and 4 in particular are for the most part relatively "major" projects involving several firms, large capital expenditures, and often government sponsorship, whereas the majority of cases of cooperation for innovation in Japan have consisted of small-scale cooperative efforts between firms and their affiliates, their customers, or other independent firms without government sponsorship. Most of these relatively small-scale cases of cooperation involve firms in *different* industries: it is estimated that four-fifths of all cooperative research is conducted by firms in different industries, and that the vast majority of these projects are relatively small-scale and involve no government funding. Small-scale cooperative research involving firms in the *same* industry (with no government funding) tends to be limited to cooperation between firms and their more specialized affiliate in that industry, which may be a former division that has been "spun off" (these are usually not direct competitors).[1]

Rather than focus on the more numerous small-scale cases of cooperation, the relatively large-scale cases were selected for closer examination because of their significance as late catch up and early frontier projects, and because the problems to be overcome for this type of interfirm cooperation are similar to but are far more severe than in the relatively small-scale cases. As will be seen, most of the firms in these case studies are among the largest and most important (dominant) firms in the industry.[2]

Regarding sources of this empirical data: the information contained in the discussion of general changes in firm structure and behavior and of inter-enterprise cooperation in particular is drawn primarily from extensive interviews carried out by the author, as well as from published data, company histories, journal articles, and other published and unpublished sources. The descriptions presented here are based on the consensus drawn from the above-mentioned sources, but differences of opinion or conflicting data are noted wherever found. (The overall evaluation and analyses are, of course, the author's.)

Of the published data available, twenty volumes of information collected by the Keizai Chosa Kyokai research group, extending from 1971 through 1990, were particularly helpful for the study of interfirm cooperation. These volumes were published yearly under the title *Keiretsu no Kenkyu: Kigyo Teikei* (Studies of Intermarket Groups: Cooperation between Firms).[3] They give examples of many different types of cooperation, including cooperation between producers and users and among several producers, for innovation, sales, import of technology, and other purposes. Despite the title's implied emphasis on business and industrial groups, the data covers both affiliated and unaffiliated large and small firms in all major industries, and systematically includes cases of cooperation reported in major economic journals and other publications during those years. The cases included in these volumes can therefore be taken as representative, although not absolutely exhaustive.

The data contained in these volumes were important in providing preliminary information regarding many of the cases that were later investigated in far greater detail as case studies. Moreover, these volumes provided the breadth of information across industries and across types of cooperative ventures that, together with other sources to be discussed below, allowed this study to begin to generalize beyond the computer and telecommunications case. It is clear that interfirm cooperation for a wide variety of purposes is a prevalent feature in the Japanese economy, and that interfirm cooperation for innovation occurs on a regular basis in all major industries in many different forms.

These published sources of data were therefore a good starting point for a study of cooperative technological ties. However, because of the lack of detailed published or unpublished data, extensive interviews proved to be necessary to give depth to the case studies. Questionnaires were used as a basis from which more detailed discussions of both general trends and particular cases could begin.[4] (These questionnaires are included in translation in the Appendix.) The respondents to the questionnaires and participants in the interviews are not cited by name unless their views have already appeared in a published form, but in all cases were persons in a position to give reliable information about and analyses of the general changes in firm structure and behavior and of the cooperative research projects. In some cases the information is second-hand rather than first-hand, and for this reason some inaccuracies are inevitable.

Interested readers are encouraged to make comparisons with other published accounts of the large-scale projects, as different observers and even different participants often tell the "same" story differently, from their own point of view. Surveys of this literature can be found in, for example, Buckley (1994), Vonortas (1991), Fransman (1990), Kodama (1991), Gregory (1985), Nihon Keizai Shimbunsha (1980), Nikko Research Center (1980), U.S. General Accounting Office (1982b), Granovetter (1993), and other sources. Congressional hearings in the U.S. regarding cooperative R&D and other cooperative ties in Japan and in the U.S. were also conducted over a period of several years, and provide interesting perspectives.[5] It may be very helpful to compare the empirical findings of this study with those in Fransman (1990) in particular; even though Fransman's concerns and those of the present study are different, regarding case studies of common interest the conclusions are similar.[6]

As can be seen from the list above, a large body of literature has appeared in recent years addressing the question of cooperative R&D from the perspective of advanced industrial countries. Most of these studies have focused on the large-scale intra-industry cooperative projects in Japan, and were designed to learn from these projects so that firms in other advanced industrial countries can "gain back the competitive edge." The assumption thus tends to be that individual for-profit enterprises at the technological frontier need help (from the government and/or other firms), particularly when it comes to very risky and costly research. This perspective, then, is somewhat different from that of developing countries whose enterprises and organizations—public and private—are still far from the technological frontier. Policy makers in a late development context often *tend* to be much less concerned than are their counterparts in advanced industrial countries with helping individual firms gain a "competitive edge" at the forefront of the international economy, and instead (in the best of circumstances) may be more concerned with creating a responsive and responsible technology base to meet a wide variety of local needs.

The case studies in this chapter will be analyzed in the following sequence. First, the DIPS program and other NTT-sponsored projects will be examined to illustrate clearly successful cases of applied intra-industry cooperative research. These projects will then be compared to the relatively unsuccessful MITI-sponsored program—also of a more applied nature—that attempted to reorganize the computer segment of the industry for purposes of commercial computer development; this case study illustrates well the limitations to applied intra-industry cooperative research. Other applied intra-industry projects are also cited, although they are not explored in detail.

General Characteristics of the Applied Intra-Industry Research Projects

In the 1960s a number of major computer and telecommunications projects were undertaken that involved not only university or government labs and individual private firms, but also cooperation to differing degrees between firms in the *same* industry, i.e., competing firms. The changing modes of cooperation in these programs, the different degrees of success, and the ways in which cooperation was used are very instructive.

One characteristic of these large cooperative programs was government sponsorship. For example, the joint FONTAC (computer) project of the early 1960s was sponsored by MITI's Agency for Industrial Science and Technology (Kogyo Gijutsuin); the Super High Performance Computer and its successor, the PIPS (Pattern Information Processing System) programs of 1966-1971 and 1971-1980, respectively, were sponsored by MITI's Electro-Technical Laboratory under the Agency for Industrial Science and Technology; and the DIPS (Dendenkosha Information Processing System) program that began in 1968 was sponsored by Nippon Telegraph and Telephone (formerly Public) Corporation (NTT, or "Dendenkosha").

The "sponsor," whether the more basic research-oriented Electro-Technical Laboratory of MITI or the more developmentally-minded NTT labs, played an important role in specifying the goals to be met, selecting and organizing qualified participants, and coordinating their activities. In the DIPS case, the sponsor was also the sole initiator of the project, whereas the Agency for Industrial Science and Technology and the Electro-Technical Laboratory initiated the other projects in response to the recommendations of both industry and government advisory committees. NTT projects were commissioned on a procurement basis (procurements were made in a manner to be described below), whereas projects sponsored by government agencies varied in the proportion and form of government financial support.

The two main types of projects sponsored by government agencies were those funded through "grants" and those funded through "subsidies."[7] The former term indicated projects that were fully underwritten by the government, and the latter indicated projects that were partially funded by the government and required repayment of these government subsidies out of profits resulting from the project.

Grants were usually given for projects that were by nature very far from commercialization (even though this was not "pure" research), whereas in the subsidies case, the commercialization stage was somewhat closer, but costly, risky and/or difficult research was judged as a major stumbling block to reaching this stage. In the grants case, patents usually went to one or more of the companies involved, whereas in the subsidies case the research association—i.e., the firms, and possibly the government—received the resulting patents. The Super High Performance Computer and PIPS projects were funded through grants as part of the National Research and Development Program, whereas the Computer Industry Reorganization program (or 3.75 Generation project), the VLSI project, and the other parts of the Fourth Generation Computer Program (to be discussed below) were funded through subsidies.

In the early stages these projects were intended to allow enterprises and organizations in Japan to rise up to the international standard in the new computer and telecommunications industry, and then begin to go beyond it. With the exception of DIPS (particularly in its later years), these early projects were designed to raise the level of the participating firms' technology without producing dramatically new or commercially-viable results—no product was made, although pilot models were usually constructed.[8] According to persons interviewed, cooperation was carried out essentially through periodic meetings for the exchange of information on the technology as it developed, as the actual research was done separately in each company's own lab using their own staff and equipment in consultation with researchers from government labs and the other companies involved. Because the DIPS case had a functional system as a goal, cooperation tended to be somewhat closer from the start, but even here cooperation in the initial stages consisted primarily of exchanging information to coordinate the development of the hardware and software.

Persons interviewed indicated that in most of the early applied cases of intra-industry cooperation (again, involving cooperation between competitors), the participating companies were assigned a specific task by the government "sponsor" based in part on the company's technological strengths, and frequent meetings were enough to coordinate work that was done essentially separately within each participating company. In some cases, the tasks were divided up and each assigned to a different company: this approach allowed the different abilities of the participating companies to be combined. In other cases, two or more firms would be assigned to work on the same task: this approach allowed a number of different "paths" to the same goal to be explored, at least until one or more satisfactory results was achieved.

In the larger of these early applied projects, tasks were usually divided up. In the FONTAC program, Fujitsu was responsible for software, and NEC and Oki Electric were responsible for hardware development. In the Super High Performance Computer case, Fujitsu, Hitachi and NEC were asked to develop computer mainframes; Mitsubishi, Oki Electric and Toshiba were to develop optical character recognition (OCR) technology, kanji (Japanese language) display and graphic cathode ray tube technology; Fujitsu and Hitachi were responsible for disk drives; Hitachi and NEC were to develop computer language compilers, operating systems, and utility programs; and a University of Tokyo team was assigned the task of researching high-speed logic circuits. In the PIPS program, NEC was assigned responsibility for voice recognition technology, Hitachi the technology for recognizing three-dimensional objects, Toshiba and Fujitsu the character recognition segment, and Toshiba and Mitsubishi Electric the picture recognition part of the project. In the case of the DIPS program, which will be discussed below, each firm was assigned a different task and their respective contributions were combined into an integrated system.

Which approach was used—dividing up tasks, or assigning the same or similar tasks—depended on the technological requirements and goal of the project. In general, several companies were assigned the same task if alternative paths were to be followed, but this same approach may have been used as well if it were felt that more than one firm should participate in the development of the technology (MITI was concerned to include all of the major companies, and NTT often wanted to include several suppliers in the research it sponsored).

It should be kept in mind that these projects involved only applied and developmental research in the early years, as the firms attempted to catch up to the international standard. It was only when the technological frontier was approached and altogether original innovation had to be undertaken, as increasingly occurred in this type of project as time went on, that inter-enterprise cooperation began to shift toward areas of relatively basic research as well. In addition, "joint development" began at this later stage to take on the meaning of not only planning, developing and fitting together different parts of a system, but of jointly deciding on the goals to be met and working together closely to find the most effective way to meet them.

The degree of cooperation necessary between participating companies therefore varied between these projects, between different parts of these projects, and between the earlier and later stages of these projects. In *all* cases, however, problems of developing the technology and coordinating the different assigned tasks (problems of "interface") existed, requiring frequent meetings.

The type of cooperation between firms in the same industry that characterized the earlier projects described above continued as well in the early "frontier applied" research projects. These projects used essentially the same methods of cooperation, but with a closer degree of cooperation, and a firm-centered (rather than university or government lab-centered) location of research. This type of cooperation for relatively applied research may not be as dramatic as the MITI VLSI-type of cooperation among competitors for relatively basic research, but the importance of this type of cooperation should not be overlooked. The ability to work together closely in this way to generate new products and technology allowed the technology to be developed more rapidly; moreover, it appears to result as well in better technology than would otherwise have been possible due to the range of resources that can be drawn upon and the intensity of research that can be achieved through cooperation.

This is not to say that in some frontier applied, as well as more basic projects, cooperation is always possible: in some cases, close cooperation may not occur, and firms might simply "participate" as a way to receive funds from the government, as will be illustrated below. However, given the right conditions, it appears that meaningful cooperation is possible. The incentives to cooperate are certainly there; moreover, firms would also risk not being included in future projects if they were unwilling to share information, especially when there are pilot models and viable systems to be built. Particularly in the case of important research, close cooperation appears to be more of a likelihood, and there may be less of a possibility of the firms participating simply as a way to receive government funds (although this is always a possibility, particularly when large sums are involved).

To illustrate the case of applied cooperative research involving cooperation between competitors, it is worth examining the DIPS project and other projects sponsored by NTT more closely: this will constitute the first case study. As in all the case studies, the information contained here was drawn primarily from the author's questionnaires and from extensive interviews, as well as from published data, journal articles, company histories, and other published and unpublished sources.

It should be kept in mind that the DIPS program and other NTT-sponsored projects were different from the other relatively large-scale projects in having been initiated by NTT rather than having come as a response to industry and government agency concerns, and in that they had a functional product as a goal. Nonetheless, the research procedures are representative enough of other applied intra-industry cooperative projects, including the later applied projects of the 1970s and 1980s, and their success noteworthy enough to justify close attention to these projects.

Here again, we need to keep in mind that the most numerous cases of cooperation involved small-scale projects in different industries (i.e., *inter-industry* research) with no government assistance; in the case of *intra-industry* research, small-scale efforts generally took the form of individual firms cooperating with one or more specialized firms (particularly affiliates) within the industry—i.e., not direct competitors. However, it may be worth repeating that where direct competitors were involved—specifically, in the *large-scale basic and applied intra-industry projects*—government or public corporation sponsorship has been the norm throughout the late catch up/early frontier period. Projects of this type involving completely independent *competitors* without any "outside" intervention have definitely been the exception, rather than the rule.[9] This may change, however, as firms become more international, and may choose to link up with other national or foreign companies in the same industry. An example of this might be NEC's tie-up with Samsung for the development of next-generation 256-megabit DRAMs.[10]

Although this particular case does not appear to involve much cooperative R&D, it indicates the type of long-term relationship that *could* form between competitors without "external" sponsors for purposes of frontier innovation; this might come most easily to firms that have worked together for some time in overseas markets (e.g., Japanese competitors in different industries that cooperate as they expand their operations into South Asia, or Japanese and U.S. competitors in the auto industry that form tie-ups for their operations in Southeast Asia); this will be discussed in more detail in Chapter 5.

NTT-Sponsored Applied Intra-Industry Cooperative Research Projects

Nippon Telegraph and Telephone Corporation has for decades made use of cooperative research projects to develop a wide variety of products. Originally these projects were carried out for purposes of production alone, as NTT has not maintained its own manufacturing capabilities and has had to work with firms in order to produce the equipment it needs. Cooperation between firms in the same industry for such purposes actually began in the prewar period when the Ministry of Communications (Teishinsho) acted as a leader and worked with NEC, Oki Electric, Fujitsu, and later Hitachi, both singly and together, in order to modify and in some cases to improve on the equipment imported separately by each of those companies. The cooperative efforts increased during World War II when equipment could not be imported into Japan, but these projects were cut off when the war became too intense. Interviews indicated that during the early 1950s the companies decided to continue making equipment—initially the *prewar* type of equipment— jointly by themselves rather than rely heavily on imports, and NTT continued to act as a leader in order to develop new equipment.

By the late 1960s, NTT was interested in moving away from the earlier technology and was already beginning to initiate cooperative research projects in order to develop altogether new technology in the shortest period of time and in the most effective manner possible, as NTT products and technology moved toward the technological frontier. Besides DIPS hardware and software, to be discussed below, cooperative research during this period was carried out in such areas as electrical exchange systems, switchboard equipment, transmission equipment, microwave equipment, optical communications equipment, and VLSI (Very Large Scale Integration: this involved research of a generally more applied nature than the MITI-sponsored VLSI project, but overlapped with it and individual company research projects in this area; this will be explained further in Chapter 4).

In each of these cases the procedures were approximately the same. According to persons interviewed, NTT laboratories initiated new joint research projects based upon their own research together with information from outside the company (customer request, and a general perception of international developments; supplier companies never went directly to NTT to propose this type of project). The NTT labs involved then selected the companies to participate in the projects based on the companies' research abilities with respect to the needs of the projects.

In the past the participants have often been drawn from among the NTT "family" members (the "big four," and other members of the "family" and their affiliates that have worked with NTT, as discussed in Chapter 2), but exceptions have always been made, depending upon the technological needs of the project and the abilities of possible participants. A high level of technological ability and the ability to cooperate appear to be increasingly more important than "family" membership.

In the facsimile case, for example, NTT asked Matsushita Denso, an outsider to the "family" but which has strong technology and an extensive sales network, to cooperate with Tamura Electric (a subsidiary of NEC, one of the "big four") and Toshiba (the latter, which also has an extensive sales network, had moved closer to NTT by the time of the project). These three were chosen because they were considered to be at the top of the field in some aspect of the technology required for developing facsimile equipment.[11] In general, firms were eager to participate in NTT projects because NTT's level of technological expertise is very high, but under no circumstances were companies allowed to participate in NTT projects if they did not have the relevant technological know-how, as will be seen in the DIPS case discussed below.

In general, it appears that during this period "outsiders" were incorporated as participants in NTT projects most often when cooperation did not have to be very close. Very important projects involving close cooperation tended to be restricted to "family" members, given their record of successfully cooperating with one another and the atmosphere of mutual trust that had developed over time.

According to persons interviewed, the procedures were as follows: after the initial selection of participants, the project was carried out by either assigning different tasks to each of the participants, or by having them work on the same tasks. During this period, most of the research for NTT projects was carried out separately rather than jointly, but frequent consultations with researchers from NTT and the other companies involved made these into cooperative research projects, rather than simply cases of subcontracted research. On aspects of a problem that required more fundamental research, researchers from the participating companies worked together on the problem; this occurred, for example, in one stage of the development of facsimile equipment. However, the amount of time spent on this type of research tended to be relatively small in NTT projects due to their generally more applied nature.

The next step was to either make small experimental samples or draw up technical reports detailing the fruits of research, depending upon the project. These were then evaluated by NTT staff members. Originally several different possibilities might be explored, but if a particular company was found to be following a promising lead or achieved a break-through, the other participants were directed to follow or adapt their own efforts to that lead unless other paths were seen as being worthy of further exploration. In some cases each participating company would be directed to supply the technologies it had developed to the other partici-pants without charge for further integration, development and produc-tion, as occurred in the facsimile case.

The project would then continue with a mixture of independent research and frequent consultations through each stage until the goal was met. After the goal had been reached, NTT paid the companies involved; this stands in contrast to the MITI-sponsored projects in which the subsidy or grant came first before each stage of the project began. Firms apparently accepted this procedure because of the expected benefits of working on successive NTT projects over time: funds spent on developing products were regarded as investments that would on balance pay off very well over time. Patents were generally assigned to NTT so that the patents could be used by NTT or any of the other participating companies, no matter which company was chiefly responsible for the innovation.

These, then, were the general procedures that were followed in NTT-sponsored research projects during this period, as related by persons interviewed who were very familiar with NTT research. The specific way in which each project was carried out and the degree of cooperation necessary depended on the nature of each project, how much basic research was involved, and how difficult and/or complex the technology was ("complex" in the sense of requiring the coordination of many different parts or combining different areas of knowledge).

NTT's program to develop optical fiber technology provides an example of these procedures in a relatively simple case involving a moderate amount of cooperative research. In this case, the participating firms were asked to work on the same tasks so that different paths might be simultaneously explored. The basic concepts and general techniques were learned from Bell Labs' research, but NTT researchers then modi-fied this technology for their own use. The project goal was specified by NTT personnel, and three companies (including Fujikura Cable, Sumitomo Electric Industries, and one other participant) were chosen and allowed to work on the project; others were not allowed to even compete in the pre-purchase stage, as it was said that this would give them access to information about the other companies' research activities in this field, according to persons interviewed.

The project combined relatively basic research related to materials and information loss problems with more applied research. All three companies worked on the same tasks, working separately using their own research facilities unless NTT's were needed, but still working closely with NTT researchers and meeting periodically with each other. In this case, if one company found that it was finding success with a particular approach, the others were directed to follow.

Each company then made samples of what they had developed. NTT researchers evaluated the samples and when a specific type was approved, the entire technology involved was transferred to all participants for its manufacture, and later to NEC and other companies that would be participating in projects using the optical fiber technology. The actual production of the fibers was done separately by each firm; once the technology had been developed, continuing cooperation would be necessary only for the actual assembly of the system unless further modifications were required. Then, after the research was completed, the companies were compensated for their work.

The general procedures, as illustrated in this example, have been more or less the same for all of NTT's applied cooperative projects, but the *degree* and *form* of cooperation in research have not been the same for all. Where the technology is fairly *simple* and *well understood* (i.e., requiring relatively little basic or frontier applied research), the degree of close cooperation has depended on the severity of interface problems. According to persons interviewed, for much of the optical communications equipment, for example, very little cooperation was necessary as NTT decided on the specifications for all of the parts of the system once the basic technologies (e.g., optical fiber, pulse-code modulation and laser technologies) had been developed. After the basic technologies were known, researchers from the participating companies did not need to work very closely together; they may have met only once a month, for example. Similarly, transmission and microwave equipment had relatively simple interface problems. Switching equipment, in contrast, posed very difficult problems due to the time element involved, and cooperation had to be far more close and systematic.

Where the technology is *difficult, complex* (i.e., involving the coordination of many parts and/or combining different areas of knowledge), or is *not well understood* (i.e., when it is closer to the technological frontier), close cooperation between firms has often been used in NTT projects to work through the problems that develop on a wide range of basic and applied levels. Private firms were increasingly able to bring expertise from their own and from the MITI-type joint research projects to bear on the questions regarding technology close to the frontier, as NTT was not able to specify what needs to be done as thoroughly as had been the case with well-known and standardized technology. Participating companies could help to some extent in identifying research paths to be followed, working together to develop the software, and then working separately on the hardware while remaining in constant contact with each other. Finally, they would come together again to combine what they have developed into an integrated system.

This is the procedure that was followed in the DIPS case, particularly in its later phases. Although primarily an applied research project, the DIPS project throughout involved the development of complex technologies that were not well understood. Because it stands as a clearly successful case of cooperative intra-industry applied research, it is worth examining in some detail.

The project to develop and construct the Dendenkosha (NTT) Information Processing System (DIPS), to be used as NTT's standard high-speed, large-scale computer system, began in 1968. In addition to NTT personnel, Fujitsu, Hitachi and NEC researchers worked together on this project. These companies were selected on the basis of their historical ties to NTT (as part of the NTT "family") and therefore their expertise in the communications field and general good relations with NTT and each other, and on the basis of their work in the field of data processing. It is notable that Oki Electric, the fourth member of the "family," was not included in the project due to its financial difficulties and lack of expertise in the computer field at that point in time. The choice to exclude Oki Electric was presumably to allow research to proceed more smoothly and to avoid a "free rider" problem.[12] The companies that participated therefore all had high, and more or less equal, levels of technological expertise. A firm with much greater technological know-how would probably not have participated because of disclosure problems, and companies with much less expertise were not allowed to participate.

The goal of the project was to develop a powerful time-sharing system that would be connected to NTT's electronic exchange and transmission systems. As such, it was designed for NTT internal use only and was not intended to be sold commercially as a computer system. However, as the system was at the heart of telecommunications technology, the development of this advanced technology was judged as being critical for NTT's ability to meet the demands of the rapidly changing telecommunications field and for its ability to keep its competitive standing in the industry.[13]

In planning this project, NTT did the preliminary work and specified the goals to be met and then divided up the responsibilities between firms based on their relative areas of expertise, leaving the means to these goals up to their best judgment. The degree of cooperation necessary for a project of this magnitude resulted in a joint effort involving applied, and to some extent basic, research and development, with firms cooperating not only with NTT personnel but with researchers from the other firms as well as work progressed.

Because NTT did not have manufacturing capabilities, it would have had to work closely with manufacturers under any circumstances on this project. Nonetheless, one of the main reasons (besides the obvious political and second sourcing reasons) NTT chose to work with several firms on this project instead of with just one or two manufacturers had to do with in its perception of the different strengths of the companies involved. Combining these different resources in the development of a major new computer system was seen as allowing access to the different firms' technologies and the general knowledge and experience of each company. In addition, this approach also allowed a reduction in the cost and risk to each participating firm in a way that could not be done if the development of the entire system were left up to just one or two companies. Because NTT paid firms only for completed work, the cost and risk to a single firm would have been very high in a large project such as this (equipment costs associated with this type of research were said to be very great).[14]

In the DIPS case, then, tasks were divided up and assigned on the basis of NTT's perception of each company's strengths. Because Fujitsu was considered to be good at technology related to the "heart" of the computer—the central processing unit—it was assigned the task of developing this part of the system. NEC was considered to be particularly good at communications technology, and it was instructed to focus on the connections between computers and with the rest of the system. Hitachi was given the job of developing drum, disk, and other mass memory equipment in view of its experience in large-scale memory systems. Therefore, the division of labor was made according to the different parts of the system, and consequently according to the size of the equipment: large, medium and small, respectively.

Organizationally, the DIPS project was carried out with each company doing the assigned research separately in their own laboratories, but also working in NTT labs when NTT equipment was needed. According to persons interviewed, researchers would then come together periodically at NTT—e.g., once a week—to discuss problems, exchange ideas, and coordinate developmental aspects. For DIPS hardware and software and the development of other electronic exchange software this type of "separate but together" approach (basically, but not entirely, a "division of labor" approach) with frequent meetings and consultations was found to work well. In this way, firms could maintain a sense of autonomy but cooperate closely as well.

As mentioned before, DIPS was designed in its early years to help Japanese companies catch up to the international standard, and in its later years to begin to go beyond it. By 1973 the project was said to have developed a system three times as powerful as any other in Japan, and continued to become more powerful as time went on, incorporating improvements into new models as new technology was developed. The initial emphasis was on DIPS hardware, but in later years DIPS software became a focus of attention as well.

Given this understanding of the procedures by which the DIPS program was carried out, we must ask why the DIPS program and other NTT projects were able to conduct cooperative research successfully and without major difficulties. Although some attribute the success of cooperative ventures such as these to aspects of the "Japanese character" (i.e., cooperative in nature), it is more likely that the participating companies were able to cooperate easily because of several factors.

First, it appears that cooperative research can be a success only when it is important for *technological* and *timing* reasons: it must be clearly superior to research done without cooperation, or will not be used due to the difficulties that arise in cooperative efforts. Technological reasons for cooperation center around the need to *combine technological resources*, whether to (1) attain the necessary range of knowledge by combining researchers with diverse backgrounds, or (2) attain a "critical mass" by combining a large number of people with the same expertise. The "timing" side of this centers around the fact that the innovative effort can be speeded up by combining technological resources, rather than waiting for a single firm to pull together or develop the skills necessary for the successful completion of the project.

The technological and timing reasons for cooperation were apparent in the NTT-sponsored projects. In the DIPS case there was a need to combine the different technological resources of several firms to make a single, more advanced system in as short a time as possible. In this case, the new knowledge relevant to each company's task would be transferred among firms. In other NTT cases researchers with similar types of technological expertise might be asked to work toward the same general goal, but would follow different approaches, and then receive technological information from each other as breakthroughs occurred; in this way, they shared the knowledge of the new technology entirely, and each could produce the required product. (The DIPS case is more representative of complex systems, and the latter description more representative of specific commodities and simple systems.) The timing aspect became increasingly important as the effort moved toward the frontier innovation stage, and competition in telecommunications equipment as well as company pride (in this case, a public corporation's pride in its accomplishments) pushed for the rapid development of new technologies.

In addition to technological and timing reasons, there are also purely economic reasons for cooperation. These include the need to cut down on costs to each firm through a sharing of research-related equipment and facilities, although this sharing was relatively limited in the case of applied projects. Costs and risk were also reduced by abandoning unpromising approaches once a better one was found, as described above. According to persons interviewed, these reasons for cooperation were somewhat more important considerations in the case of relatively well-understood applied research, whereas for frontier types of research, technological and timing reasons were often of greater importance. In other words, for important "breakthrough" technologies, cost and risk appear to become less important considerations than making sure that the desired technologies are achieved in the first place; cutting down on cost and risk appear to become more important thereafter, in the more predictable applied stages.

Other factors that appear to have contributed to the success of these cooperative efforts include the fact that the firms had a clear goal to attain and a sense of the economic importance of the project. For these reasons, firms were willing and more able to put aside rivalries and work effectively on the research.

NTT's leadership and also clearly helped to make this type of cooperation successful. Regarding NTT's role and the division of research tasks in NTT projects: in general, private companies concentrated primarily on applied research, and most of the more basic research necessary for NTT projects was done by the NTT labs themselves. In the DIPS case, the research undertaken for this project of both a relatively basic and applied nature stood on the base laid by earlier research done in several countries, including Japan. Information and experience gained in earlier Agency for Science and Technology and MITI projects, for example, fed directly into the DIPS project. Drawing on this knowledge, NTT began using its own substantial research facilities to do preliminary research and developmental work in the computer field as well as in telecommunications for some time as the fields moved closer together. Through this effort, NTT accumulated its own software and did all the preliminary work necessary to outline, without specifying all the details, the type of system to be developed. NTT therefore had decided on the architecture and language to be used before discussing its needs with the companies involved. This allowed NTT to guide and coordinate the companies effectively as they progressed toward their goal.

NTT's role was therefore far more than simply that of an agency procuring a product, or even a manager/coordinator of a project. Like MITI's Electro-Technical Laboratory (ETL), NTT's resources for basic research complemented well the resources of the private companies. Moreover, unlike ETL projects, NTT's position as a public corporation at the center of the telecommunications industry dictated that NTT-sponsored projects be designed to not only further relatively basic research, but also to push through the applied stages and develop functional products that NTT would then purchase. Without this type of guidance, competitors certainly could not easily work together through all of the stages of these relatively large-scale intra-industry projects to come up with functional products, as will be seen in the following case study.

Finally, one of the most critical factors that appear to have contributed to the success of these projects is the nature and attitudes of the participating firms. First, these firms had a high and more or less equal level of expertise. Second, and of equal or even greater importance, these companies had a long history of cooperating with each other to various degrees on NTT and other projects, and found these projects to be beneficial to them for several reasons. They were therefore capable and willing participants.

From the point of view of the participating companies, NTT projects were ambitious undertakings offering them a chance to gain experience in developing a specific product rather than just the general expertise offered to them in other projects. (It should be remembered that these same companies participated in projects initiated by private firms, and in MITI- and other government-sponsored projects as well.) Consequently, they derived knowledge and expertise from the earlier projects and from their own research, and then gained additional experience by working together with NTT researchers and with researchers from other companies on large applied projects.[15] Although the research done for this system could not be transferred and sold separately—NTT's hardware needs and software (which was not compatible with other systems) were too specialized for that—the knowledge gained from this ongoing project formed an important part of the knowledge base of these companies that would allow them to engage in greater product and technological innovation in the future. Specifically, the knowledge gained from this project could be used in such commercial applications as the computer series developed jointly under the MITI-sponsored "Reorganization of the Computer Industry" program (to be discussed in detail below) and in other applications. For these reasons, the firms involved had both the ability and incentives to participate in major cooperative projects.

Regarding early frontier projects: the degree of close cooperative research in NTT projects has depended in large part upon the amount of basic or frontier applied research necessary, the technological difficulties, the timing requirements, and the interface problems that arose as different areas of NTT's research and development efforts moved closer to the technological frontier. In contrast with the MITI-sponsored projects, NTT's research on such frontier areas as VLSI and fifth generation computers was generally smaller in scale and more application-oriented, and according to interviews, most of the basic research was carried out in the NTT labs themselves where small teams (e.g., of five researchers) concentrated on specified topics and worked together with and transferred that information to the companies involved. Nonetheless, it appears that the more NTT strove to meet and surpass the state-of the-art technology and the more *basic* research was required for technology NTT considered to be of importance, the more NTT adapted its standard procedures as circumstances required. (The general requirements for relatively basic research will be taken up in the following chapter.)

With respect to *applied* research projects, the "separate but together" procedures continued to be utilized into the early and later frontier stages both because the new technology in this industry has been complicated and not well understood, and because the products and technology in the industry have been increasingly integrated into larger "systems" of products.[16] In Japan this has been referred to as "systematization," which has been recognized as an important trend both in the nature of products and technology and in enterprise strategy. As a general rule, the field of telecommunications, involving computer/electronic exchange, satellite, and optical technologies, among other new and complex technologies, have required a great deal of cooperation on many levels due to the interface problems and the increasing sophistication of the technology as it moves up and down through the entire technological complex from devices and fibers through whole networks. As the fields of computers and telecommunications increasingly merge and produce new related industries (new areas related to information systems, new medical equipment, and others), these problems will undoubtedly intensify.

These observations have thus far been directed toward NTT applied research projects and, by extension, to other applied projects involving coordination by a public corporation, government agency, or other "central coordinator." These considerations regarding conditions that allowed successful cooperative research projects of this type (i.e., *involving direct competitors*) would appear to hold true as well for (1) large-scale applied intra-industry projects that are *not* commercially-oriented, but rather are coordinated by a central body and are designed to generate preliminary information or pilot models; and (2) selected projects that are directed toward the development of a *single* well-specified and coordinated commercially-oriented product (these need not be centrally coordinated by a third body, but all important questions must be clearly worked out before the project is started).[17]

In contrast, even if all the conditions necessary for cooperative research as outlined above are met, it may be very difficult, if not impossible, for firms that are direct competitors to cooperate on this type of applied project at a stage close to *general* commercialization (i.e., producing an *ongoing* stream of products, as opposed to a single commercially-oriented product). In order to illustrate this point, we will examine in the following case study the attempts of MITI to reorganize the Japanese computer manufacturers into pairs of firms (NEC-Toshiba, Hitachi-Fujitsu, and Mitsubishi Electric-Oki Electric) that would cooperate to produce commercial computer equipment, and discuss why these attempts were not very successful, in contrast to the cases analyzed above.

Computer Development
Under the MITI Reorganization Program

Persons interviewed indicated that the government-sponsored applied intra-industry projects discussed above came as a response to concerns on the part of both industry and government that Japanese companies would not be able to rise up to the international technological standard in these important fields. These projects were, then, largely *industry-initiated* in order to raise their own level of technology. It was also noted that although the DIPS and other NTT-sponsored projects discussed above were initiated by NTT, they were clearly projects that private firms could benefit from in the sense of raising their level of expertise and technological know-how. The MITI-sponsored program to reorganize the computer part of the industry into cooperating groups of firms, however, was initiated solely by MITI, and was *not* perceived by the private enterprises involved as being clearly in their own best interests. Why this attempt to initiate cooperative applied research between competitors was less than successful will be discussed in some detail, as it is instructive in pointing out the limitations to this type of cooperative research.

According to persons interviewed, the original plan to reorganize the major computer manufacturers into one or more groups arose from MITI's concern that the manufacturers were spending too much of their resources producing similar products that were not internationally competitive, and might not even be able to survive the changes associated with capital and trade liberalization anticipated for the mid-

1970s and 1980s due to the threat of competition and takeovers by foreign firms. According to interviews, MITI originally wanted the firms to merge their divisions into a single large company in order to compete effectively with IBM. Failing this, MITI thought they should at least cooperate closely to eliminate unnecessary duplication in their research and production efforts, and moreover should expand production, specialize and diversify their products so that they might be more competitive in both the international and domestic markets.

The incentives for reorganization into cooperative "groups" were generous subsidies, low-interest loans and, of course, the possibility of continuing good government-industry relations. The legal basis for these policies was given by the 1971 Kidenho (Law for Provisional Measures to Promote Specific Electronic and Machine Industries). This law was intended as a temporary measure to support the development of "state-of-the-art" technologies in certain "critical" fields in which Japanese companies were either (1) far behind the international standard, (2) producing at a volume that made it impossible to derive economies of scale, or (3) producing with outdated or expensive techniques. It also allowed for corporate mergers and tax benefits as was judged necessary to achieve these goals. The Kidenho was in effect from 1971-1978, and was followed by the Kijoho (Law for Provisional Measures to Promote Specific Machinery and Information Industries), which was in effect from 1978-1985. The latter was different from the former in that it emphasized software as well as hardware development, and cooperative efforts rather than mergers—which indicates something about the success of the earlier period's merger policy.

In 1971 the manufacturers agreed to pair up into three different groups in order to develop and produce a more advanced computer series. It was decided that NEC and Toshiba would cooperate, as would Hitachi and Fujitsu, and Mitsubishi Electric and Oki Electric.

These pairings were made on historical and technological criteria. It is said that NEC and Fujitsu could not be paired because although they had the same goal, they had two different approaches, with Fujitsu moving toward a strategy of compatibility with IBM software whereas NEC maintained a strategy of non-compatibility (NEC has since moved in the direction of IBM-compatibility as well, given IBM's power to set the international standard in software). According to official reports, NEC and Toshiba formed one group because the computer division of General Electric, Toshiba's U.S. licensee, had merged with Honeywell, which was NEC's licensee. Hitachi and Fujitsu had come to share the same strategy of developing IBM-compatible equipment, and therefore made up the second of the pairs. Mitsubishi Electric and Oki Electric then formed the third group.

After the industry was divided into three cooperating groups, the government provided 50% of the expenses for the development of the more advanced computer series; this was referred to as the "3.75 Generation" project. From 1972 to 1976, the groups received about 57.47 billion yen for research (about $195.9 million), and produced the NEC-Toshiba ACOS series, the Mitsubishi-Oki Electric COSMO series, and the Hitachi-Fujitsu M series.

On paper, the cooperative ventures proceeded well. However, according to interviews, the projects were in fact less than ideally cooperative and accomplished less than the desired technological goals. The Mitsubishi-Oki Electric grouping, for example, found that it could not attain the level of overall technological expertise necessary to compete in this field, and in 1975 Oki Electric decided to specialize in the development and production of terminal equipment in view of financial difficulties and limited technological resources in this field. Mitsubishi Electric also decided to withdraw from the large-scale, high-speed computer business. (It remained in other segments of the computer business, however, and joined with Hitachi and Fujitsu in the establishment in 1975 of the Computer Development Laboratories, Ltd. (CDL), a "joint venture" that participated formally in the VLSI project, to be discussed below.)

Hitachi and Fujitsu might seem a more suitable match, given their roughly equivalent technological and financial resources in the field, but it appears that this very equality of resources produced a contentious atmosphere, with neither company acceding easily to the will of the other. As an example, they originally decided that Hitachi would develop the M-170 and M-180 models, whereas Fujitsu would concentrate on the M-160 and M-190 models. However, Fujitsu came out with an M-180-2 model, prompting Hitachi to retaliate with its M-162 model, and so on as each countered new products with its own models. According to persons interviewed, there were always arguments and more competition than cooperation overall.

To a limited extent, it appears that Hitachi and Fujitsu were able to decide on a division of labor and carry it through. However, it is not clear how much actual cooperative research was done beyond working out software compatibility problems between the equipment developed by each company. Some persons interviewed speculated that Fujitsu's strength in computers and relative weakness in materials and parts complemented well Hitachi's strength in materials and parts and relative weakness in computers, making cooperative research in certain areas an important justification for this joint effort. However, for most of this "collaboration" each company did the research for and developed their assigned products separately, with a minimum of cooperative research.

Therefore, we get a very mixed picture of this effort with respect to cooperation for innovation: there may have been some genuine cooperative research that facilitated innovation in certain aspects of computer development, but for the most part a simple (and tenuous at that) division of labor without real cooperative research appears to have been the norm.[18]

The third pair, the NEC-Toshiba collaboration, is regarded by some as the most successful of the joint ventures. It produced the ACOS series in which Toshiba is credited with developing the medium-sized computer series and NEC with the very large and small computer series.[19] Moreover, NEC and Toshiba appeared to cooperate closely in doing research as a "team" for the VLSI project and other projects that followed.

However, what is not as well known is that NEC and Toshiba "cooperated" easily because NEC apparently took over the venture, which involved some Toshiba personnel but NEC management. Toshiba's division was essentially given up to NEC; according to some persons interviewed, this was in order to streamline Toshiba, which found that the project taxed it financially and diverted its resources from other important projects, such as its large generator (including nuclear) projects. Another factor was undoubtedly that NEC had been in the computer business a long time whereas Toshiba was new, making this a very unequal arrangement. According to one person interviewed, NEC at one point did not seem to want to continue on with Toshiba, but the problem was solved when Toshiba decided to withdraw from the large-scale computer business that it originally had intended to pursue. It appears that the cooperative effort continued largely because of Toshiba's strength in marketing rather than its technological expertise in this field. Through this arrangement, Toshiba gained access to the low-priced large-scale computer technology that it lacked (and potentially, a greater share in NTT's business), and NEC in turn gained access to Toshiba's extensive sales network.

The company that grew out of this association—the NEC-Toshiba Information Systems (NTIS)—was established in May 1977 and was capitalized at one billion yen on a 60/40 basis. (One person interviewed remarked that this was because 50/50 ventures of this sort are rarely successful, citing the Hitachi-Fujitsu case as an example.) Each company contributed funds and personnel, and brought in its own customers.

NTIS was originally set up to handle marketing and servicing of the ACOS series, but it soon officially began to concentrate on the development of VLSI technology as well. A VLSI section was set up within NTIS, but one person held that there had never at any point been technicians working in NTIS, and others stated that the section was set up for administrative purposes and to act as a conduit for government funds. According to these reports, it had always consisted of NEC managers and some Toshiba personnel from sales and systems engineering divisions, and that it continued essentially as a sales organization to handle the hardware and software produced (presumably mostly by NEC). In general, it appears that the intention on the part of the two companies was not to combine the technological resources of NEC and Toshiba by pairing up to develop a computer system or its components jointly, but rather was intended as a way to maintain good government-industry relations, receive government funds, and possibly divide up a product line. This is not to suggest that they did not do real cooperative research in other contexts, as in the examples given above and below; it is simply to emphasize that the reorganization program apparently did not result in much cooperative research.

Whether these reports are wholly accurate or not, it is clear that these joint ventures were less than the close cooperative efforts envisioned by MITI planners. One person interviewed indicated that within a short period of time of the establishment of the NEC-Toshiba (NTIS) and the Hitachi-Fujitsu-Mitsubishi Electric (CDL) joint ventures, Toshiba was thinking of withdrawing its employees from NTIS, and Mitsubishi Electric was indicating that it might not participate in any more joint ventures with Hitachi and Fujitsu after both the VLSI and Next Generation Computer projects were completed. (Recall that Hitachi and Fujitsu formed the Computer Development Laboratories, or CDL, which was their equivalent of NEC-Toshiba's NTIS. Mitsubishi joined CDL for the VLSI project after its collaboration with Oki Electric broke off.) Hitachi and Fujitsu did establish, in addition to CDL, a joint venture known as Nippon Peripherals, Ltd. (NPL) on a 50/50 basis to conduct research, manufacture and market terminals and peripherals; however, this is a field that has become standardized and less innovative, and it is unclear to what extent cooperative research for innovation was actually a central concern of the organization. The relative unimportance of these cooperative ventures to the firms involved is indicated in the low level of investment made in them by each participant.

It is clear that these collaborations were much less successful than were the NTT cooperative projects analyzed above despite the fact that the latter were also intended for applied research of a technologically similar nature. The main difference was that the NTT-type projects involved cooperative research designed to produce in each case a single product (or pilot model) that was well-specified and coordinated (in the NTT case, this was done by the procurer). The reorganization project, in contrast, was intended to produce a *continuous stream* of products to be sold to various different markets, and therefore involved research that was close to commercialization of a far more wide-ranging sort offering a larger potential market. This posed the problem of not only disclosing proprietary information, but also of deciding on the products to be developed and the ways to develop them, including the division of responsibilities between firms—i.e., strategic issues and territorial problems. (Additional problems centered around such matters as dividing up patents and revenues according to each company's contribution; this was often difficult to do, but these potential sources of conflict could be more easily worked out.)

Given these difficulties, the firms were unable to work together effectively, and were unable to take full advantage of the technological benefits of cooperation. In the DIPS case it was necessary for the companies to work closely together because the parts were inseparable as elements of one system, whereas in the computer development case the firms ended up dividing up the tasks and working essentially separately. As mentioned before, it may be that a certain amount of technologically useful cooperative research was done between Hitachi and Fujitsu utilizing their different strengths, but even in this case the problems appear to have outweighed the potential benefits.

Cooperation may continue for non-technological reasons as well, e.g., due to the benefits of combining one company's technological abilities in certain areas with another company's marketing abilities, or because of the complementary nature of the two companies' markets (Toshiba and Hitachi are more consumer goods-oriented, for example, whereas NEC and Fujitsu are relatively producer goods-oriented). Cooperation undertaken in order to link one firm's technological abilities in a certain field with another firm's marketing abilities may in fact stimulate the innovation process by opening up a wider and somewhat more "assured" market (assuming that there is consumer loyalty to a particular company or group's products). Similarly, cooperation in order to develop a larger product line by essentially combining two separate firms' complementary products may stimulate innovation because of the range of applications for new technology in this larger combined market.

It may be, for example, that computer and telecommunications-centered firms will need to cooperate in the future with consumer goods or small equipment manufacturers as the range of applications of this technology expands into new areas and the need grows for developing integrated product lines that include these goods. However, cooperation to expand product lines would most likely only be undertaken on a case-by-case basis, as firms would ultimately prefer to add on divisions and undertake research and production by themselves if the products were important.

For example, although it does *not* appear that the computer reorganization program was undertaken and the pairings made because of the complementary nature of the different companies' product lines and technologies, one potential result might be that their different emphases would allow them to extend their product lines. However, company rivalry prevents this in most cases: for example, persons who are familiar with NEC's case reported that NEC appears to be intent on developing its own products whenever profitable, including small equipment and consumer products divisions, and would not be inclined to leave these goods to Toshiba (or any other competitor) to develop except on a temporary basis. Moreover, the pairings for cooperation do not cover the entire range of company products: Toshiba, for example, is strong in heavy electrical equipment, but NEC was reported to be more likely to cooperate with a Sumitomo group member or another technologically strong firm unless Toshiba's technology was exceptional. Therefore, although cooperation either for combining technology and marketing skills or for combining complementary product lines might be undertaken on a case-by-case basis, it is unlikely to lead to more profound ties between two separate companies.

More to the point of this discussion, such collaborations, even when they occur, involve very little interfirm cooperation for *innovation*. Combining product lines or different firms' technological and marketing skills can be used as competitive techniques, and might indirectly stimulate innovations. However, this is quite different from the type of cooperative research that speeds up the innovation process and makes it more effective, which is the focus of attention in this study.

Conclusions:
Conditions that Allow Successful Applied
Intra-Industry Cooperative Research

In this chapter we noted that many of the larger firms in the industry chose to undertake cooperative research through the FONTAC, Super High Performance Computer, PIPS, DIPS, and later applied projects in order to help extend their own technological know-how—and, of course, to receive compensation for their efforts, the relative importance of each incentive depending upon the project. The firms have done this in spite of the problem of disclosing company secrets and the expenses incurred.

From this survey, we saw that the most apparently successful cases were those that:

1. showed a clear technological and "timing" need for cooperation—this need generally arose from the newness (and attendant uncertainties), difficulty and/or complexity of the technology, and was

made more urgent by the need to solve the technological problems as quickly as possible; and

2. showed a clear economic need for cooperation involving the reduction of cost and risk to individual firms; this allowed research projects to be undertaken that might not otherwise have been possible.

These can be considered to be the primary reasons for firms—public and private—choosing to cooperate in order to carry out both relatively "routine" as well as the more ambitious projects of the late catch up and early frontier period. Again, the *technological requirements* coupled with the need for the *rapid development* of new products and technologies, together with the *cost* and *risk* involved (the latter considerations being the primary ones in the case of relatively "routine" cases of innovation), act to drive firms in this direction. For these reasons, it is said that the more advanced and difficult the desired technology is, the more incentives firms have to cooperate, and the closer firms may have to cooperate in order to arrive at the desired goal quickly (as they approach and move beyond the technological frontiers, they are once again not just dealing with interface problems).

In addition to these considerations, other conditions that contributed to the success of these relatively large-scale intra-industry projects were found in the cases that:

3. involved the participation of firms having a *history of cooperation* with other firms for a wide range of purposes (this is a crucial point, as is discussed throughout this study);
4. involved the participation of firms having high, and more or less equal levels of expertise;
5. had a clear goal and sense of the economic importance of the project;
6. had a *central coordinator*, particularly (but not necessarily) a procurer (a government laboratory, government agency, a public enterprise, or—in rare cases—one of the competing firms might play this role, providing that the participants recognized the usefulness of the projects);
7. were part of a *general innovative effort*, on the part of both public and private organizations, to develop a broad range of complementary technologies pertaining to a particular field (e.g., computers and telecommunications); and
8. maintained some distance from the stage of *general* commercialization, particularly if a large, diverse and fast-growing market was at stake. Individual cases of procurement or cooperative development

of specific new products may be successful, but an ongoing relationship between direct competitors for the development of an unspecified stream of new products is not likely to be.

Regarding this last point: it appears that close cooperation on a long-term basis for general commercial purposes is very difficult because of problems of inter-enterprise rivalry that reappear throughout and make the division of authority and responsibility, as well as patents and revenues, a matter of ongoing contention. Conflicting personalities, policies and general attitudes also tend to hinder cooperative efforts unless clear lines of authority are drawn and a clear rationale for cooperative research is present.

Finally, it appears that one should not underemphasize the importance of the firm's history of cooperation, and the importance of the development of mutual trust over time. Cooperative efforts are a form of "learned behavior" (to use Richard R. Nelson's phrase), and it appears that firms feel more at ease with inter-enterprise cooperation the more time they have spent on such projects and the more experience they have had with a wide range of cooperative efforts. This implies that interfirm and other types of cooperative behavior can be learned, but it also implies that new forms of cooperation will come more naturally to firms that already have had a long history of different types of joint efforts, as has been true in the case of Japanese firms.

Further Discussion

The cases discussed in this chapter were the relatively large-scale intra-industry projects of the late catch up/early frontier period in Japan. They can be seen as supplementing the more common, small-scale applied projects involving firms and affiliates or independents within the same industry. In the relatively large-scale efforts, a "central coordinator" (e.g., a public enterprise, government agency, or—under very restricted conditions—even an individual large private firm) often brought direct competitors together in a series of projects in order to utilize their respective skills and expertise, create (in most cases) a viable system, pilot model, or product as a result of the cooperative efforts, and at the same time help pull up the technological abilities of all the participants.

Moreover, although it is conceivable that procedures similar to those described here could be put to use in advanced industrial countries, the circumstances allowing this type of cooperation—as illustrated in the Japanese case above—would appear to be more "natural" to the political economic setting found in other late developing economies. For one thing, most of the smaller-scale applied forms of cooperative research involve a private firm and one or more specialized affiliates in the industry, which is a form of research that can be easily facilitated by the use of formal and informal group ties, as are often found in latecomer countries. Moreover, since the larger projects tend to be organized by public enterprises and government agencies, latecomers having strong public enterprises may have a significant advantage, particularly in the catch up period when rough "blueprints" regarding the path of and requirements for technological advance exist. Rather than lose this advantage through indiscriminate privatization (often as a reaction to very real problems associated with public sector institutions), late developing countries may find it preferable to try to transform these institutions and put this potential advantage to good use in the new competitive context, e.g., in some of the ways indicated here.[20] The stated intention in Japan was to bring all enterprises in key industries—public and private—to the point at which they would not simply master and operationalize imported technology, but could also go on to adapt and improve upon it. This was done with a good deal of protection and guidance, but in Japan's case there was a clear-cut sense of the need to face stiff international competition sooner or later, and both private and public enterprises had strong incentives to learn from a wide variety of in-house and cooperative research projects, rather than become stagnant oligopolies or rent-seeking institutions behind protected markets. Moreover, firms were not allowed to become free riders in the government-sponsored cooperative projects: if they did not pool their strengths, knowledge and resources and pull their own weight, they would be left out of subsequent government-sponsored projects.

These projects resulted in both "hits" and "misses," and no doubt involved more uncertainty than would be true if local enterprises simply continued to rely on international firms for ideas and technology; however, the result of the two "national" versus "international" strategies are obviously quite different. In an era characterized by the globalization of economies, efforts to pool and pull up the general technological capabilities of *domestic* private and public enterprises within the framework of a *national* economy may seem anachronistic; however, the importance of the nation-state as a protector and promoter of enterprises with a predominantly national identity is likely to continue for some time.

In the Japanese case, the attempts to develop research and technological linkages in key sectors of the national economy, including through the use of cooperative applied R&D efforts, contributed to the relative technological self-reliance that is a key characteristic of Japanese enterprises in recent years. Such attempts are being pursued in several of the more industrialized latecomers at the present time and are likely to be duplicated in many others in the years to come, as will be discussed in more detail in Chapter 6.

Nonetheless, in certain cases there is a significant potential for abuse that must be monitored carefully. One of the cases discussed in this chapter clearly illustrates the possibility of spending public funds on "cooperative research" projects that end up involving little or no actual cooperative research.

There is no doubt that cooperative applied projects can help to raise the technological capabilities of domestic firms. However, in many late-comers (as well as in the early industrializers), public as well as private funds have a way of being spent in a manner that never shows any meaningful results, and cooperative cases that result only in a pilot model (or less) may be good candidates for such abuses. Particularly in cases that involve large public expenditures, whether directed toward private or public enterprises, there is a strong possibility that more socially useful results would have been achieved if the funds had been used elsewhere.

It is also important to be aware that large-scale cooperative projects may simply reinforce the political and economic dominance of a limited number of enterprises within the country. The relatively large-scale projects of the type detailed in this chapter would not be controversial to the extent that they are seen as being truly instrumental in bringing up local technological capabilities to meet local needs, and in avoiding a complete dependence on international enterprises. However, to the extent that such large-scale projects are seen as merely benefiting individual large enterprises in their own profit-seeking endeavors, they will be highly controversial in a late development context. These issues will be taken up again in Chapter 6 in our more detailed consideration of the public policy implications of cooperative technological ties.

For now, we may turn our attention to the issue of inter-enterprise cooperation for relatively basic (or "fundamental") research and projects that helped to mark the turning point in Japan's postwar experience of technological advance, as firms moved decisively into frontier research. We will continue to focus on cooperation between competitors (*intra-industry* cooperation) for these new innovative efforts, and then take up the questions of *inter-industry* cooperation in Chapter 5 below.

Notes

1. As an example, NEC transferred much of its small-sized medical electronics equipment operations to San-ei Instrument Co., Ltd., a "specialized firm" in the NEC group. Similarly, Hitachi has worked with Hitachi Medico Co., Ltd. and Toshiba has worked with Toshiba Medical Systems Co., Ltd., when their projects

required technical input from this branch of the electronics industry. Cf. Masuda (1977) for detailed examples of cooperation with specialized affiliates in this industry. (Very often, if a division grows large enough, it may be separated off to form a new company—a specialized subsidiary—and the parent company will then continue to work closely with the newly created firm. This separation can occur for a number of reasons. For example, divisions are sometimes separated off for tax purposes, or to save on labor costs, as subsidiaries may not give the benefits parent companies do. Separation is more likely if the division represents a field that is not very important to the parent company's main industries.)

2. There have been very few large-scale government-funded projects involving *only* small firms. Groups of small firms (e.g., a number of sub-contractors) may get together on their own in order to carry out cooperative research, but these have not been the focus to date of the large-scale cooperative projects in Japan. Regarding relatively small-scale cooperative ventures involving small firms exclusively, cf., for example, Gerlach (1992a). In postwar Japan, cooperative ties among small businesses (i.e., small business groups) take such forms as producer and purchaser cooperatives, traditional and "high tech" (technopolis-type) industrial estates, and neighborhood associations.

3. Keizai Chosa Kyokai (1971-1990); these volumes are subtitled *Kigyo Teikei no Bunseki* (Analysis of Interfirm Cooperation) and *Kigyo Teikei no Doko* (Trends in Interfirm Cooperation).

4. See the Appendix for English translations of the questionnaires used in this study. The questions were sent ahead, and the answers were discussed (usually in Japanese) in the first 2-3 hour meeting. Subsequent meetings followed up on particular points raised in the initial meeting and in discussions with other persons interviewed.

The first questionnaire was intended to discern general trends with respect to changes in the organization and behavior of these firms as they attempted to innovate more effectively in new fields. The second questionnaire focused on the issue of interfirm cooperation in particular, using examples drawn from the responses to the first set of questions and from the *Keiretsu no Kenkyu* volumes, as well as from other published articles and documents. The persons interviewed included company executives, managers and engineers that had participated in or had direct knowledge of the research projects, university professors, government officials, economic journalists, and others knowledgeable about particular cases of inter-enterprise cooperation. By following up on and counter-checking points made by each person interviewed, the author found that a clear and consistent picture of the projects emerged over the course of the study.

5. These include hearings and reports carried out by a number of different Congressional bodies (see U.S. Congress 1983, 1984, 1987, 1989, 1990a, 1990b, 1991a, and 1991b, among others).

6. Vonortas and Fransman are good places to begin in surveying this literature. In addition, Kodama (1991) discusses many of the larger cooperative projects up to the early 1990s (PIPS, VLSI, other NTT projects, and more recent developments) through short descriptions and analyses, reviews the history of Engineering Research Associations in Japan, and discusses quantitative studies of

cooperative research in Japan (cf. also Kodama, 1986). Granovetter (1993), among other sources, discusses the important role played by group banks and trading companies in coordinating group activities, including projects involving cooperative R&D.

Fransman's excellent study focuses primarily on several large intra-industry projects, involving cooperation between the dominant firms (direct competitors) in the industry, usually with government or a procurer's support. He begins with a periodization of the development of the computer and electronic devices industry in Japan from 1948 to 1979, and then examines the following projects: the VLSI Research Project (1976-80); the Optical Measuring and Control System Project (1979-85); the High Speed Computing System for Scientific and Technological Uses Project (the Supercomputer Project, 1981-89); the Future Electronic Devices Project (1981-90); and the Fifth Generation Computer Project (1981-90). Finally, he presents the results of a survey of four of the largest electronics companies. The study does not look into *inter-industry* cooperative technological efforts, or the more applied and development-oriented *intra-industry* projects involving large firms and small affiliates (this he considers to be intra-firm), or large and small "independents," or two or more relatively small firms (in other words, the most common and widespread forms of inter-enterprise ties for cooperative technological advance). Still, regarding the important projects under consideration, Fransman's findings and those of the present study are very compatible, and interested readers are directed toward his detailed study.

7. These were also known as "research contracts" or "consignments" (referring to *itakuhi*), and "matching grants" for "industry-government research projects" (referring to *hojokin*), respectively.

8. One person interviewed commented that these pilot models were often made as simple as possible for demonstration purposes, and therefore did not show the full scope of research accomplishments.

9. With respect to this point, Fransman found that "Japanese corporations are just as cautious as their Western counterparts in entering into cooperative research agreements. It is significant in this connection that there are only two examples of spontaneous research cooperation [found by Fransman in the course of his inquiries] between the largest competing Japanese industrial electronics companies, that is research cooperation agreed in the absence of facilitating measures taken either by government or a large procurer."

Given Fransman's primary focus on large-scale projects, this finding is not surprising. However, if one widens the focus to include smaller-scale research efforts within an industry (including affiliated firms, and also between firms and informally tied "independents") and the vast range of inter-industry projects that form the majority of cooperative technological efforts in the late catch up/early frontier period, the conclusions will naturally be different.

10. "The deal illustrates the growing interdependence of the world's large semiconductor manufacturers. Two years ago, there was a bitter rivalry between Japanese and Korean chipmakers in an oversupplied market. Today, with demand for semiconductor memory growing at 60% a year, companies need to pool their resources to meet a growing need for computer power, and for

research and development. . . . The two have already agreed to exchange information on developing next-generation 256-megabit D-Rams—four times the capacity of the existing biggest chip—to reduce the burden of development costs." ("NEC–Samsung Link-up Will Produce Chips for Europe," *Financial Times*, February 7, 1995.)

11. In the facsimile case, cooperation was used not only because of the technology involved, but also to shorten the development time as tasks could be divided up, parts exchanged, and production of the same type of equipment undertaken by all three firms. Because this effort involved only applied and developmental research, periodic meetings were usually sufficient to work out interface problems.

12. There are conflicting reports about why Oki Electric was not included; however, its perceived weakness in the computer field (for whatever reason) is likely to have been the most compelling reason.

13. NTT has always prided itself on its resources and technological expertise, but the need to innovate became even more pressing due to the inroads into its communications and data transmission markets by private companies: NTT's virtual monopoly in these fields was eroded as the fields themselves changed and new entrants appeared in both new and old markets.

14. It may be that NTT helped finance particularly costly research "up front" under certain circumstances, but this was not mentioned by persons interviewed regarding the projects discussed here.

15. NEC, for example, is credited with many achievements in research, both in its independent work and in its earlier work with universities and government labs. One of these projects was with NTT for the development of the NEAC computer, the forerunner of the DIPS program. In addition, it was one of the three companies charged with developing mainframes and was one of the two companies to develop computer language compilers in the Super High Performance Computer project before becoming responsible for one entire section of the DIPS project.

16. Other NTT projects of the 1980s included such projects as NTT's joint research with NEC, Fujitsu and Hitachi on the next generation optical transmission systems, and with NEC, Mitsubishi Electric and Oki Electric on work stations (cf., for example, the 1987 volume of *Keiretsu no Kenkyu*).

17. An example of the first type of project may have been the decision of three "old Furukawa (zaibatsu) Group" members (that later became members of the Dai-ichi Kangyo Bank's keiretsu) to undertake joint research in the fields of optical fibers, semiconductors, and other related areas. In this case, Furukawa Electric, Fuji Electric, and Fujitsu planned to begin by using Fuji Electric's central research institute as their locale for cooperative research. (On this, cf. *Keiretsu no Kenkyu*, 1984, p. 7.)

An example of the latter type of project, drawn from outside of the computer and telecommunications industry, might have been the joint development of nonmagnetic manganese steel by Daido Steel (affiliated with Nippon Steel) and Toshin Steel (affiliated with the Fuyo Group) for the Japan (formerly National) Railways-sponsored linear motor car project. (This *portion* of the project may have involved *intra-industry* cooperative research to some extent, whereas the entire project would be considered *inter-industry*, as will be discussed in Chapter 5.) Regarding this project, cf. Nikko Research Center (1980), p. 68. More information is needed to indicate to what extent these examples were truly cooperative and how basic or applied, as opposed to simply developmental, the research actually turned out to be.

18. The strategy of a simple division of labor without much, if any, cooperative research appears to have been extended to cases of international "cooperation" in this field, at least up through the early 1990s. Many international "joint ventures," for example, seem to have involved two firms dividing up a product line and supplying each other with the necessary equipment, rather than doing any substantial cooperative research (although this now appears to be changing). This will be taken up in more detail in the following chapter.

19. It may be significant that although sales and other statistics for Hitachi and Fujitsu were typically listed separately, statistics for NEC and Toshiba often combined the two companies under the "ACOS group" label.

20. The important role that can be played by public enterprises in fostering technological advance in the private sector in late developing countries is shown in studies ranging from Nigeria (Chukwujekwu, 1991) to Japan (Anchordoguy, 1988, Fransman, 1990, and others). It should be kept in mind that private sector institutions in a late development context—without incentives or requirements to do otherwise—may tend to be equally or more rent-seeking, opportunistic, and corrupt as public sector institutions. "Sick" industrial units may occur as frequently as a result of individual "milking" of private firms as they do of public sector negligence. Changes in both public and private enterprise behavior comes when the prevailing incentives and requirements change.

4

Cooperation Between Firms in the Same Industry: Case Studies Involving Relatively Basic (or "Fundamental") Research

General Characteristics of the Basic Research Projects

In the preceding chapter we have examined the important role cooperative technological ties can play in the case of relatively applied research. We found that, according to many observers, the combining of different technological resources allowed firms to develop what they could not do as *quickly* or as *effectively* on their own. Moreover, we found that cooperation was in some cases said to help reduce cost and risk factors that can act as barriers to innovation.

In this chapter we shall see that many regard cooperation among enterprises and organizations for relatively "basic" research as being even more important than in the applied case. This is because, according to persons interviewed, the technological difficulties and need for rapid innovation, together with cost and risk factors, may be even greater in the case of relatively basic research. Basic research is also seen as being more amenable to cooperative efforts than applied research, as the latter is closer to the stage of commercialization, which creates major barriers to cooperation. Therefore, the shift over time toward an increased emphasis on basic research has opened up the possibility of a wide range of new forms of cooperative efforts. (Again, "basic" or "fundamental" research is used here in the sense commonly employed by industry, in contrast to "pure" research that has no commercial applications in mind. The latter is rarely undertaken by industry, but is usually left to universities and government research institutions.)

In Japan's case, once the leading firms had caught up technologically in most fields related to computers and telecommunications, they were faced with the need to do far more basic research in order to advance the frontiers of technology than they had ever been required to do up to that point. In the 1970s and 1980s a number of large-scale cooperative projects that were focused on relatively basic research goals were taken up by major firms in this emerging "combined" industry. This chapter will examine several of these large-scale intra-industry basic research projects.

One characteristic of these projects is their greater variety of forms of organization of research, as compared with the applied research projects. The most *common* form of organization for relatively basic research is the "separate but together" approach described in the applied research case: firms conduct their assigned research primarily in their own labs, but consult each other frequently in order to move the project along. The firms work on either the same or complementary research, depending upon the technical requirements, and the frequency of consultations depends on the difficulty of the project. Very difficult, new and/or complex technologies are said to require extensive joint efforts to shorten the development time, eliminate overlapping research, and make the basic research efforts more effective. These points will be illustrated below.

Although this "separate but together" approach has been the most common organizational pattern, we will see that certain types of cooperative basic research go beyond this, to the extent of establishing cooperative research laboratories, as pioneered in the MITI-sponsored VLSI project. This attempt to get firms to cooperate closely and in a fully integrated manner has no equivalent in the applied research cases we have seen so far; even in NTT-sponsored applied research, cooperative work and frequent meetings in the NTT labs simply served to supplement and coordinate the work done essentially separately in each company. It is the "joint research institute" form of (at least potentially) intimate cooperation that has attracted the most interest world-wide.

In this chapter we will be concerned primarily with cooperative research efforts that make use of joint research laboratories. However, the requirements for and perceived benefits of cooperation for basic research will be discussed in more general terms as well.[1]

The MITI-Sponsored VLSI Program
and Other Cooperative Basic Research Projects

The Very Large Scale Integration (VLSI) story is by now well known, although different observers have related the story in different ways. The

VLSI case represented the first major attempt to bring resources from competing firms together in a joint research institute designed to allow those firms to work closely on different problems of a relatively basic nature.

Based on the positive results of this pioneering case, more recent research projects in Japan have been characterized by even more ambitious attempts to push out the frontiers of technological and scientific knowledge, and have taken on research of a far more challenging nature (albeit with very uneven results thus far). For the purposes of illustrating the next stage of research once firms in a late development context have caught up technologically, we will include details regarding this early frontier project. This will be based primarily on the author's interviews with project participants, together with published and unpublished sources.

The VLSI program began in Japan as one of Nippon Telegraph and Telephone Public Corporation's many ongoing projects. NTT wanted to attain the state-of-the-art technology in integrated circuits, and considered it very important to anticipate future developments in technology in this rapidly changing field. It considered LSI and then VLSI technology to be of central importance for its computer/exchange systems in the future, and initiated a joint research effort with Hitachi, Fujitsu and NEC in April 1975 to develop this new technology. (The distinction between LSI and VLSI was based on the number of transistors that can be implanted in a silicon board: LSI included 4K, 16K and 64K bit memories, and VLSI included 128K and 256K bit memories, with 4K indicating approximately 4,000 implanted transistors.)[2]

It should be kept in mind that this technology was very new and difficult. Research was being conducted worldwide to develop this technology, but it was only in its early stages at the time the NTT project was begun. The project was therefore not only a case of original innovation rather than an attempt to catch up to the existing state of knowledge, it was also an undertaking that involved a great deal of difficult and relatively basic research. VLSI may be considered "evolutionary" in the sense that it was an extension of existing knowledge of integrated circuits (and was not as ambitious as more recent projects in Japan), but the new technological problems confronted in this research were substantial and attempts to develop this technology were expensive, risky, and very time-consuming.

For this and other reasons, NTT decided to invite the three companies to participate in this project and allocated 20 billion yen for it (approximately $100 million). In the earlier applied projects, such as the DIPS program, NTT would outline its needs and coordinate the research and development efforts, leaving the means to achieve the research goal up to the companies themselves. However, given the difficulty and poorly understood nature of VLSI technology, it was reported that NTT researchers initially had to specify everything and work closely with each of the manufacturers as they progressed in their research.

As in many of the earlier projects, the firms were asked to work on the same problems, again separately, but with frequent meetings for the exchange of information as the research progressed. According to persons interviewed, the firms soon found that the difficulty and newness of the research made closer cooperation a necessity, and the frequency and intensity of consultations were far greater than in the earlier case of simple integrated circuits where the technology was relatively well-known and uncomplicated.

At first the firms did not want to work this closely together because of problems of disclosure. However, several persons interviewed said that they were eventually convinced to do so in view of the opportunity the NTT project presented to work on the development of a technology they perceived as having great importance, and as ultimately having applications far beyond those NTT had in mind.

Meanwhile, MITI (which was reported to be under pressure from politicians) became concerned with the overall development of computer technology in Japan. According to official reports, MITI and the Japanese public and private enterprises were caught by surprise when they heard of IBM's "future systems" plans based on VLSI and other fourth generation technologies. (Some persons interviewed thought that the program to help Japanese firms catch up may not have been actually affected by this announcement, but that the announcement was politically useful.) MITI decided to stimulate research of a similar nature that would allow Japanese companies to compete at least domestically and hopefully internationally; Japanese firms were strong technologically in several fields, but semiconductors was not one of them in the mid-1970s. Because MITI's Electro-Technical Laboratory (ETL) had also been doing preliminary work on these problems together with five manufacturers (the same three that were working with NTT, plus Mitsubishi Electric and Toshiba), MITI decided to suggest to NTT that they combine their efforts into one large project.

NTT was at first not interested in doing this as its research was geared specifically to its own needs, and not to the needs of manufacturers wanting to develop general computer systems; however, it ultimately agreed to the plan. It appears that the firms themselves were also initially resistant to the idea of another MITI-sponsored project aimed at a general commercial market, possibly because of their experiences in connection with the reorganization program, as discussed in Chapter 3. According to observers, these hesitations were overcome when it was decided to stick strictly to relatively basic research and let each firm apply and commercialize the research results individually. (Government financial assistance helped to overcome this resistance as well; however, persons interviewed felt strongly that—contrary to what some think—government financial assistance was definitely not the only reason firms agreed to become involved in this project.)

The VLSI Technology Research Association was formed under MITI auspices in March 1976, including as members Fujitsu, Hitachi, Mitsubishi Electric, NEC, Toshiba, Computer Development Laboratories (CDL, the Fujitsu-Hitachi-Mitsubishi Electric "joint venture," as discussed in Chapter 3), and NEC-Toshiba Information Systems (NTIS, the other collaborative organization), together with technical staff from ETL and additional help from NTT. The Association was to conduct research over a four-year period, beginning in April 1976 and ending in March 1980. From then on the Association's role would be to handle patent requests and the repayment of government loans (or "subsidies"). These loans totaled over 29 billion yen (approximately $145.49 million) out of the total four-year budget of 70 billion yen (approximately $350 million), and it was stipulated that the loans be repaid out of profits resulting from the research successes of this project.[3]

By the end of the four years over 1,000 patent applications came out of the project, and the project was considered a success by technical experts the world over, including observers in the United States. For this reason, the VLSI project received international attention and became the most controversial of the national projects. Projects that allowed firms to "catch up" had not been given much attention, but the frontier VLSI, Fifth Generation Computer, and subsequent projects have been given extensive coverage in the advanced industrial countries.

The MITI-sponsored VLSI project was significantly different from both the NTT-sponsored program and previous MITI-sponsored national projects in several ways. First, the NTT VLSI program was designed specifically for DIPS and other NTT equipment, and was therefore more applications-oriented from the start. According to persons interviewed, the results of the project could not be used for general computer development without expensive conversion procedures due to its particular input-output and interface characteristics. In contrast, the MITI project was far more ambitious and attempted to further the basic research aspects as much as possible by selecting certain fundamental research themes and then pursuing these goals in a comprehensive way. For example, MITI was said to be concerned with examining several alternative methods for fine pattern generation and establishing which was best, whereas NTT was more concerned with developing a practical technique at an early date. The MITI project results could be incorporated into NTT technology, but the reverse was not as easy without undertaking a difficult conversion process.[4]

Second, besides being far more oriented toward basic research, the MITI VLSI program was different in that it was the first to employ a joint research institute in order to promote very close cooperation between firms. According to reports, MITI decided to try this approach because the rapid development of the technology appeared to be critical if Japanese firms were not to fall further behind, and the technology appeared to require very close cooperation if the goals were to be achieved. Most observers at the time doubted that the joint research institute form of organization would be successful, and the companies involved at first preferred to do the research in their own labs, citing the difficulties in carrying out very close cooperative research. However, on MITI's insistence the joint research approach was adopted.

The formal organization of the MITI project was as follows: the Association was subdivided into (1) the "Cooperative Laboratories" made up of all five single company members plus ETL, (2) the Computer Development Laboratories (CDL), and (3) NEC-Toshiba Information Systems (NTIS). The Chairman and Vice Chairman of the board were the presidents of Toshiba and Mitsubishi Electric, respectively. NTT's Director of the Plant Engineering Bureau and the presidents of Fujitsu, Hitachi, NEC, CDL and NTIS acted as directors. A former MITI official who had previous experience with other national projects was named Executive Director, and a former ETL engineer was appointed as Director of the Cooperative Laboratories. Research and clerical staff were contributed by participating companies, and were paid their normal salaries by the parent companies.

Although some have questioned whether firms sent their best researchers, Sakakibara and others noted the uniformly high level of the personnel's expertise. Sakakibara also pointed out that the Director of the Cooperative Laboratories personally selected the researchers and asked the companies to "lend" them.[5]

Regarding facilities, the Cooperative Laboratories were able to carry out their research at the newly-constructed NEC Central Research facilities and used NEC's technical library, saving them the expense of establishing these themselves. New equipment was purchased as needed, and was distributed among participating firms at the end of the project.

The Cooperative Laboratories are the key to the research institute's success or failure because, as was pointed out in Chapter 3, the function of CDL and NTIS in *this* project even more than in the earlier computer development case appears to have been solely administrative. It is said that the "Cooperative Laboratories" handled "fundamental" technologies, whereas CDL and NTIS were responsible for "application" technologies. However, it is again unclear whether CDL and NTIS in fact facilitated any cooperative research or played any important technical role in this at all. It appears that the application technologies which were developed and patented as a result of this project were essentially developed in individual companies, but were considered to be products of the Association in order to qualify for subsidies.[6]

Given that CDL and NTIS have been strictly applications-oriented, the interesting part of the project for present purposes is the organization and conduct of research done in the "Cooperative Laboratories." This institution, which again focused on the more "basic" research aspects of VLSI technology, contained at its height about one hundred researchers, including five or six from ETL. It consisted of six laboratories located within the same research complex, each of which was headed by a director. The six directors came from the five participating companies and from MITI's ETL.[7] According to the project's Executive Director, Masato Nebashi, the researchers in each lab were predominantly from the lab director's company, but other companies were represented in each lab as well; in other words, each lab had a company "coloring" (there was a "Hitachi lab," a "Fujitsu lab," and so on) in order to have a "critical mass" for decision-making, and was predominantly but not exclusively made up of that company's researchers.[8]

Each laboratory was assigned a specific research theme. These assignments were based upon prior negotiations and resulting agreements. According to one person interviewed, because microfabrication technology was considered to be important but very difficult, three labs were assigned to work on this (the "Hitachi," "Fujitsu" and "Toshiba" labs). Crystal technology was researched in the "ETL" laboratory. The "Mitsubishi" lab was assigned the responsibility of developing process technologies, and the "NEC" lab was given the task of developing device and "testing/evaluation" technologies.

According to Nebashi, during the first two years the labs were secretive about their research, and researchers tended to act as if they were working only within their own separate companies. Researchers from different firms did not mingle easily, and each lab stuck closely to its assigned task without much exchange of information (one laboratory went so far as to install equipment to keep the door leading from other labs locked). However, according to Nebashi, as work progressed the exchange of information became less difficult, and by the last two years of the project real cooperative work was done and technical information was readily exchanged. This exchange of information was done both informally through visits to other laboratories and discussions with researchers, and formally through "announcement meetings" (symposia)—about fifty in all—and the approximately 300 papers that were presented at those meetings. Communication was encouraged by eliminating doors between labs, setting up common rooms to be used by all researchers, organizing interlab discussions of general interest, and organizing year-end and other parties.[9]

At the close of the project the laboratories were disbanded and staff members returned to their respective companies. However, this does not necessarily mean the end of all exchanges of information: Nebashi noted that a "graduates' group" was organized and that these researchers "agreed on regular meetings to exchange corporate information," presumably general information relating to VLSI technology.[10]

The success of the Cooperative Laboratories in promoting technological innovation is indicated in the number and quality of patents that resulted from the four-year effort. The Cooperative Laboratories alone accounted for approximately one-half of the total number of patents produced during the four years. These were all patents reflecting new technology of a more "fundamental" nature, and they attracted world-wide attention, indicating their quality. Even IBM reported that the Association had surpassed it in certain areas of VLSI technology (e.g., electron beam technology). It is said that this accomplishment in basic research allowed Japanese firms to take the lead in developing 256K VLSIs and begin moving toward one megabit VLSIs.[11]

Of the approximately five hundred patents developed by the Cooperative Laboratories, it is said that 59% were developed by single individuals, 25% by several individuals from the same company, and 16% by several individuals affiliated with different companies.[12] About 5% of the patents were developed together with ETL researchers; presumably this would be part of the 16% mentioned above. The fact that a majority of patents were attributed to work done by individuals does not imply the unimportance of a joint research facility, just as the predominance of joint patents attributed to researchers from a single company over joint patents held by researchers from different companies does not imply a lack of cooperation between researchers from different organizations, but rather reflects the overall organization and mode of conduct of research.

Nebashi emphasized the importance of information exchange and the meeting of (and struggles between) diverse ideas and approaches as making these successes possible. According to him, the joint research institute form of collaboration was successful mainly because of (1) the long history of cooperation between competitors in Japan, which he referred to as the "coexistence of competition and cooperation in Japanese industries": this helped not only in the actual research, but with patent management and other administrative matters as well; (2) the sense of the clear importance of the project (recognized by everyone "from top executives to first line researchers"); (3) the existence of competition between labs to obtain better results (though not competition in the sense of "winners and losers"); and (4) the clarity of research themes, which were decided upon through discussions a year before the actual research was begun, and which were reevaluated throughout the four years. Nebashi also emphasized the importance of (5) the strict adherence to a timetable and (6) the facilitation of an easy flow of information, as other important factors contributing to research success.[13]

The first two points are obviously important for any type of cooperative research effort. The specific methods that help to make the joint research form of cooperative organization successful (points 3-6) serve to further differentiate the VLSI project from earlier applied projects. First, the earlier applied projects did not specify the research themes as clearly at first, and although there was a general expectation that the projects would end or a pilot model would be made by a certain date, the work did not have a strict timetable and was often carried on through subsequent projects that essentially extended the amount of time and money devoted to the initial endeavor. (It might be argued that this was an appropriate way of conducting the earlier projects, which were more applied in nature and which often took the form of passing through several "stages" as firms mastered and integrated increasingly complex knowledge.)

Second, there apparently was less of a spirit of "cooperative competition" and less of a flow of information in the earlier projects. The clear and limited goals of the VLSI project and the limited time period in which the research could be conducted appear to have facilitated this "cooperative competition," and caused researchers to work overtime and work together more systematically in order to reach the set goals by the end of the designated time period. Moreover, if the project had been designed to involve competitors in a series of joint ventures that were not clearly laid out from the start, the project would probably have been far less successful. As one person interviewed noted, even if cooperation is restricted to basic research, it is difficult to participate in *ongoing* undefined joint ventures with competitors due to problems of trying to coordinate two or more different ways of thinking. (However, it should be noted that these observations apply to *relatively* basic research. As the "pure" research end of the spectrum is approached, a clear and limited goal and a limited time period may be neither possible nor desirable.)

Opinions differ greatly regarding exactly how much close cooperation actually took place in the MITI-sponsored VLSI project, or how different the results would have been if firms had undertaken the research strictly on their own (i.e., how much delay there would have been). However, persons interviewed suggested that this project can be seen as another step by which competing firms *learn* new ways to cooperate with each other: overcoming barriers to cooperative research would have to be learned through a trial-and-error process, and it is very possible that, as Nebashi indicates, this project made a big step in that direction. It certainly made possible the *idea* of relatively ambitious joint research involving competing firms, both in Japan and elsewhere. For better or worse, this in itself puts into motion forces that favor the development over time of new and more ambitious forms of inter-enterprise cooperation: for example, as firms outside of Japan try to do this (with varying results), Japanese firms may be pushed even harder to find ways to reap the technological benefits of actual close intra-industry cooperative innovation.

Alternatively, firms the world over may just learn to use this as a way to get more government funding; many consider this to be the case with the development of research consortia in the U.S. (again, opinions vary tremendously). Certainly, a great deal of caution and a much closer examination of proposed and ongoing projects appear to be needed in order to prevent potentially significant problems from arising. More will be said about this below.

Comparisons with Applied
Intra-Industry Cooperative Research

In order to evaluate the role of cooperative research for basic research in general, and the role of the joint research institute form of cooperation in particular, we must now return to the more fundamental question addressed previously for the case of applied intra-industry research: under what conditions is cooperative research of this sort possible and desirable, from the enterprise's point of view, and what are the implications of this? To answer this question, it will help to review the conditions that were found to be important in allowing cooperative research to be carried out in the applied case (as discussed in Chapter 3), and compare these findings with the case of relatively basic research projects. Some of these preconditions are clearly more important in the basic research case, and some less so. Moreover, some of these points would apply just as well to cooperative research involving non-profit organizations, but all of them apply to private and even a large proportion of public (particularly commercially-oriented) enterprises. To take them point by point:

Technological and Timing Requirements. The clear technological and timing reasons that drive enterprises and organizations toward co-operation are very important in both relatively basic and applied cases, but are potentially even more important for basic research projects because, at least in many industries at the present time, basic research is one of the main areas of competition, and new knowledge and technologies can have wide-ranging effects. Moreover, the technological necessity for cooperation is likely to be even greater than in applied cases because the technologies are less well understood, more difficult and more complex. Finally, the need to be "first" or at least keep abreast of innovations of a more basic nature are at least as great as in the applied case, once the frontier is reached. In a rapidly changing and developing industry such as that of computers and telecommunications, basic research must be done not only effectively, but rapidly as well. In every case cooperative research has been said to shorten the development time, which tends to be long in the case of basic research (the longer the time period before the new technology can be developed and used, the less firms desire to undertake the innovation).

As in the case of applied research, the technological reasons for cooperation may stem from either the need to combine different types of expertise or the need to have a large number of researchers working on several different approaches. If the basic research is so "new" that all researchers will have more or less the same relevant knowledge, it may be particularly important (assuming that the goal is a desirable one) to allow researchers the chance to pursue indirectly several different approaches to a problem by having each firm or laboratory do research on a different alternative, and then report their results and exchange ideas as research progresses.

Whether researchers work on the same or different (complementary) problems, this type of division of labor should make research more focused and manageable and it should cut down significantly on the uncertainties facing each organization. The very fact that a major research program progresses in a coordinated way gives even private firms the incentive to invest and attempt to develop their assigned tasks in view of the promise of a scientific exchange of research results at the end of the program.

Many argue that this is important because firms are often not confident enough to pursue ambitious and highly risky, time-consuming basic research on their own. As noted above, there are usually many alternative approaches and parts to a project and firms cannot afford to explore them all, but the selection of an approach or a particular segment is a difficult process in itself. As one executive and technical manager interviewed put it, "For manufacturers, the most frightening thing is to go off in a bad direction." This lack of confidence means that ambitious projects would probably not be undertaken in the individual firm and the technology, and products and other technologies that might have resulted from it, would have to be developed over a much longer period of time (slowly, cautiously) if they could be developed at all. Thus, persons interviewed contend that cooperative basic research appears to be able to raise the overall pace and effectiveness of technological innovation.

Economic Aspects. The economic reasons for cooperative research are similar to those cited in the applied case, but are said to be even more acute because the costs and risks are usually much higher in the case of basic research. The skyrocketing costs and short lifespan of research equipment are important reasons why basic research is moving out of universities and is coming to be increasingly centered in firms, but according to interviews, when the burden becomes even too great for individual firms, cooperative research is increasingly proposed as an answer. (The alternative, according to one person interviewed, would be more government-funded research in university and government labs, but this is often not feasible.)

The risks to each firm include important technological uncertainties, which can be shared or reduced through cooperative research in the way described above. Again, many argue that the sharing of risks and costs is said to make projects possible that would otherwise not be undertaken.

History of Cooperation. Regarding the nature of participants, a history of cooperation among participating firms is undoubtedly even more important than in the applied case, given the close cooperation that is often called for and the potentially wide range of applications of the knowledge produced. In general, cooperation is easier in the case of relatively basic research than in applied research close to the stage of commercialization. However, the fear of disclosing new important information will tend to deter close cooperation for basic research unless the cooperative efforts take place within a strong atmosphere of mutual trust. This sense of mutual trust cannot be written into a contract, but rather must be developed slowly and carefully over time.

Levels of Expertise. The condition of high and more or less equal levels of technological expertise also appears to be far more critical for successful cooperation in the case of basic, as opposed to applied, research. The "free rider" problem of the participation of firms with relatively low expertise is avoided through the preselection process. Moreover, once selected, the firms are unlikely to assign researchers that are poorly trained to these projects both because the research results are considered to be very important to the firms and because they know that if they act as "free riders" they will develop an unfavorable reputation, and will not be included in future projects.

Clear and Important Goal. Even if cooperative research is justified for technological, timing, and economic reasons, there must still be a clear goal and sense of the economic importance of the project for this type of cooperative effort to be undertaken. This point was made very clearly by the Executive Director of the VLSI project. In the applied case, the eventual uses of the technology were relatively well known. As one moves toward the basic end of the research spectrum, however, the exact types and range of uses and the market are not as well known, making an explicit sense of the *potential* economic importance of this new technology far more of a concern than in applied research. Moreover, an understanding of the significance of the project appears to be particularly important in overcoming problems when researchers have to work closely together on the same themes rather than dividing up tasks, given the researchers' reluctance to cooperate this closely. A clear target or "threat" can give a sense of this significance.

Central Coordinator. The role a central coordinator can play is important but not as crucial as in the case of applied research; for basic research, firms appear to be able to govern themselves if they can manage to agree on a division of labor and a timetable. However, it appears that the larger the number of participants and the greater the importance of the proje t in terms of the resources that are to be devoted to it and its potential value, the more important a central coordinator becomes in order to resolve conflicting interests. Moreover, many contend that the *financial* assistance provided by an external organization—e.g., through government subsidies or grants—may be more important in the basic research case if the costs are very high and the risk is great due to the difficulty of developing the technology. However, whether government funding is appropriate or justified by these higher costs is, as noted above, a highly controversial issue, and needs to be considered carefully in view of the specific circumstances that are involved.

On the role of procurement in basic research: the element of procurement, which directs research toward a specific goal, usually has a positive effect on applied research, as in the DIPS case, whereas it could have a negative effect on basic research under certain conditions. The contrast between the MITI-sponsored VLSI project and the U.S. Department of Defense-sponsored Very High Speed Integrated Circuits (VHSIC) program illustrates this point. MITI's VLSI project was aimed at relatively basic research that would have a wide range of commercial applications, whereas the VHSIC program was oriented specifically toward the Defense Department's needs. In view of this, firms willingly participated in the VLSI project despite the anticipated problems, whereas many firms initially chose not to participate in the VHSIC program because its specialized needs were perceived as diverting their research staff and other resources from the pursuit of more generally commercially-applicable approaches to the technology. It appears that firms agreed to join the VHSIC project only when they were allowed to do research that *would* be commercially applicable.

The nature of competition and technology in the industry—e.g., how rapidly innovations must be developed, and how wide-ranging their applications may be—therefore affect the degree to which contracts, as opposed to subsidies or grants, can be used to encourage the development of a new technology. In general, basic research is more likely to be undertaken if the results are broadly commercially-applicable, whereas "broad commercial application" in the applied intra-industry case may make cooperative research more difficult, as this research is too close to competition at the product stage to allow for anything but relatively restricted efforts for a particular end result.

Innovative Environment. The need for a general innovative effort that includes a broad range of complementary projects is particularly important in the case of basic research. Without a wide range of projects being undertaken simultaneously, the relatively high failure rate of individual basic research projects may discourage further research in the field. It is said that this can be avoided if complementary projects contribute to each other and "spur" each other on, helping to make this type of research more effective and systematic.

Distance from Commercialization. The condition of the technology not being too close to commercialization holds by definition in the basic research case. However, basic research that is *too* far from commercialization may present a problem, as firms usually prefer to leave "pure research" to universities or government laboratories while they wait until a clearer commercial potential emerges before getting involved in the research.

To summarize, then, we find that intra-industry cooperative research must be neither too close in the applied case nor too far from commercialization in the case of relatively basic research, and that applied research usually requires a specific, limited application, whereas a broad commercial application is more important for basic research. (These, of course, are general principles, and exceptional cases may be found.)

Regarding the specific procedures for conducting cooperative research: it was seen that in the case of applied intra-industry research the most successful procedures involved dividing up tasks and instituting frequent consultations. This may work well for some, and perhaps even most types of basic research. However, for other types, many contend that having researchers from different firms work in very close proximity and prompt each other all along the way can actually speed up and make more effective their attempts to develop a particularly difficult, new and/or complex technology.

For this type of basic research, the organizing of a joint research institute, as occurred in the MITI-sponsored VLSI case, is said to be very useful. This type of organization appears to be most effective when the technical staff requirements of a particular project are large relative to the resources of individual firms. In the case of the crystal technology part of VLSI, for example, each company had very few researchers in this field relative to the number of specialists required and found that it helped to cooperate in order to speed up and make more effective the development of this technology. In other cases, a company may find that the experience and know-how of its technical staff is not diverse enough to cover the areas of knowledge required. In both of these cases a clear technological rationale exists not only for cooperative research in a general sense, but for a specific organization of research that allows for very close cooperation between researchers—e.g., in the form of a joint research institute.

Depending upon the requirements of the research, a joint research institute is said to be desirable from a capital and equipment point of view as well. By arranging to purchase and share expensive research equipment and eliminate research that overlaps with that carried out by other firms, individual public and private enterprises can make a very expensive research proposal somewhat more manageable financially, and therefore more likely to be undertaken.

Despite these advantages, we find that one of the main disadvantages of this type of organization is that it is very expensive to establish a research institute, buy equipment and supplies, and staff the institute. Only if the technology favors close cooperation, the timing of research results is important, the research to be undertaken is very expensive and risky for individual firms to do on their own, and the research is not only clearly important economically, but is also likely to be a success, is this form of organization likely to be adopted due to its cost. For projects that do not meet these criteria, the goal may be attained more economically if a special research institute is *not* established, and research is done on either an individual or cooperative basis, but is conducted primarily separately in each enterprise's existing research institute.

Besides the cost considerations, other potential problems that this form of organization can encounter include the difficulties involved in selecting appropriate goals and handling resulting patents. In the VLSI case, as the first attempt of this kind, the original goals were set too low by the firms, causing MITI to ask them to raise their research targets. (Goals were set too low presumably because firms initially had strong reservations about this type of close cooperative research and wanted to minimize the importance of the project. They may have been concerned about what could be achieved and about how much would be disclosed in such close quarters.)

Patent problems also had to be discussed in detail through frequent meetings. For example, there was pressure to open the patents to outsiders (other Japanese companies or foreign firms). It was finally decided that the patents could be used by all members of the Association, and that a patent invented by a particular member's researcher could be used without charge by third parties (e.g., IBM) that had a cross-licensing agreement with that particular firm. If the patent were developed together with government employees, however (as happened in about 5% of the cases), even firms that had cross-licensing agreements with member companies would have to contract for the patent through the Association. In general, all of the patents would be available to outside firms through contracts with the Association.

Given these difficulties and the expense involved, many have wondered whether the MITI-sponsored VLSI project would have been more economical, and whether the technology could have been developed just as effectively if research had been conducted in each enterprise and organization's lab separately. As noted above, there is no simple answer to this question, as it depends on the extent to which the sharing of technological know-how and equipment in this way speeded up the process by overcoming technological, psychological and other barriers that would have been encountered if the research had been conducted in separate laboratories. To some, the decision to duplicate this form of organization in the national project for research on opto-electronics (optical integrated circuits) and other projects indicates that it was considered successful enough under certain conditions to justify the expense of setting up a joint research laboratory.[14] Some see this as further evidence that the joint research lab can be much more than simply a means to get around the Ministry of Finance's reluctance to fund individual companies, and as being both technologically and economically justified for certain types of relatively basic innovative efforts. (This form of cooperative research could conceivably be used even in a few "frontier" applied projects, but it is not very likely because frequent meetings are usually sufficient in the case of frontier applied research until the pilot model or the actual product is put together. If researchers work very closely together only at the final stage, a joint research laboratory would probably not be economically justified.)

Leaving aside the question of the specific organization of cooperative basic research, there are also significant questions regarding whether the research could have been carried out just as effectively without government subsidies of any kind. In the VLSI case, each firm had done some research and continued to do relatively applied work on VLSI technology in their own separate research divisions, but it was reported that they did not feel capable of carrying out on their own the more fundamental and high-level work that was envisioned in the MITI-sponsored proposal.

In general, persons interviewed thought that for very expensive and very risky projects, it appears that without government assistance, firms will advance the research only as each aspect of the technology becomes better understood. Thus they contend that both cooperative research *and* government subsidies are being used in Japan as well as in other countries to quicken the pace as well as make the basic research efforts more effective. In the VLSI and in subsequent projects, they generally felt that the combination of cooperative research together with government subsidies of a "pay back out of profits" type helped to ensure the movement forward of these more ambitious basic research efforts.

Again, others are not so sure this is so. They are keenly aware of the degree to which firms use these arguments in order to receive government subsidies, and would prefer that private enterprises in particular fund their own research efforts, even if the pace of innovation is somewhat slower. In their view, the joint research lab approach may simply cover up the fact that public funds are being used to support individual powerful for-profit firms that are already technologically advanced, and are no longer justified (if they ever were) in receiving government assistance. In addition, some would argue that the "psychological barrier" that many described as a lack of confidence had a great deal to do with the end of the catch up period, and that firms simply needed to become used to competing at the technological frontier.

At the moment, we do know that a large proportion of both government policy makers and their industrial counterparts in Japan continue to favor government assistance for very ambitious cooperative research projects. According to one executive and technical manager, cooperative basic research in the form of "national projects," as an example, have been (justifiably, in his view) conducted in a form significantly different from the national projects of the past. The earlier "large-scale" (*ogata*) projects to develop the computer field were far from commercialization, but were simply evolutionary rather than being dramatically forward-looking (i.e., attempts to master entire new areas of knowledge). In contrast, the frontier projects have tended to be much further from commercialization, and have been decidedly more risky, long-term and ambitious in nature. These projects were thought to represent a new philosophy on the part of government policy makers: that universities and government laboratories alone should no longer bear the responsibility for relatively basic research, but rather that firms should also be involved in this forward-looking effort, with the government supporting those firms in their efforts. It is the government support that remains most controversial. (Interestingly, government support for explicitly commercially-oriented technologies—as opposed to defense purposes—has now become far more commonly accepted in advanced industrial countries than it was at the time of the VLSI project, in large part due to the perceived technological successes in Japan and to some extent in the East Asian NICs in recent years.)

Further Discussion

The intra-industry "basic" cooperative research discussed here is the form of cooperation that has drawn the most attention internationally, even though in the total realm of cooperative research practices it is the exception, rather than the rule. Even in developing countries that already have a number of different forms of cooperative research being undertaken within business or industrial groups, or between private firms and universities, government laboratories, or public enterprises, it is the idea of "R&D consortia" that has attracted the most attention.

This is understandable, given the high costs, risks and technological requirements associated with relatively basic research and the importance of this type of research, particularly as firms attempt to move toward the later stages of technological advance and embark on frontier innovations. Moreover, in the Japanese case, these late catch up/early frontier projects had the important psychological effect of proving that firms in this non-Western country had tremendous potential for innovation, and not just "imitation" or relatively limited improvements on existing products and technologies; a similar type of recognition is desired by many policymakers in other late developing countries.

Nonetheless, it is important to emphasize that in both advanced industrial and in developing countries these relatively basic research projects also have the potential of being very controversial, even more so than in the case of applied intra-industry research. Public expenditures may be greater in the case of "basic" research projects, and in some cases the beneficiaries may be limited to firms that are already economically and politically dominant.[15] Moreover, because of the nature of relatively basic research, meaningful results may not be immediately forthcoming, and the potential for spending large amounts of public funds on projects that enterprises eventually would have taken up on their own becomes a strong possibility.

There tends to be less controversy in countries whose public and private enterprises are farther from the technological frontier. Typically, in these countries the public enterprises and institutions do the bulk of "basic" research and transfer it to other enterprises and organizations, but over time public and private enterprises tend increasingly to work together as the latter increase their technological capabilities.

(We find very little controversy, and in fact much less discussion of cooperative R&D or "research consortia" in any form, in the least industrialized countries. This is due not only to the fact that relatively basic research is of much less immediate concern to them, but also because there has been more of a tendency to rely on international enterprises for new ideas and technologies. For this reason, the question of *when* cooperative intra-industry "basic" research might be of relevance to the least industrialized countries is a matter of pure speculation at this point.)

In advanced industrial countries, government-supported large-scale "basic" cooperative ventures may be controversial, but they are not likely to disappear anytime soon. For example, with regard to the future of cooperative "basic" research projects in Japan, recent indications are that as the Japanese economy slows down leading firms may attempt to seek out even more government support for their research efforts. The prolonged recession of recent years has cut private funds available for research (whether relatively basic or applied) that will take years before becoming commercialized; in response, companies in Japan have tended to rely more heavily on government-funded programs. For example, Sumitomo Electric is reported to have cut its research staff in superconductors from forty-two scientists to thirty-five, and according to one report, "instead of searching by itself for materials able to achieve superconductivity at higher temperatures, it will rely on the International Superconductivity Technology Center, a consortium largely financed by the Japanese government."[16]

If such reports are any indication, it appears that regardless of whether one thinks that public funds should or should not be spent to support large-scale "basic" research projects of this type, in the current international climate they are likely to continue to be promoted through government initiatives, both in advanced industrial as well as in many of the developing countries. In the U.S., for example, cooperative research has been encouraged in the 1980s and 1990s by such institutions as the Department of Commerce, e.g., through its Advanced Technology Program (ATP), and the Defense Department through its procurement and other policies; much of this has been of an intra-industry, relatively basic (or "generic") nature.[17] The Congressional hearings and other sources noted in Chapter 3, as well as numerous other studies, have dealt in part with a description and assessment of cases of cooperative R&D projects carried out in the U.S. in recent years.[18]

Intra-industry cooperative research of both relatively basic and applied types are also increasingly pursued on an international basis— i.e., involving enterprises of different national origins.[19] (In fact, there is a large and rapidly growing literature on the "new organization," and the need for networks and strategic alliances—including those extending across international boundaries—in order to compete in the "new" world economy.) Cooperative research projects that involve firms of different national origins have also become highly controversial, particularly when government funding has been involved. As an example, objections started to be raised when U.S. firms benefiting from the federal funding program began sharing their expertise with foreign companies and building factories abroad. (One such case occurred when Advanced Micro Devices allied itself with Fujitsu and set up a joint development program with a manufacturing facility in Japan, and IBM began doing joint development activities with Toshiba and Siemens in 1992; at this point many began to wonder about the wisdom of taxpayers funding cooperative research done by companies—e.g., via Sematech—that use their newly acquired skills to operate increasingly outside of the country. As the president of Sematech put it, "Clearly, the biggest concern is spending tax dollars to create jobs in other countries. But we are entering an era when nationalistic issues will continue to decline." He noted that even Sematech itself "gradually will become an international organization."[20])

Under these circumstances (i.e., that of the globalized advanced industrial economies), we can expect that cooperative projects increasingly will be used—controversial or not, and with or without government financial assistance—to help individual international firms with an increasingly tenuous national identity gain a competitive edge as they attempt to conquer international markets in their profit-seeking endeavors. However, this use of cooperative technological ties again takes us far from the issue of cooperative projects in a *developing country context* that help to broaden the technological base across a wide range of organizations and enterprises, benefiting the local communities. Of course, cooperative projects in developing economies could equally end up benefiting only *individual* economically and politically influential firms seeking to conquer international markets, but these projects are likely to be as controversial as are their counterparts in advanced industrial countries. In either case, more socially useful applications of cooperative techniques are clearly both possible and desirable; we will return to these controversies in Chapter 6.

For now, we will turn our attention away from the well-publicized cases of *intra-industry* research, and take up the question of different forms of *inter-industry* cooperative research—i.e., that involving firms in *different* industries—in the following chapter. Inter-industry cooperative research is notable as being not only far less controversial, but also far more common, than are the intra-industry forms of cooperation discussed up to this point. Inter-industry cooperative research has particular relevance to a wide range of late developing countries, including those characterized by "groupings" (through family, regional, or other networks) of domestic enterprises, as will be discussed in both Chapters 5 and 6.

Notes

1. According to estimates based on a Japanese government survey, less than 14% of interfirm collaboration was directed at basic research in the early frontier period; one-third of cooperative projects were defined as "applied," and over half were considered "developmental" (from Rokuhara, 1985, p. 40). This conforms with the idea the vast majority of collaborative efforts have been small-scale and applied in nature. However, the relative amount of basic research in the later frontier period (i.e., in more recent years) tends to be larger, as the importance of basic research has become increasingly recognized across a broad spectrum of industries, and firms have found it increasingly difficult to provide the necessary funding without pooling their resources with others, particularly in a slow growth economy. These trends may tend to boost the proportion of relatively basic research (as distinct from "pure" research, which is likely to undergo a decline in slow growth economies even though its importance will increase in the long run), but this depends on political conditions in individual country contexts.

2. More specifically, each "k" represents the capacity to store 1024 bits of information.

3. Government subsidies were 3500 million yen the first year, 8640 million yen the second year, 10052 million yen the third year, and 6906 million yen the fourth year, totaling 29098 million yen. The VLSI project represented the hardware part of the Fourth Generation Computer program; under this program, subsidies of 20 billion yen were also given to CDL and NTIS to develop the "Operating System," or software, part of the program, and 3.5 billion yen was given to these five and three other companies—Matsushita Communications, Oki Electric, and Sharp—to develop new peripheral equipment. Sakakibara pointed out that this average annual outlay was approximately two to three times the normal annual research expenditure for semiconductors of the five major companies, but it was not more than some U.S. companies spent alone each year for this purpose. Cf. Sakakibara (1983), pp. 14-15.

4. VLSI research continued within NTT alongside the MITI-sponsored project. These efforts resulted in the world's first 128K device (designed for use in telecommunications), among other achievements (cf. Gregory, 1982, p. 3). Persons interviewed also noted that although NTT would not duplicate the Fifth Generation Computer project sponsored by MITI, NTT labs planned to carry out research on aspects that were clearly related to NTT's needs and interests. This "overlap" of research themes does not necessarily lead to a duplication of research, but instead often produces results that are complementary, as noted above.

5. Cf. Sakakibara (1983), p. 14.

6. In the "Operating System," or software, part of the Fourth Generation program, NTIS and CDL may have played a more significant role as their staffs are said to have included systems engineers as well as sales personnel. However, it is also possible that these organizations once again simply served as a means by which government subsidies were given to the five firms involved, which then developed the software separately. As noted above, it is difficult to cooperate this close to the point of commercialization.

7. According to Sakakibara (1983, p. 9), approximately fifty additional companies (including Toray Industries, Canon, Olympus Optical, and Toppan Printing) worked with the Cooperative Laboratories in making machines on an experimental basis.

8. From Nebashi (1980, 1981), and interview with Mr. Nebashi. Some journalists reported at the time that only the members of the lab director's company were present in each lab. This appears to be incorrect, but even if it were correct, the more important question is how closely the different labs were able to work in order to integrate the different aspects of the VLSI technology they were assigned to develop.

9. In addition, researchers were encouraged to go out drinking together, participate in Saturday meetings to "deepen mutual understanding," and join the Association's sports club. Cf. Nebashi (1980) and Sakakibara (1983).

10. Nebashi (1980).

11. For details on these successes, see Sakakibara (1983), p. 11, and Gregory (1982), p. 3.

12. Sakakibara (1983), p. 13.

13. Nebashi (1980).

14. The cooperative laboratory for research on optoelectronics was established in 1981 (the project extended from 1981 to 1989). Participants included ETL and nine other companies (the "Big Six" and Sumitomo Electric, Matsushita and Furukawa), and research was conducted on six themes in six research laboratories. In contrast, it was decided not to use it, at least in the initial stages, for research on fine ceramics as was originally proposed, presumably because it was not either technologically or economically justified in that case.

15. As an example, there has been extensive public debate in recent years regarding the use of government funds and policies to aid the chaebol of South Korea, and by extension the use of public funds to aid leading firms (often chaebol members) involved in R&D consortia.

16. "Japanese, in a Painful Recession, Trim Industrial Research Outlays," *New York Times*, November 29, 1993, p. D1.

17. New ideas for cooperative R&D involving the dominant firms in an industry continue to be pursued in the U.S. For example, in the mid-1990s the "Partnership for a New Generation of Vehicles" program was said to embody "an exclusive R&D arrangement between the U.S. government and Detroit's Big Three auto makers." ("U.S. Study Faults Japanese Multinationals," *Asian Wall St. Journal*, October 19, 1994.) In the same month, a collaborative venture, with U.S. federal funding—involving IBM, AT&T, Motorola and Loral—was announced

with the goal of developing X-ray lithography for future chips ("The Incredible Shrinking Chips," *Financial Times*, October 29-30, 1994).

18. Studies of cooperative R&D in the U.S. have increased enormously over the past years. A sampling would include Bozeman, Crow and Link (1984), Dimancescu and Botkin (1986), Link and Bauer (1989), Radtke and Ponikvar (1984), and Vonortas (1991), among others; a list of references up to 1990 are also cited in Vonortas (1991).

19. Regarding case studies of *international* cooperation for R&D, cf., for example, Roehl (1987), Mowery (1988), and Mowery and Rosenberg (1985, 1994); see also Cowhey and Aronson (1993), particularly as regards alliances for cooperative R&D across international boundaries.

This type of international cooperation—among equals, rather than unequals as in the earlier technology transfer case—appears to be a growing trend. It is difficult to tell how close this cooperation actually is; however, such joint efforts as Hitachi's "wide ranging cooperation" with Control Data on terminals, Fujitsu's joint development of numerical control equipment with Siemens, and NEC's cooperation with Data Communications Corporation to develop a wide range of digital equipment could in principle be cases of actual joint *intra-industry* research between (more or less) equals. The joint venture involving IBM, Toshiba and Siemens to jointly develop higher capacity memory chips, and Advanced Micro and Fujitsu to develop flash memories, could also be cases of actual cooperative intra-industry R&D. (The Toshiba, IBM and Siemens alliance is said to have developed "the world's smallest and fastest" microchip of its kind—the 256-megabit DRAM—in IBM's research facility; see "Hi-tech Powers Design Superchip," *The Asian Age*, June 7, 1995.) In addition, several Japanese companies have set up short-term "information exchange" relationships with foreign companies (e.g., Hitachi with Motorola for five years) in order to keep both companies aware of new developments that occur in either company, or in the industry in their respective countries. Finally, increasing numbers of international joint ventures to "design new products" appear in daily business newspapers. For example, on October 18, 1994, on p. 9 of the *Asian Wall St. Journal*, entries included "Beijing, Seoul to Work on HDTV," "Sony, Microsoft and Phillips Ally to Create Interactive Music CDs," and "Silicon Graphics Units Plans to Unveil Chip to Rival Digital's" (the latter involving Silicon Graphics working with Toshiba, and NEC designing the chip). These "development"-oriented joint ventures presumably involve relatively little basic or applied research.

Inter-industry cases of international cooperation have also become plentiful in recent years. For example, "Sumitomo 3M" (involving 3M, NEC and Sumitomo Electric Industries) and "Mitsubishi TRW" (involving TRW, Mitsubishi Electric, Mitsubishi Heavy Industry, Mitsubishi Trading Company and Mitsubishi Bank, to do software for space development) are joint ventures that were said to have been established for purposes of joint research, although it is not clear how "joint" the research actually has been. Fujitsu's cooperation with Furukawa Electric and Corning Glass has been one in which Corning Glass supplies both companies commercial-use optical fibers, Fujitsu supplies Corning with the technology to connect the fibers up with telecommunications terminal equipment, and Furukawa Electric supplies Corning with information on developments in their telecommunications group. In the international arena as well, it appears that in order to do close cooperative research, a long learning process is necessary.

20. "Rethinking the National Chip Policy," *New York Times*, July 14, 1992, p. D1.

5

Cooperation Between Firms in Different Industries for Purposes of Innovation, and Comparisons with Intra-Industry Research

Forms of Inter-Industry Research

The development of altogether new products (serving new markets or needs), as opposed to simple product differentiation, is very often made possible through the incorporation of "new" scientific knowledge and "new" techniques (new to the firm) into the design of existing products. This knowledge or technical know-how often comes from scientific or educational institutions, or is adopted from other industries.

When knowledge and techniques from one industry or several industries are required for the development of new products or processes in another industry, cooperation between firms in different industries can provide the most effective way to transfer and combine the knowledge and techniques quickly, given the time it takes to acquire the technique or set up a new division embodying those techniques within the enterprise or organization. This use of the inter-industry form of cooperation for the development of specific new ideas, products and processes is far more widespread and frequent than is the intra-industry form of cooperation discussed in the two previous chapters. (The very large number of inter-industry cases cited each year in the *Keiretsu no Kenkyu* volumes, as opposed to projects involving intra-industry cooperation, give some indication of this.) The intra-industry case may be more "dramatic" than the inter-industry type of cooperation, but it is also much harder to organize and carry through, particularly when direct competitors are involved. It is also much less clear how much cooperative research is actually done in intra-industry projects, as opposed to the inter-industry case, where cooperation is far more pervasive and open and there is much less controversy surrounding the cooperative projects.

One question that arises is: how is the case of cooperation between one large firm and one or more small firms different from that of cooperation between divisions within a single large diversified firm? (For example, what is the difference between Hitachi cooperating with smaller companies and different divisions of TRW pooling their resources and cooperating with each other?) Cooperation between firms in different industries might be equivalent to interdivisional cooperation within a single firm if that firm has already diversified into the different relevant industries. However, when the firm does not "cover" the fields or industries necessary for the specific products or processes in question to be developed, cooperation between two or more separate firms in different industries can provide a means to gain access to information, knowledge and technical know-how that has no equivalent in even the most diversified multiproduct firm.

This type of cooperation has taken on a variety of forms in Japan, ranging from informal consultations, "research groups" to explore potential new areas of innovation, and research projects that involve no change in organization, all the way to more formal research joint ventures. It has allowed for a great deal of flexibility in terms of being able to combine a very wide range of experience and technical expertise. It also has had the advantage of being able to draw on enterprises and organizations that have developed a good working relationship, a sense of mutual trust, and a relatively long-term commitment to working periodically with each other, without these necessarily becoming ties that are too restricting.

In addition to this relationship between enterprises for the development of specific new products, a looser, more general and ongoing relationship between firms and organizations in different industries has served to provide a stream of *information* over a long period of time concerning new opportunities and new knowledge and techniques that would be of interest to other firms. This looser form of cooperation between firms (and other organizations) in different industries has been particularly helpful to enterprises seeking to enter into new fields. The content of information will differ according to whether firms are in growing industries and are aggressively looking for new investment opportunities near or at the technological frontier, or whether they want to diversify out of declining industries into "established" industries.

In either case, this "information group" principle has allowed enterprises to share information about potentially important new technologies and new product areas throughout the period in question. In addition, this exchange of information has acted as a means to arrange the more *specific* form of inter-industry cooperation discussed here—i.e., cooperation for the development of new products and ideas through the combining of knowledge and techniques (technological cooperation). This loose, ongoing cooperation of the "information group" type also has no functional equivalent in even the highly diversified multiproduct firm: divisions can, of course, relay information to other divisions within the firm, but given the relatively limited scope of any one enterprise or organization, the "information group" with members in a wide range of industries and technical fields can at the very least be an important supplement to other means of obtaining this information.

Cooperation between firms and organizations in different industries can therefore be either of the specific or more general "information group" type. It can be used both for the development of new products and industries and for the firm's attempts to move into established industries that are new to the firm, but not new to the world.

This chapter will focus on the more specific type of cooperation, i.e., cases of inter-industry technological cooperation for new product and process development. The emphasis will be on the ways in which firms in different industries in Japan during the late catch up/early frontier period have cooperated to produce new knowledge in an effort to generate new products or new industries, either by combining existing knowledge and techniques and developing them further, or by doing more basic and frontier applied cooperative research (again, "basic" is used here in the sense of relatively fundamental research with a general commercial goal in mind). This chapter will not deal with inter-enterprise cooperation in the sense of cooperation to establish a new product area or industry based solely on imported technology, or cooperation to help a firm move into a well-established product area or industry, although these efforts can in some cases act as precedents to the type of innovative activities discussed here, affording both experience and linkages.[1]

Examples of inter-industry cooperation will again be drawn primarily from the computer and telecommunications industry (and related industries) in Japan. Because this industry is still in a dynamic, emerging state, inter-industry cooperation in recent years has served mainly as a means to combine and develop the previously separate fields of computer and telecommunications technology into a new, transformed industry, and then to extend the new technologies into additional product areas, "spinning off" new industries from the combined industry.[2]

General Characteristics of Inter-Industry
Cooperative Research Projects

Because of the combined nature of this industry and related fields and the rapidity with which they continue to develop, we find that firms have had to ensure access to a very wide range of knowledge and technical know-how to remain competitive over time. This required knowledge has included not only that of computers and tele-communications equipment per se, but also such diverse technologies as those involving lasers, optical fibers, satellites, and new materials. In addition, these firms, either through their own efforts or through cooperation with other firms, found that they needed to have at least a working knowledge of such fields as numerical control, medical, and automotive technologies in order to develop applications of computer and telecommunications technology in these fields. According to persons interviewed, staff researchers in these firms ranged from pure mathe-maticians to physicists to linguists and psychologists as well as electronics engineers, but firms still found that the range of knowledge and/or experience necessary for the desired innovations was greater than that possessed by their own staff members. The "complexity" of the industry thus has invited cooperative efforts, under conditions to be discussed below.

Not every new technology requires cooperative effort, but the firms in this industry in Japan found that cooperative research was occurring frequently enough that the choice of a research partner became an important issue. Informal research partnerships have tended to develop over time between firms in different industries. In the late catch up/early frontier period research partners were drawn from within the same industrial or business group for certain types of inter-industry research, or from outside the ranks of these groups whenever a particular firm's technological know-how was needed.

As in the case of intra-industry research, if the development of a new field required a series of cooperative projects, it was important to develop an ongoing relationship with cooperating firms in such a way that a good working relationship could be established and maintained. This type of relationship was particularly important the closer the research was to the technological frontier because of the potential problem of research partners disclosing proprietary information to out-siders. Moreover, the need to innovate quickly in a highly competitive field favored firms that have developed a good working relationship, if cooperative research was involved: working out the details of cooperation may otherwise take a great deal of time. Japanese firms have found in the past that this type of relationship was easiest to establish with domestic firms, but such a relationship could—and undoubtedly increasingly will—be worked out over time with international firms as well as the need arises. Moreover, although certain types of inter-industry projects have historically been conducted within industrial or business group boundaries, over time firms have increasingly tended to cross group lines in order to gain access to specific new technologies and other resources (i.e., to develop new ongoing relationships outside of traditional group boundaries); this is consistent with the overall pattern of crossing group lines as is necessary or desirable now that firms have caught up and face new challenges (including the full internationalization of the economy).[3]

In general, inter-industry cases of cooperation for innovation involve mostly applied and developmental research, although a small amount of basic research may be done as well.[4] In the case of firms from different industries cooperating to develop specific new products, the usual procedure has been for a firm seeking to improve its established products to attempt to integrate the knowledge held by a firm in a different industry into its *existing* products, thereby transforming those products. (An example of this might be the addition of computer-based controls to existing equipment.) For this type of cooperative effort, very little basic research was needed.

In some cases, the two firms would work together to develop an entirely new product, as when a general electronics firm worked with a camera firm on new types of copying equipment, or when an electronics firm and an aerospace firm pooled their researchers to develop new types of sensing or monitoring equipment. This would involve far more intensive cooperative work. The question was one of how to combine and develop the knowledge the firms have about their respective fields. This effort usually involved more than simple developmental work, but it appears that only in exceptional cases did problems arise that required a substantial amount of basic research.

This has also been true in the case of cooperation for the development of "systems"-types of products. Here, the developmental component tended to be stronger than in the individual commodity case, but this depended upon the type of system to be constructed. The putting together of a system may involve only the linking up or simple combining of existing products, in which case not much original research was required. However, the further development of such a system may involve the integration of new products and functions in a way that transforms the "existing" products into something quite different; this type of effort would call for applied and sometimes relatively basic research.

For example, in the case of Toshiba's effort to develop "office automation," the first step was to develop individual products: the plain paper copier, facsimile, word processor, small business computer, and other office equipment. This involved both relatively basic and applied research (relatively *basic* for devices such as integrated circuits and, even more so, their successors, and *applied* for each piece of free-standing equipment). The second step was to begin integrating these products into a system that exists within a single office, modifying and further developing them so that their functions could be enhanced. This involved a good deal of applied and developmental research. The third step was to move toward eventually integrating this system (which operates within a single office or firm) into a larger system that links firms and other organizations through a variety of means, including optical fiber-based and satellite communication networks. Depending upon the problems encountered, in this type of multistage effort firms found that applied and possibly even relatively basic research might be needed. Moreover, the more new, difficult and diverse technologies are required to be integrated and developed further, the greater the incentives would be for the use of interfirm cooperation in this effort.

At each stage of the further integration and expansion of the system, the component products must be reevaluated and replaced or modified, and new components added. The new functions envisioned as the system expands, making more services possible, often are not technologically practical without further research. Thus the progress from the simple combining of existing products through the development of a fully integrated system creates the conditions for the generation of new knowledge and new commodities in its wake.

The firms found that the more elaborate and original the new products or systems, the more planning and coordination was required. The development of very "advanced" systems, for example, involved a very expensive, risky and time-consuming process. The most ambitious "systems"-type projects were generally undertaken through business, or in some cases industrial, group efforts, or through the sponsorship of a government agency or public corporation. (Less formal "groupings" that developed a mechanism for making and carrying out group decisions could also undertake such projects.) Groups or government agencies may act according to the suggestion of individual firms, but the projects that these groups or agencies organized were usually those that individual firms had difficulty organizing by themselves.

Individual firms tended instead to initiate cooperative projects that were relatively small-scale, inexpensive, and "paid off" quickly. They tended to be projects to develop individual commodities or simple systems, and involved only a small number of firms. (A "simple" system here indicates one that is small in scale and scope.)

In this way, we can distinguish between two main types of co-operation between firms in different industries: (1) cooperation between two or more firms for the development of specific new products, processes and simple systems, and (2) business or large industrial group or government–sponsored cooperation for the development of more ambitious systems. (One should nonetheless keep in mind that the difference between these two types is often just a matter of degree.) In all of these cases inter-industry cooperation was chosen over development within a single firm for reasons that are similar to intra-industry cases of cooperation: the need to combine knowledge and develop the commodity or system effectively and in as short a time as possible, as well as to share costs and risk. The form of cooperation simply changed according to the circumstances of each case.

Cooperation for the Development
of Individual Products and Simple Systems

Most cases of cooperation for the development of specific new products and simple systems were initiated by a single firm. The participants in the project may have received small government grants or designed the new commodities to be sold to government agencies or public corporations, but these cases of inter-industry cooperation were virtually never organized or coordinated by either group or government bodies, apart from individual cases of procurement.[5] Instead, the initiating firm chose one or more partners, making the selection according to the technology needed and the ability of the firms to work together; the former reason often drove them to seek partners outside of "group" ranks, whereas the latter drove them to select partners from within the group.

Examples of this type of cooperation between firms that are members of the same industrial or business group include Fujitsu's cooperation with Furukawa Electric Company's cable division for the development of optical technology, and Toshiba's cooperation with Ishikawajima Harima Heavy Industries and Sanki Engineering for joint research on freight shipping and discharging systems.[6] Fujitsu is a member of the Furukawa group, which is part of the larger Dai-ichi Kangyo Bank (DKB) group, and Toshiba is a member of both the "Toshiba-Ishikawajima Harima Heavy Industries Group" (an industrial group) and the more general Mitsui group (a business group). For this reason, Fujitsu has tended to work with Furukawa members (e.g., Furukawa Denki Kogyo) and sometimes DKB group members, whereas Toshiba tended to cooperate with Toshiba affiliates and Mitsui members (e.g., Sanki Engineering) whenever possible.[7]

Interviews indicated that the preference has been for cooperation with industrial group members first, business group members second, and others after that.[8] Firms within the group would be selected not only because of the mutual trust and good working relationships that have developed over time, but also because of the obligation on the part of the smaller affiliates to accept the large firm's request for participation—it was difficult, although not impossible, to turn down such a request. Nonetheless, when the level of technological expertise needed was not available within the group, firms would seek cooperative partnerships outside of it. This would tend to occur more when the technology needed was very new, difficult or specialized, whereas relatively simple, standardized or widely-available technology could usually be supplied by a group member.[9]

The usual procedures for cooperation of this type involved the "separate but together" approach described in the intra-industry cases of cooperation above, except that inter-industry cases usually involved the dividing up of tasks, and rarely involved several firms being directed to work in different ways on the same task. Typically, there was only one firm representing a particular industry or type of technology in these cooperative efforts. Firms therefore cooperated to define the problem and divide up tasks, and met often in order to develop the new technologies necessary for the individual parts and then the entire integrated product or system. As in the intra-industry cases, the degree of close cooperation depended on the newness, difficulty, and complexity of the new products and technologies: again, relatively basic research required more intimate cooperation, whereas the simple fitting together of existing products, on the other extreme, usually required only periodic meetings.

Most cases of inter-industry cooperation during this period fell in between these two extremes. The most common case was that of an individual company working with one other firm (whether a subsidiary, affiliate, or unaffiliated company—sometimes a "user," or customer) to develop a particular product. Examples of this include, in Hitachi's case, Hitachi working with Unitika, a textile and plastic engineering firm in the same Sanwa Group, on an "anti-disaster" system; with Teraoka Seisakusho, an unaffiliated large commercial scale manufacturer, on a new type of electronic scale; with Nagoya Kiko (unaffiliated) for stacker cranes; and with Nippon Kokudo Kaihatsu and Hitachi Kenzai, a Hitachi affiliate, on underwater bulldozer systems. Small and medium-sized companies have also commonly engaged in this type of cooperative activity. For example, Yaskawa Electric Manufacturing cooperated with Shinto Kogyo for the development of a fully-automated casting plant, and Pentel (formerly a stationary company) worked with medium-sized Murata Data on facsimile equipment.

Moreover, in the late catch up/early frontier years this type of cooperation was used by practically every large firm in the computer and telecommunications industry in order to develop new applied fields. In the case of developing control machinery for shipping, for example, Mitsubishi Electric worked with Mitsubishi Heavy Industries, Hitachi worked with Hitachi Shipbuilding, NEC worked with Sumitomo Heavy Industries, Toshiba worked with Ishikawajima Harima Heavy Industries, and so on (i.e., they tended to work with their own group affiliates in shipbuilding/transportation equipment). Similarly, in the case of developing small-scale control systems, Toshiba worked with Tatung Signal Company (an affiliate) and Hitachi worked with Nippon Signal Company (unaffiliated) on control systems for trains, oil pipelines, and other uses. In the case of the development of new transportation systems, NEC worked with Niigata Engineering (a DKB member), Hitachi with Tokyu Car Corporation (a Tokyu Group member), and Toshiba with Anzen Sakudo (a cable and ropeway manufacturer; the latter project is interesting in that it was not aimed at either particular users or an immediate market, but rather was an experimental attempt to develop the technology for a small monorail, with an eye to a future market).[10]

When the undertaking was designed to meet the needs of a specific customer, as opposed to being sold on the general market, the "user" and possibly other companies were brought into the cooperative effort. The "user" was very often in the same business or industrial group. For example, Toshiba worked with Honshu Paper—also a Mitsui member— to develop a fully automated paper-making process for the company's own use, and Fuji Electric worked with Kawasaki Heavy Industries and Isuzu Motors (all DKB members) for the application of control machinery technology for Isuzu's use.

All of these cooperative projects were initiated either by one of the main potential participants in the development of the new technology, or by a potential user of the new technology. They were not large-scale "group projects" coordinated through a presidents' club, bank or trading company, in the sense that will be discussed below.

The way in which tasks were divided up is seen very clearly in the collaboration between Fujitsu Facom, Kawasaki Heavy Industries (both DKB members), and Yamatake Honeywell (unaffiliated, but which also works with NEC), for a robot system to be sold to Fujitsu Fanuc and Hino Motors (a Toyota member). For this project, Fujitsu Facom developed the machinery group control system, Kawasaki Heavy Industries developed the industrial-use robot, and Yamatake Honeywell concentrated on the all-purpose hand for the robots. They had to work closely together to design the project and work out the details of the development and fitting together of the different parts as the project progressed. For this type of applied and developmental research a joint research institute was not required, but frequent meetings were.

Regarding the question of whether this type of cooperation would be limited to a single point in time or would be ongoing, this depended upon such factors as the rapidity of technological change in the field of knowledge required by the initiating firm and the importance to that firm of the technology to be obtained. According to persons interviewed, if the technology required were "singular" in the sense of being identifiable existing knowledge held by the other firm, cooperation tended to be limited to a single point in time. Occasionally, however, the knowledge required was of a less identifiable, "ongoing" sort because of rapid technological change in that field of knowledge. The firm might then choose to develop an ongoing cooperative relationship with the other enterprise in order to be kept up on new developments that could potentially benefit the initiating firm's products. If the field of knowledge were important enough to its products, however, persons interviewed indicated that the initiating firm would eventually set up a new division within the firm itself in order to have that technology and know-how readily available.

Cooperation for the Development
of Large-Scale Systems

The procedures for carrying out inter-industry cooperation for the development of "complex" systems were somewhat different from the case of individual new products or simple systems, although there was a considerable amount of overlap and the distinction between these was not always an easy one to make. As discussed above, a system usually integrates individual products into a "whole"; a complex system refers here to one that is relatively large in scale and scope. In their most developed forms, systems (particularly complex systems) not only combine products, but integrate them in such a way that they become capable of carrying out functions that are not possible either as individual products or as a simple combination of products put together into a coordinated whole. In the office automation example referred to above, the system that links offices, libraries, data processing facilities and other institutions involved more than a simple combination of existing products (copiers, word processors, and others). The new needs to be met and functions to be carried out required that the integrated system allow more than the simple sum of the functions of each of its parts—i.e., one could not simply link together a few pieces of existing equipment and call that "office automation."

Cooperation for the development of complex systems often involves several firms representing several different industries, in contrast to the usual relationship between a restricted number of firms that characterizes inter-industry cooperation for the development of individual commodities and simple systems. For example, although Mitsubishi Electric's or Toshiba's cooperation with Japan National Railways (JNR, the formerly public enterprise) for the development of the superconductive magnet for a "linear motor car" could be considered cooperation for individual commodity development if the vehicle alone were the object of cooperation, the need to integrate the vehicle into a new, coordinated system of transportation would eventually require the collaboration of firms with several different types of expertise, taking it out of the individual commodity category.[11] Whether this could be considered a "simple" or "complex" system would depend upon the ambitiousness of the project—i.e., the scale, and the range of fields that must be coordinated. Similarly, although cooperation between electronics firms and rocket body manufacturers for the rocket alone was for the most part similar to cooperation for the production of an individual commodity, the more complex requirements of the entire rocket-based space effort required cooperation with several other enterprises representing several other different fields.

For these large systems, greater planning and coordination has been necessary due to the range of enterprises and industries involved in the development efforts. Although small-scale systems-type projects were often successfully carried out within a single diversified firm or through cooperation between a firm and one or two other enterprises, complex projects were usually large enough in scale and scope to require a central body or agency that planned the project in outline (specifying the "need" in detail), selected the participants, and coordinated the carrying out of the project. For example, new weaponry and defense systems, telecommunications systems, and hospital systems all have required extensive inter-industry cooperation in order to develop the new technology; because of the costs, risk and coordination problems, a central organization or agency must commission and coordinate this type of effort if it is to be undertaken at all. The new technology may *later* "filter down" to individual homes or offices (e.g., laser technology incorporated into new types of audio equipment, or advanced medical equipment in private doctors' offices), but if the technology is radically new rather than simply combining existing products or technologies, a large purchaser/ coordinator usually has been required for its development.

In Japan, this "central organization or agency" has tended to be either

(1) the coordinating body of a business group or a large industrial group (or a new informal grouping), or (2) a government agency or public enterprise. The research projects coordinated by groups of private firms have been directed toward relatively quick commercial gains, whereas the government agency and public enterprise–sponsored projects have had somewhat different ends in mind. In addition, each of these selected the participants for joint research projects in different ways, as will be explained below, beginning with the group-centered research projects and then going on to non-group based projects.

Regarding group-based research: when a group's coordinating body (usually the leading firm, the presidents' club, the group bank, or the group trading company) organized large-scale systems-type projects, participants were drawn, with rare exceptions, from among group members. As noted in Chapter 1, this type of group-sponsored effort was particularly pronounced beginning in the late 1950s in such fields as nuclear power, ocean development, and urban development. Although many of these early projects anticipated a faster growth of demand for their integrated services than actually developed and were not as successful as expected, group-based projects continued to be important throughout the period. This has been true particularly in cases where very large amounts of capital were required, the project was naturally "inter-industry" in the sense that it was not a clear outgrowth of a particular industry, and the project was close to commercialization and did not involve a great deal of risk with respect to the development of the technology and the securing of a market.

In the 1970s and 1980s business and large industrial group projects were also undertaken in such areas as business consulting, metals development, manganese development, coal liquefaction, and computer services.[12] The "computer services" projects, for example, involved up to thirty members of a business or industrial group in the provision of systems engineering and software services (one such example would be NEC's NEAC Information Processing Service group, which in the early 1980s was composed of twenty-three affiliated companies).

Smaller and more specialized service groups also arose at this time, including those offering environmental engineering services (e.g., the Hitachi Water Management Group, made up of Hitachi, Hitachi Metals, Hitachi Chemical Company, Hitachi Plant and Engineering, and occasionally Shin Meiwa Industry and Horiba, all Hitachi affiliates), and cable television software groups (e.g., Nippon Cable Television, which brought together Hitachi, Nippon Educational Television, Tokyu Agency, and Asahi Evening News information services).[13]

As noted above, not all of these group projects were successful. For example, Mitsui Seiyaku Kogyo, which was established by Mitsui Toatsu Chemicals and was made up of the twelve Mitsui companies that were to work together to develop new medical products, found that the field was not expanding rapidly enough and ran into severe financial difficulties. Finally, Mitsui Toatsu took over the company and one-third of its employees were transferred into other divisions.

Nonetheless, in new fields characterized by a growing market, these group-sponsored projects were said to have been very successful. In fact, a number of "think tanks" for business and industrial groups, including Mitsubishi, Hitachi, Furukawa, Tokai, and Sanwa, were established under such names as "information planning centers" and "general planning research institutes" with the purpose of providing an information source for possible group projects and new products. Moreover, several persons interviewed and other published sources (including the *Keiretsu no Kenkyu* volumes) noted the apparent strengthening of group connections in the 1970s and 1980s, judging from the increase in inter-corporate shareholding, the participation of new firms in presidents' clubs, and the increased participation in group projects.[14] This was also a period in which new members were brought into both business and industrial groups for technical reasons (i.e., their technological capabilities in particular fields), thus enabling them to participate in group-sponsored projects.[15]

Because of developments in science and technology and the perceived need for large-scale "systems" in the future, including "social systems" related to such fields as city planning, transportation, and health systems, many firms in Japan have anticipated the need to cooperate with firms in other industries. For this reason, from the 1970s on, many firms without sufficient industrial or business group connections sometimes have appealed to large banks, securities firms or other institutions to act as central coordinators for large-scale systems-type projects in which they could participate; this essentially has amounted to the establishment of new "business groups" coordinated by that institution. Such a trend indicates the importance of business and large industrial group membership, together with newer, less formal groupings, for the organization and execution of large-scale commercial inter-industry projects.

These business and industrial group projects are to be contrasted with efforts, particularly smaller-scale ones, whose desired goal fell obviously within the bounds of a particular industry: in the latter case, the project was usually organized by a large firm within that industry, which invited firms in the other required industries to participate in a cooperative effort. (These firms might belong to the same group, a different group, or be independent of all group ties.) The group projects are also to be contrasted with projects that were judged to be socially beneficial, but were risky and further away from the stage of commercialization, or were expected to be unprofitable for a long period of time: projects of this kind were seldom undertaken without government agency or public enterprise supervision and support.

These latter types of government-sponsored projects typically involved frontier applied research of a complex systems-type in defense, energy production, urban planning, transportation systems, and other "infrastructural" fields. Grants and subsidies were typically bestowed on these research projects, ranging from small-scale grants to large-scale grants or subsidies for national projects. Public enterprises have also promoted research of this sort, not only when the object of research was expected to be immediately commercially successful, but also when the research was judged to be necessary for "infrastructural" (including social) investments, requiring large amounts of capital investment without the possibility of returns in the near future.

With respect to the selection of participants, both government agencies and public enterprises have tended to ignore industrial and business group membership and have selected the firms that appeared to be most qualified for the project, although a public enterprise may favor firms it has worked with in the past (in essence, its own "group" members), and both have historically favored domestic firms, for a variety of reasons (including the desire to bring up their level of technology). Industrial and business group membership has entered in only if a contract is awarded to one company and that firm is allowed to choose other participants, in which case it may select its own group members.

Even here, technical considerations have usually prevailed: for example, Mitsubishi Heavy Industries chose to do joint research with NEC, a Sumitomo member, on the AAM2 (air-to-air) missile project rather than with a Mitsubishi group member. This project was sponsored by the Defense Agency, and included Mitsubishi Heavy Industries as main contractor, NEC as manufacturer of the homing system, and Daikin Kogyo as manufacturer of warheads, among other firms. Mitsubishi Heavy Industries chose NEC (perhaps under Defense Agency pressure) because the latter had been working for some time on a homing system with the Defense Agency—even before Mitsubishi became the main contractor for this project.[16] In general, group membership was not a major consideration for government-sponsored research projects for complex systems; in the case of grants, for example, the usual practice has been for one firm to be named as prime contractor, and other firms are given contracts on the basis of their bids.

Complementarity of Different Types
of Inter-Industry Cooperative Projects

Despite the fact that the type of research project undertaken tended to differ depending upon whether it was initiated by an individual firm, a group coordinating body, a government agency, or a public corporation, there was in fact a certain amount of overlap in terms of research goals, and a definite complementarity in these efforts. This has promoted the simultaneous following of different paths to the same general goals by using a variety of methods and by pursuing different "subgoals."

For example, in the case of optical fiber-based television and communications systems, which combined elements of inter-industry and, to some extent, intra-industry cooperation, research was carried out not only by (1) large firms and their affiliates, but also by (2) firms organized under NTT (public enterprise) sponsorship and (3) firms participating in an experimental program coordinated by a government agency and funded by government grants. To some extent, this apparent duplication of research efforts seems to have been caused by in-fighting between the Ministry of Posts and Telecommunications (and NTT, its affiliate) and MITI, both of which wanted a strong foothold in the future of this industry. However, the research emphases and participants were in fact very different in each of these three programs:

1. The large electronics firms concentrated mostly on the equipment ("hardware") aspects of relatively small-scale systems.
2. In contrast, because NTT envisioned the eventual laying of an optical fiber system throughout the country, it brought together firms from different industries to do the initial research for the eventual development of a large-scale system.
3. Finally, the "Hi-OVIS" (Highly Interactive Optical Visual Information System) project to create an actual working "interactive video system" based on this technology was established through the process of firms bidding for government grants administered through MITI. This project involved firms that are not affiliated with one another. It essentially allowed them to put their ideas into operation in the form of a simple working system, which in turn allowed them to focus as well on the range of possible *uses* (the "software") for such a system (this was true even though the project was still very far from commercialization, as it would probably depend upon NTT's optical fiber "lines").[17]

Therefore, in the case of the optical fiber-based television and communications technologies, the efforts of large firms and their industrial groups concentrated on developing products that they could sell individually or as part of a small-scale (essentially self-contained) system, whereas the firms organized by NTT focused on the development of large-scale as well as smaller systems that would utilize NTT's "lines" (infrastructural investments of whatever nature). Finally, the firms brought together under a government grant concentrated on exploring the possible uses of these systems. There may have been some overlap in these different projects, but their emphases were clearly different, and as we will see, appear to have been complementary in nature.

Regarding the type of cooperative research in these optical fiber-based cases: as was true for most systems-type projects, the research was primarily applied and developmental, as the basic research on optical fiber technology had already been done by this time. However, it tended more toward developmental work in the grant case and more toward frontier applied research in the NTT and industrial group cases.

Close inter-industry cooperation was very often necessary only in the early stages of a project. In the optical fiber-based television and communications case, cooperation was necessary primarily at the experimental or applied stages of research, but not at the developmental stage. In NTT-sponsored efforts, for example, once these optical fiber-based systems had moved closer to the stage of general commercialization, NTT could simply specify the type of equipment it desired of its suppliers based on these experimental projects. Similarly, firms could simply make specifications and purchase the necessary equipment from their group affiliates once the initial work involving close cooperation was completed. The more difficult the technology, the more research was necessary before this developmental stage, involving only a small degree of cooperation, could be reached.

We have seen that inter-industry research often has been carried on both within the company, and in various forms of cooperative projects, which may overlap with each other. This "overlapping" approach to commercially-oriented research can allow a new technology to be developed from a number of different angles. As was true in the intra-industry case, the same large firms were often involved in several complementary cooperative projects, including those that they initiated, those they were invited to join, and those that they were allowed to join by winning a contract or grant.

Moreover, these joint research efforts complemented the research done exclusively within the firm itself. One person interviewed estimated, for example, that of the total research that Toshiba engages in for its efforts in the "space development" (aerospace) field, about 30% represented the firm's own research, whereas joint research accounted for about 35% and purchased technology another 35%. Other rough estimates of the contribution of joint research to the firms' total research efforts in the fields that make use of joint research ranged from 10% to 40% of the total (these estimates pertained to major firms in the computer and telecommunications industry).[18] Thus, although a firm's research on a particular technology may have been conducted primarily in its own laboratories, it might also have had access to the staff and equipment of public enterprises or government labs, and it might coordinate research with work going on in the laboratories of other firms according to the requirements of the project.

This leads us to the question of the eventual "internalization" of research, eliminating the need for joint research as the firm becomes more established in a new field. As discussed above, in the case of individual commodities and simple systems, interviews indicated that if the new field were important enough to the firm, it would eventually establish a new division and attempt to carry out most of the functions necessary for the further development of new products in that field within the firm itself. (However, even after a new division had been established, the "former" research partners might still maintain cooperative ventures with and sales to the company establishing the new division, given that the new division was not likely to duplicate the entire range of products and technologies of the research partners; rather, it would internalize only those fields that were found to be important in view of the firm's own plans for expansion.)

In the case of complex systems, the total internalization of research was much more difficult and was unlikely to occur because of the extremely wide range of know-how and facilities required for such complex systems. As in the case of simple systems, "ongoing" joint research might be used indefinitely for applications outside of the firm's main product lines or for specific unimportant components of a system that were thought of as being "best left to specialists." (One example that was cited is that of the furniture that would house the components of a "home information system": in this case, firms were expected to continue to cooperate with other firms rather than take on these responsibilities themselves.) In the case of complex systems, however, ongoing joint research would probably be necessary even if the field proved to be a key area of concern to the firm.

The inter-industry projects discussed above were conducted primarily in the late catch up/early frontier period, as public and private enterprises in Japan continued to learn to use new forms of cooperative technological ties in order to strengthen their technological capabilities. Cooperative efforts of this type have remained important, and in the future systems-type cooperative projects in particular are expected to multiply as commodities are combined and then extended in the form of more complex systems. This represents an outgrowth of both developments in science and technology and a calculated effort to develop new products in this manner. Judging from these trends, we can expect that inter-industry cooperation between firms will remain important not only for the development of individual new products, but for the development of both simple and complex systems as well.

Inter-Industry and Intra-Industry Cooperation: A Comparison of Main Points

In this chapter, we have seen that during this period there were two main types of inter-industry cooperation between firms: cooperation for the development of individual commodities and simple systems, and cooperation for the development of complex systems. We found that the bulk of the joint research conducted for both types of projects has been in the "frontier applied" to developmental range; a small amount of basic research may have been necessary for these projects, but this only supplemented the primarily applied body of joint research to be carried out.

It is useful to recall that *intra-industry* cooperation (often involving cooperation between competitors) has been generally successful only in the cases of (1) relatively basic research for the development of technologies that serve as "elements" of individual commodities and systems, and (2) relatively applied research for individual commodities or even systems-type products if done on a procurement basis, or for very specific and limited projects. Intra-industry joint research was found to be very difficult (except in the procurement case); inter-industry joint research, in contrast, has been mostly applied or developmental and close to commercialization, and has faced far less of the difficulties of disclosure and rivalrous behavior.

Regarding the initiation or "sponsorship" of inter-industry cooperation, we found that cooperation for the development of individual commodities and simple systems was usually initiated by individual firms. Cooperation for the development of complex systems, however, was most often initiated either by the coordinating body of a group or a government agency or public enterprise.

In contrast to this, it should be remembered that there were virtually no cases of group sponsorship of *intra-industry* research for the simple reason that there is usually only one major firm representing a particular industry within a single business or industrial group. (At the most, there might be smaller, more specialized affiliates in the same group: cooperation between the larger firm and its smaller affiliate did not require group "sponsorship" in the sense used here. It should be kept in mind that groups with two major firms in the same industry were strictly the exception during this period.) Just as in the inter-industry case, there may be overlapping research in the efforts sponsored by different organizations having different emphases; however, in the intra-industry case, the overlap was between (1) the internal efforts of individual firms, and the efforts of (2) public enterprise-sponsored and (3) government agency-sponsored research. As discussed in Chapters 3 and 4, the first tended to be relatively small-scale and commercially-oriented, the second was generally more ambitious but with specific applications in mind, and the third was ambitious but concentrated more on relatively basic research. In both the inter- and intra-industry cases, persons interviewed contended that these diverse efforts usually proved to be complementary and contributed to the firms' overall knowledge base.

Regarding the form of cooperation, it was noted that cooperation in the inter-industry case usually involves the dividing up of tasks between participating firms, whereas in the intra-industry case tasks might be divided up, or several firms might be asked to work together on the same tasks, following similar or different approaches. In both inter- and intra-industry cases, the closeness of the cooperative effort (i.e., the frequency of meetings and the necessity for the physical proximity of researchers) appears to have depended upon the newness, difficulty and complexity of the products and technologies; cooperation was "closer" for basic and frontier applied research, and "looser" for purely developmental research.

The reasons for undertaking inter-industry cooperative research were similar to the reasons cited for intra-industry cooperative research. In both cases, the *technological* requirements of the research (the knowledge and expertise necessary, or the need for a large staff of qualified personnel), together with the requirements of rapid development (the *timing* aspect) were among the most critical factors that pushed firms to undertake cooperative research rather than carry out research exclusively within the firm or "through the market." The technological and timing considerations were particularly important in the case of frontier research. In addition, the *costs* and *risk* associated with certain types of research were contributing factors leading to the decision to engage in cooperative research. This technological flexibility gained by the public or private enterprise is enhanced by the fact that research teams can also be disbanded once their usefulness has ended; the *long-term* affiliations and *ongoing* cooperative technological ties may operate through teams that are formed and reformed as required by technological and timing considerations, and—in certain cases—by cost and risk factors.

On the question of whether research would remain in the realm of inter-enterprise cooperation or would eventually be internalized within the firm, persons interviewed indicated that the tendency was to eventually set up a new division and internalize the research if the new field were judged to be important to the firm's main efforts; this applied to both inter-industry applied research and intra-industry basic research. However, in the case of large complex systems, research would most likely continue to be conducted on an interfirm basis even if the field is a key area of concern to the firm.

These, then, are some of the main findings and comparisons that have emerged from our study of both *intra-industry* and *inter-industry* forms of cooperative technological ties. It may be worth noting that a very interesting study conducted by Niwa and Goto (1993) complements and reinforces many of these findings. Based on their sample of 474 companies that responded to their questionnaires regarding collaborative (cooperative) R&D, including intra-and inter-industry R&D projects of all "sizes" (but primarily the typical, relatively small-scale forms), the authors found that 89.5% of the enterprises had experiences with collaborative R&D in the preceding five years, whereas only 7.8% had no such experiences.[19] Moreover, 67.7% of the responding enterprises reported that collaborative R&D had been increasing, while only 4% reported a decrease in such projects.[20]

Jumping to the authors' conclusions (on p. 208), we find the following points:

1. Collaborative R&D has been increasing, and will increase in the future.
2. The purpose of R&D of this type depended upon the type of partners involved. "The factor of economizing R&D resources seems to be a primary and basic purpose of R&D collaboration, but it does not have an active function. One active function of R&D collaboration is the so-called synergy effect that companies conducting collaborative R&D can create new ideas, new technology, and/or new product concepts during the collaborative process. This effect seems to have become a strong expectation among participants. One effect of synergy is to reinforce corporate technology. For this purpose companies did not select partners of collaborative R&D from companies of the same industry."
3. Respondents thought that in the near future, the "social contribution" type of R&D (e.g., "contributing to solving social problems based on technology development, contribution to the solving of global environmental problems, and international technology transfer") would increase. Here, governmental and

national organizations typically select and organize participants in cooperative projects. (In the present study, these are referred to as social "infrastructural" types of projects.)

4. Finally, according to the authors, "the responses to R&D management regarding collaboration revealed the four most successful management items, that is, clarity of the project target, leadership...[qualities] of the project leader, ...[periodic] information exchange and progress control, and having influential supporters of the project."

These findings, along with other such surveys and quantitative studies, reinforce the idea that the most typical cooperative projects are the multitude of relatively small-scale and intra-industry applied and developmental efforts, and that the bringing together of resources from different fields of technology (what the authors call "synergy effects") may be equally or, under certain conditions, even more important than cost and risk considerations. The study also indicates an increasing trend with respect to cooperative R&D, suggesting that its usefulness continues beyond the late catch up/early frontier period, well into the stage of competing at the international technological frontiers as enterprises in a "mature" advanced industrial economy. (A follow-up analysis of trends in the context of an economy in recession—e.g., in the mid- to late-1990s—would allow interesting comparisons to be made.)

For all of the reasons cited above, some forms of inter-industry as well as intra-industry cooperation involving enterprises and organizations can be expected to continue into the "later" frontier period to be an important source of innovation, just as they were in the late catch up/early frontier period. Inter-enterprise cooperation can be seen as one way in which public and private enterprises and other organizations in Japan attempted to form technological networks that helped establish the knowledge and technology base necessary for technological catch up, including technological adaptation and innovation, and then begin the movement into frontier areas of research.

Further Discussion

The examples of *inter-industry* cooperative research cited here took place during the late catch up/early frontier period in Japan, and to a large extent they represent the use of cooperation for purposes of technological catch up. However, it appears that this form of cooperation can be used as well for the development of frontier technologies—e.g., for altogether new forms of transportation, as the linear motor car example cited here illustrates.

We find some parallels to these cases in other advanced industrial countries. For example, defense agencies throughout the world organize inter-industry "cooperative" projects (again, drawing expertise from a number of *different* industries) to develop new defense-related technologies, particularly when complex systems are involved. However, to the extent that such projects are one-time events, it will be difficult for truly cooperative behavior to emerge, involving more extensive sharing of information and expertise in ways that come more easily when the participants regularly engage in collaborative efforts of one form or another over a period of time. Some of the projects discussed here did involve participants that worked with one another one time only, but to the extent that even unaffiliated (independent) firms found themselves cooperating in a *series* of projects of different types (with different initiators or sponsors), cooperative behavior in the sense used here was more likely to emerge.

Given the types of inter-enterprise ties and relatively close government-industry relationships that exist in many late developing countries, it appears that the political economic circumstances of many late entrants will be far more conducive to these types of cooperative relationships than would be true of enterprises in most of the early developing countries. We have noted the importance of formal and informal affiliations between individual enterprises (e.g., as ongoing "partners" or subcontractors), as well as the roles played by public enterprises and government agencies and laboratories in initiating and coordinating cooperative inter-industry projects (i.e., as "central coordinators").

Because potential central coordinators of this type (public enterprises, government agencies and others) often play a very significant economic role in the more industrially advanced of the later entrants, and because cooperative ventures already exist in such areas as marketing, finance and services (e.g., as used by group or business network members and their affiliates), it is very likely that cooperative projects for *technological purposes* will increase over time as well as the catch up/early frontier efforts of enterprises become more intense. To the extent that enterprises—both public and private—in late developing countries find it useful to cooperate domestically rather than rely solely on foreign suppliers of ideas and technologies, they are likely to use these institutions to increase the sources of information and the range of knowledge, skills and other resources they can draw upon in order to increase their collective technological strengths. (As will be discussed in the following chapter, this generalization would not appear to hold true in the case of the least industrialized countries.)

In contrast, we are unlikely to see the breadth and depth of cooperative efforts of this type arising in other advanced industrial countries because the precedents and institutions are largely lacking—for example, it is much easier to form Sematechs in these economies (involving firms in the same industry brought together for limited purposes) than to build MITI-type organizations, public enterprises, industrial and business groups, family and other inter-enterprise networks, and other economic institutions—including ongoing inter-industry affiliations used for initiating cooperative research—that are more closely associated with late developing economies.[21] Again, *individual* inter-industry cooperative efforts are likely to be successful in other advanced industrial countries (and in the less industrialized countries as well, particularly those with kinship, regional, or other ties that help to link up modern sector enterprises); however, the *widespread, overlapping and complementary* forms of inter-industry cooperation discussed here are not likely to be duplicated easily in advanced industrial countries with their histories of atomistic and individualistic competition, and the prevalence of a "winner takes all" ethic.

Thus, with regard to *inter-industry* forms of cooperation as well, it appears that the more industrialized of the late developing economies, rather than the advanced industrial economies, may make greater use of inter-industry types of cooperation, specifically in order to increase the speed, flexibility and effectiveness of technological catch up and early frontier efforts. This is especially true in the cases of complex or combined industries and areas in which "systematization" is occurring.

The use of this type of cooperative practice is also facilitated by the fact that there tends to be much less controversy surrounding inter-industry cooperation (as opposed to the more expensive intra-industry cases, for example), and there is likely to be much less resistance to such projects from any quarter. Keiretsu-like ties have been challenged by certain advanced industrial countries as resulting in unfair competitive practices, but for the most part group-sponsored research projects have not been targeted specifically as being unfair. This may be in part because the most high-profile cases of formal group sponsorship of such projects in Japan occurred during the late catch up, and not the later frontier, period of innovation, and perhaps because the most common forms of cooperative inter-industry research are relatively small-scale and involve no government funding.

Examples will be given in the following chapter of firms in the more industrially advanced of the late developing countries that have already begun using inter-industry, as well as intra-industry, cooperative technological institutions and practices, and of firms in other countries that appear to be moving in a similar direction. The chapter will also examine cases of latecomers in which such collective efforts are *not* likely to develop in the foreseeable future, and discuss why cooperative research efforts are unlikely to emerge in these cases in the near future.

Finally, although most of the discussion thus far has dealt with private and public enterprises that have been attempting to increase their technological powers for commercial purposes, we will also explore a theme briefly introduced in this chapter: that of cooperative research used for infrastructural and other non-commercial, socially beneficial ends. This type of research has the potential to involve a wide range of organizations—public, private, and non-governmental—and is particularly relevant to and has important implications for large sectors of the contemporary developing world.

Notes

1. Examples of cooperation to establish a new product area based on imported technology include the case of business group members cooperating in order to enter the low-density, high-pressure polyethylene industry, as noted in Chapter 1. Examples of cooperation to help a firm move into a well-established field or industry include such cases as that of Kanebo Kagaku (the chemical division of a textile company) jointly developing a drainage (pumping) system with TDK using ferrite technology in order to enter that market; Hitachi, Mitsubishi Electric, Mainichi Broadcasting, ICI (of England) and Ciba Geigy helping Teijin (a textile manufacturer) to move into the electronic video recording industry; Mitsubishi Electric working with TEAC in order to enter the audio equipment and VCR (VTR) markets; Toyota helping its associate Toyoda Spinning and Weaving move into the auto parts industry; and Toshiba cooperating with Tokyo Alarm Hochiki and Nihon Victor to enter the emergency use broadcasting equipment field. (These examples are taken from various *Keiretsu no Kenkyu* volumes.)

2. Other new fields and industries that are the focus of cooperative activities involving inter-industry research include new materials; new sources of energy; and biotechnology, "bioreactors" and "biomaterials," to name only a few of the ongoing projects of the late 1980s and 1990s.

3. An example of the firms crossing group lines to work together on overseas ventures includes the case of several Japanese enterprises from different groups working together with India's Thapar Group to develop a coal-fired electricity-generating plan in Western India. The Japanese firms include the Marubeni Corporation and Toshiba Corporation, along with Hitachi Ltd., Ishikawajima Harima Heavy Industries Company, Tokyo Engineering Corporation, a subsidiary of Tokyo Electric Power, Bank of Tokyo, Sakura Bank Ltd., and several trading companies (Itochu Corporation, Kanematsu Corporation, Mitsubishi Corporation, Mitsui and Co., Nissho Iwai Corporation, Sumitomo Corporation, and Tomen Corporation). (*Asian Wall St. Journal*, October 19, 1994.)

In addition to overseas ventures, unexpected economic difficulties may also encourage new modes of affiliation. As Suzuki observes, "The outright rivalry that has characterized inter-group relationships during the period of Japan's high economic growth waned and was supplanted by great cooperation following the oil crisis of the mid-seventies. This is clearly reflected in the proliferation of major inter-group joint ventures" (1988, p. 53, quoted in Orru, 1991, p. 250). In other words, firms may go outside of group boundaries more than in the past, which many interpret as indicating a loosening of keiretsu ties (for interviews regarding the idea of a loosening of keiretsu ties in recent years, see, for example, "Loosening of the Corporate Web" and "Mitsubishi's Extended Family," *Financial Times*, November 30, 1994, p. 13).

Such reports do not suggest that the group form is disappearing, particularly as a means of sharing information (see the *Financial Times* article cited above for interviews giving examples of continuing *intra-group* cooperative activities). Gerlach (1992a) discusses not only the benefits of inter-corporate and inter-organizational alliances, but also the perils of pursuing a "lone-wolf" strategy in an economy characterized by "alliance capitalism." As an example, he contrasts the successful reconstruction of Toyo Kogyo by Sumitomo Bank and other affiliates with the difficulties faced by Sanko Steamship when it reported bankruptcy in 1985. According to Gerlach, the latter had not only avoided long-term alliances with any particular group of firms, but had also become "alienated from the larger Japanese community in the early 1970s by its highly unusual attempted hostile takeovers of several Japanese firms" (p. 200), and suffered the consequences. Similarly, Miyashita and Russell (1994) argue that although industrial groups have come under a great deal of pressure in the slow-growth years, business group ties still offer a great deal to group members—i.e., the benefits still outweigh the inconveniences. As they put it, "And yet, we see examples of very large, independent firms (e.g., Suntory, Kyocera, Hoya), that have decided to ally themselves with the Big Six. We see Toyota, which by all rights should be pulling farther away from the Mitsui Group, holding a full member's seat on the Nimoku-kai. If keiretsu membership for the Old Three were basically a matter of post-zaibatsu family unity, and for the New Three were little more than opening a pipeline to a big bank, the whole system would seem to have little relevance in the 1990s. Why, then, would a senior executive of a fiercely independent, family-controlled company like Suntory Cement say 'We must be in a keiretsu to compete effectively?'" (Miyashita and Russell, 1994, p. 196.)

Thus, the group form is maintained, while at the same time new, *ongoing relationships* are developing for a number of reasons—technological, financial, and other—and that these trends are reflected in new affiliations for cooperative R&D as well as for other cooperative ventures, often involving non-group members. This is particularly true, but not exclusively so, when government procurement or international projects are involved.

4. It is not clear, for example, how much relatively *basic* research has been featured in biotechnology projects, which over the years have brought together firms from such diverse fields as the food industry, pharmaceuticals, and breweries. (One such example from the early frontier period would be the cooperative research involving Ajinomoto, a food industry company, and

Mochida Pharmaceutical, for the development of A-145, an anti-cancer drug. Cf. Nikko Research Center, 1980, pp. 95-96.) It is likely that most of the cooperative cases in biotechnology have involved directing technical skills toward relatively applied research tasks.

5. Examples of procurement include Fujitsu's joint research with Nippon Telegraph and Telephone (Public) Corporation and Japan (National) Railways to help develop an electronic system for trains, and Hitachi's work with Kawasaki Heavy Industries and the Sapporo City Transportation Bureau on the Sapporo subway system. For other cases of inter-industry cooperation carried out on a procurement basis, see the *Keiretsu no Kenkyu* volumes and individual company histories.

6. These and other examples cited in this chapter (unless otherwise noted) are taken from interviews and the *Keiretsu no Kenkyu* volumes covering 1971-1990.

7. As one source of additional examples of both "small" and "large" *inter-industry group* projects, cf. Fruin (1992). He cites a number of relatively "small-scale" (but, in sum, significant) cases of cooperative R&D involving group members: for example, he describes the Toshiba (Yanagicho Works) IC card project that began formally in 1985, involving a number of Toshiba divisions and research units, as well as companies within and outside of the Toshiba group (pp. 247-8). He also presents a detailed account of cooperation between Mitsubishi Motors, Mitsubishi Electric and Mitsubishi Heavy Industry, stating "The combined talents of Mitsubishi Electric and Mitsubishi Heavy Industry gave Mitsubishi Motors a leading edge in designing and producing the auto-motive subsystems that are still on the drawing boards of rival firms. The utility of interfirm cooperation is beyond question" (p. 197). In this context, he also notes, "The leading edge that Mitsubishi Electric and Mitsubishi Heavy Industry gave Mitsubishi Motors was not financial in character. Lead-time savings are far more important than cost savings in development and design activities, especially when a new model can reconfigure industry standards in rapidly changing markets. Where costs are well known or fairly estimated in advance, that is when sourcing parts and components is a low-risk activity, group affilia-tion means little or nothing at all. In such instances, Mitsubishi Motors or any other major manufacturer simply buys from the lowest cost producer. However, when close coordination between different steps in the development sequence is critical and, therefore, when ease and speed of effective communication in product development are of primary importance, the tacit, implicit, and some-times explicit ties of cooperation based on interfirm affiliation are irreplaceable. Coalitions like the one binding MMC, MHI, and MELCO offer a more rapid, less costly, and less irreversible response to market and technological innovation that internal development, provided that coalitional partners do not waste resources in excessive monitoring and governing activities" (pp. 197-198).

8. A survey conducted by Japan's Fair Trade Commission, however, found that 83% of inter-industry cooperative research projects surveyed involved firms that were *not* affiliated in the sense of formal business or industrial group ties. Cf. Kosei Torihiki Iinkai Jimukyoku (1984), p. 20; quoted in Samuels (1987), pp. 23-24. This study, and its data base, would have to be examined further in order to

explain the discrepancy between this and the impression given by the *Keiretsu no Kenkyu* volumes and interview data. New "groupings" and cooperation between formally unrelated firms are certainly on the rise, but the incidence of selecting partners from among affiliates whenever possible still seems to be a very common practice. (It is possible, for example, that the inclusion of one non-group firm in the project classified a heavily group-based project as "non-group," or that the survey focused primarily on government-sponsored projects, which usually try to avoid organizing along group lines.)

9. Once a good working relationship outside of the group is established, it tends to continue. For example, according to interviews, Fujitsu usually worked with Toyota on various projects, despite the fact that Toyota is formally affiliated with a different group (Mitsui); interviews further indicated that Fujitsu would not work on a regular basis with Nissan, Toyota's competitor. (Nissan in turn often worked with NEC.) Firms may develop long-term ties with a number of "independent" companies as well. For more on the recent tendency of firms to select partners from outside of their business or industrial groups, cf. Imai (1990).

10. Other cases of *inter-industry* cooperation involving group members would include the automobile electronic engine control systems projects—e.g., those involving (1) Nissan and Hitachi, which are historically linked through the Nissan zaibatsu and later bank ties, on the one hand, and (2) Toyota Motor, Toshiba, and Nippondenso, all Mitsui affiliates, on the other. Cases of *intra-industry* cooperation involving members of different groups and/or independent firms included the MITI-sponsored attempts to develop electric cars. The two research groups in this project include (1) Daihatsu Motor, Nippondenso, Yuasa Battery, and Matsushita Battery on the one hand, and (2) Toyo Kogyo, Hitachi, Fuji Electric, Japan Storage Battery, Shin-Kobe Electric Machinery, and Furukawa Battery, on the other. See Nikko Research Center, 1980, pp. 82-83 on the engine control system projects, and the same publication, p. 62, on the electric car case.

11. As noted in Chapter 3, the nonmagnetic manganese steel for this project was jointly developed by Daido Steel and Toshin Steel, in what is presumably a case of cooperative *intra-industry* applied research. Other parts of the project involved inter-industry cooperation for the development of separate parts (e.g., the superconductive magnet). However, the system as a whole drew together electronics, steel, rubber tire, cable, inorganic chemical, measuring/control instrument, and other manufacturing firms, as well as Japan National Railways and the Tekken Construction Company (ibid., pp. 67-68).

12. The example of coal liquefaction processes included three private sector processes, two of which were group-based: these included the "Sumitomo coal method," the "Mitsui SRC method," and a third process (the "KOMINIC method") that involved Mitsubishi Chemical Industries, Kobe Steel, and Nissho Iwai (the latter two firms are affiliated with the Dai-ichi Kangyo Bank Group, which is not connected to the Mitsubishi Group). Three other approaches were also being pursued through the government-sponsored "Sunshine Project" in this period: one was heavily "Mitsubishi-colored," one was an outgrowth of the Sumitomo efforts, and one involved firms from several different groups (ibid., pp. 28-30).

13. In the case of the development of cable television hardware, leading firms pulled together affiliates from both business and industrial groups to combine the studio equipment, antenna, cable and other technologies necessary for the projects. Typically, the large electronics company and its group affiliate in the cable industry would form the core of the group effort in this industry. NEC, for example, worked together with Sumitomo Electric Industries and Anten Kogyo (Sumitomo group members), and Toshiba worked with Toshiba Shogi (the group trading company), Nippon Antenna, and Showa Electric Wire and Cable (Toshiba group members). Hitachi worked with Hitachi Cable (and perhaps others), Mitsubishi Electric worked with Dainichi-Nippon Cables (a Mitsubishi member), among others, and Fujitsu worked with two Furukawa members. (Oki Electric cooperated with Fujikura Cable Works, a Mitsui member, however; Toshiba also worked with Mitsui Trading Company on a cable television project, but this was presumably a different type of system than in the Toshiba example cited above.)

14. Cf., for example, the introductory commentary in the *Keiretsu no Kenkyu* volume of 1974.

15. It is interesting to examine the changing lists of membership over time to get a sense of changing technological and other requirements (cf. Dodwell, various years; Toyo Keizai, various years; or other publications that periodically list group membership roles).

16. This project involved both relatively basic and applied research, and involved cooperation between Mitsubishi and each of the other firms (Mitsubishi Heavy Industries and NEC, Mitsubishi Heavy Industries and Daikin, and so on) at the start. Once technical interface problems were worked out, however, periodic meetings were enough to sustain the cooperative effort. After this project ended, Mitsubishi Heavy Industries and NEC continued to work together on a more advanced system utilizing AAM2 technology.

17. The Hi-OVIS project, which began in 1976, pooled the resources of Fuji Telecasting Company (for the relay car), Fujitsu (for computer equipment), Ikegami Tsushinki (for color cameras), Matsushita (for video, still picture, and studio equipment), Sony (for microphones), Sumitomo Electric Industries (for transmission equipment), and Toshiba (for video equipment). From Hi-OVIS Visual Information System Development Association (undated), inset.

18. All of these, including the Toshiba figures, are very rough estimates and can be thought of as representing expenditures, and perhaps results in a more general sense, as perceived by the individuals interviewed.

19. The 474 companies represented 36.9% of all companies that were sent questionnaires. According to the authors, "In the industrial sector, all the construction companies had participated in collaborative R&D. 94.6 percent of the chemical companies had participated in collaborative R&D. The lowest percentage was found in the food industry at 80 percent. Although the percentages showed only slight differences among industrial sectors, collaborative R&D was dependent on the various characteristics of the industrial sector.

We asked the companies without collaborative R&D experiences why they have never participated in collaboration. The most cited reason (54.1 percent) was that there was no need for collaborative R&D. The second most cited reason was that they could not find adequate partners (37.8%). The companies without collaborative R&D experiences conducted technology introduction (43.2%) and technology grants (21.6%) as substitutes for collaborative R&D" (Niwa and Goto, 1993, p. 212).

20. "They were also asked why collaborative R&D had increased. The answer 'technologically weak fields of the company are complemented' was dominant, amounting to 65.2 percent of the responses. This answer means the second type factor of corporate collaborative R&D background, that is, reinforcing technology. The second cited reason was 'related technology of the company is reinforced' (28.6%). This belongs also to the second type factor. 'R&D period is shortened' (27.9%) was the third and belongs to the first type factor, that is, economizing R&D resources."

According to the authors, "only a few companies point out that 'R&D costs are reduced' (9.8%) and 'risks with the increase of R&D investments are dispersed' (12.5%) as reasons for the increase in collaborative R&D. These results illustrate obviously that the main reason for collaborative R&D is to reinforce technology based on synergy effects and that economizing R&D resources is not a strong reason for R&D collaboration" (p. 215). In specific, the authors found that economizing on costs and risks used to be more important for these companies in the past—presumably when the companies allocated fewer funds for R&D purposes—whereas in later years, technological reasons tended to prevail. (Recall that the majority of these are small-scale and not the very large-scale costly efforts.)

The authors also found that timing, cost and risk considerations prevailed more in the intra-industry collaborations cited in their sample, whereas technological synergy was seen as more possible and significant in the inter-industry cases cited in their sample. Finally, the authors note that "in cases of collaborative R&D with universities and public institutions, the responding companies pointed out more frequently the purposes of expanding and reinforcing corporate technological fields, obtaining unfamiliar technology like basic technology and taking corporate social responsibility as the main purposes than in cases of other partnerships. The first two purposes belong to reinforcing technology and the last belongs to social contribution. In cases of governmental and national organization partnership, a frequently chosen purpose was keeping a good relationship with government" (*ibid.*, pp. 217-218).

21. For example, in recent years we have seen continual and systematic industry resistance in the U.S. to MITI-like organizations, in spite of early proposals advanced by the Clinton Administration to move in that direction (cf. statements, for example, quoted in "Cutting Edge?", *Newsweek*, March 8, 1993). Nonetheless, many—e.g., Ferguson (1990)—advocate the encouragement of keiretsu-like ties among firms in the U.S. (On this, see also, for example, "American Keiretsu: Learning from Japan," *Business Week*, January 27, 1992. This article illustrates a number of attempts that have been made in recent years to move toward various forms of cooperative behavior among U.S. firms, primarily involving large firms and their suppliers, but also competing firms, and reasons

why some advocate even more formal keiretsu-like ties.) Others—e.g., Miyashita and Russell (1994)—argue that both "horizontal keiretsu" (business groups) and "vertical keiretsu" (industrial group and subcontracting networks) will not be possible as institutional forms for enterprises in the U.S. to adopt. However, they do suggest that U.S. enterprises consider (1) fostering long-term relationships between suppliers and manufacturers, (2) the spinning off of non-core businesses into affiliated subsidiaries, and (3) learning to cooperate in R&D ventures.

6

Possible Implications for Other Late Developing Countries

Introduction

The preceding chapters have detailed the development of cooperative technological ties in Japan. The case studies illustrated the range and dynamics of many of the more ambitious types of cooperation undertaken in the late catch up/early frontier period, and the historical chapters were intended to indicate the conditions under which cooperative technological efforts—both large-scale and small—could emerge.

Regarding the historical background facilitating cooperative efforts in Japan: we focused in particular on three important elements that are seen as influencing the emergence of cooperative ties: (1) the degree of *industrial dualism* in Japan which affected, among other things, the possibility and form of ties between "modern" and "semi-traditional" enterprises (historically in the form of relatively large modern sector firms and small semi-traditional enterprises/units); (2) the existence of family-based enterprise networks in the form of industrial houses (zaibatsu) and later *inter-enterprise groupings* of different types, influencing ties between primarily modern sector firms (including large modern firms and their smaller affiliates); and (3) the *role of public sector institutions* in facilitating these ongoing, relatively long-term technological linkages. Although we need to keep in mind that cooperative efforts are influenced by a myriad of elements and trends, it may be useful to continue to focus on these three factors as one means of assessing the likelihood for the development of cooperative technological ties among enterprises and organizations, involving both the public and private sectors (and, increasingly, the "third sector"—i.e., the non-profit/NGO sector) in other late developing countries.

Regarding *industrial dualism*, it was argued that in Japan the *timing* of development efforts (i.e., Japan as a relatively early latecomer) was such that the technology gap, along with other important potential "gaps" of the time—e.g., having to do with financial, organizational, and marketing expertise—faced by firms earlier in the century was challenging, but was not as profound as that faced by later entrants. A relevant question would thus be: does the existence of a wider technology gap and more extreme industrial dualism facing many of the countries industrializing later in the century prevent similar cooperative technological ties and linkages across domestic enterprises (particularly between larger modern and smaller semi-traditional firms) from forming? It is important to recall that the question of industrial dualism, in our usage of the concept, is not strictly an issue of dualism in terms of firm *size*, although for simplicity's sake it is often posed in this way (and size is often, although not always, related to the nature of the enterprise in a late development context). The issue of industrial dualism is more specifically concerned with differential access to capital, markets, new technologies, and other resources and information, as well as with significant differences regarding the nature of technology and modes of operation that can be found in different types of enterprises (for this reason, many technologically advanced and well-connected small firms are best considered as incipient "large" firms). In a late development context, the question addressed here is: are cooperative ties likely to emerge across very different sectors of the economy, with the more "modern" enterprises and organizations helping the units or enterprises that are more "backward" to advance? Do these ties help set the stage for widespread and relatively egalitarian cooperative technological efforts at the near-frontier and frontier stages, as they appear to have done in Japan's case? Alternatively, will such cooperative ties will be confined to only a narrow part of the industrial spectrum and a relatively small number of domestic firms (i.e., only certain "modern," technologically advanced firms), adding to already existing tendencies toward an industrial divide, and in the process diminishing the possibilities for cooperation among domestic enterprises across the economy? This is the first of several questions that will be addressed in the discussion below.

Regarding the role of *inter-enterprise groups*: we have seen that in the Japanese case cooperation with firms in formal (and, increasingly, informal) groupings also helped create a strong basis for the more ambitious intra- and inter-industry efforts of recent years. Although historically the inter-enterprise ties within these groupings typically originated in non-technological spheres—developing, for example, in response to group members' needs for finance, marketing, warehousing, or other services—over time the *technological* component in these ties became more important as the technological challenges they faced became more pressing. As discussed in the chapters above, subcontracting and other affiliative ties within groups deepened dramatically over time, most notably as part of the creation of postwar industrial groups in Japan. Increasingly, information and technological flows began to move "up" (from small subcontractors, suppliers, affiliates and others, "up" to larger firms) as well as "down" to smaller enterprises. This occurred as both "small" and "large" enterprises caught up technologically and developed their capabilities for highly original forms of process and product innovation, both of the relatively routine (but in the aggregate very important) types as well as the more ambitious forms.

These evolving inter-enterprise groupings have interesting parallels with groupings found in other late developing countries, including the informal family-based networks of enterprises and the more formal family-based industrial houses or business groups (including those sometimes referred to as conglomerates, but which differ sharply from the conglomerates of advanced industrial countries that are often clusters of firms "united" for solely speculative financial reasons). A relevant question would be: are these and other forms of interlinked enterprises in contemporary developing countries likely to provide a basis for the development of cooperative technological ties? Could they, and are they likely to, act as central coordinators for cooperative technological projects in the catch up and early frontier period of innovation in other late developing countries? Moreover, what would be the social and economic implications of such cooperative efforts? This is the second question that will be taken up below.

Regarding the *role of the public sector*, we have discussed how the Japanese government influenced the development of cooperative ties among enterprises, although not always in ways that other countries might want to emulate (e.g., through the wartime creation of institutions facilitating government-industry ties, and the forcible linking up of small firms with larger enterprises). We have also indicated the importance of the public sector in Japan (including government agencies, public enterprises, government laboratories and other organizations) in securing a domestic orientation with respect to the development of technology—i.e., avoiding technological dependence, and promoting relative self-reliance. This was done by first creating a buffer between existing technological capabilities and international standards so that enterprises could improve their products and processes without immediately facing the full force of international competition, and then by requiring certain standards of performance (pertaining to both private and public enterprises and organizations) as a prerequisite for continued assistance.

These, and other aspects of the government-industry relationship in

Japan that evolved over the prewar and postwar periods, have interesting parallels in many late developing countries and stand in contrast to practices that characterized (at least historically) the earlier developing countries. A third question, to be taken up and explored below, would be: what is the likelihood for, and potential social and economic implications of, similar public sector practices and policies regarding cooperative technological ties in other late developing economies?

Judging from recent institutional developments in many of the Asian NICs and "next NICs," we might conclude that cooperative technological practices of different types are, in fact, quite likely to develop in a wide range of developing countries in the near future. We have already seen a number of examples of government-sponsored cooperative research in the 1980s and 1990s, including the Republic of Korea's VLSI and other projects and Taiwan's electronics industry-oriented projects, focusing on semiconductors and other technologies; such projects appear to have involved cooperative arrangements that have similarities to those found in Japan's government-sponsored projects.[1] Moreover, private firms also seem to be starting to undertake cooperative research efforts without any government assistance. For example, speaking in general terms, E.M. Kim reports that in South Korea "research and development are often coordinated between companies, and expenses and even laboratory space may be shared."[2] This may be true of loosely affiliated firms, but it is all the more likely among enterprises within established family-based networks or enterprise groups.

In addition to these signs of emerging cooperative technological ties, institutional changes that preceded Japan's postwar cooperative ventures also seem to have parallels in the developing world. For example, China's explicit policy of adopting the industrial group structure of allied enterprises and its close study of other Japanese institutions associated with the public and private sectors, Malaysia's creation of an institution with similarities to both Japan's MITI and South Korea's Export Promotion Board, and other recent institutional developments in countries already characterized by family-based networks and other inter-enterprise arrangements further suggest that cooperative technological practices may be possible and even likely in a number of countries that are attempting technological catch up and early frontier forms of innovation (how socially beneficial these policies turn out to be will vary, however, depending on the economic and political conditions in each country).

Nonetheless, this pattern may not hold for firms in all developing countries. Recognizing that each country—and even different regions within an individual country—embodies unique historical and contemporary circumstances, we may still be able to make some generalizations about which contexts are more or less likely to favor the development of cooperative ties.

In the discussion that follows, a rough distinction will be made between the "least industrialized countries" of the contemporary developing world and the more industrialized "NICs" (newly industrialized countries) and "next NICs" (or "near NICs"). Although these are very rough categories and there is considerable debate about which countries fall into which categories, these rough distinctions are maintained as a way to indicate segments along a continuum, and reiterate that both a country's *prior degree and path of development* and its *timing of efforts at rapid industrialization and technological advance* (which are, of course, closely connected) are important indicators of the extent to which cooperative ties can be formed.[3] We will begin our discussion with the example of the least industrialized countries, and then the "NICs" and "next NICs," as a way to begin to analyze the likelihood for the development of cooperative technological ties in contemporary developing countries. (As indicated in Chapter 1, Japan can best be seen as an "early" late industrializer, with a much longer sustained path of industrialization and socioeconomic transformation—i.e., capitalist development, in Marx's sense—than that found in other late developing countries. For this reason *postwar* Japan is in an entirely different position than that of current-day developing countries; nonetheless, interesting comparisons can be made between Japan's early experience of industrialization/socioeconomic transformation and the later experiences of the NICs, next NICs, and least industrialized countries.[4])

Timing and Cooperative Technological Ties: "Earlier" Versus "Later" Late Development

It may be useful to begin the discussion with an examination of the question of the *timing* of late development and the technology gap at different points in historical time. The conditions that existed in Japan earlier in the twentieth century will be contrasted with the circumstances faced by the least industrialized countries in the late twentieth/early twenty-first centuries, while the experiences of the "NICs" and "next NICs" are seen as falling in between the two.

In Japan's case we need to keep in mind that prior to and earlier in the twentieth century, Japanese firms were faced with technologies that they could master without a large-scale scientific and technological infrastructure. They even found it possible to blend relatively traditional techniques with imported technologies, which aided in the development and transformation of *both* the relatively traditional ("domestic") and imported technologies. This was the idea behind the development of

"Meiji technology," for example. (The practice of combining the best "traditional" techniques with the "application of modern science" dates back to at least the Meiji period. As Ogura noted, the concept "Meiji technology" as used in the agricultural realm involved selecting, applying and later combining the best traditional practices with applications of agricultural science to solve local problems, "not by taking over farming techniques from abroad."[5]) This desire to apply "traditional" techniques to "modern" products and processes and *vice versa* can be contrasted with conditions prevailing in late twentieth century post-colonial societies, which face both a much wider technology gap and the psychological and cultural consequences of modern colonialism.[6] (We will discuss the possibilities for and barriers to "technology blending" below.)

Even in the newly arising modern sector, in Japan the capital, research and skill requirements did not pose insurmountable barriers to the relatively large firms that were favored in these industries. These enterprises often worked with government agencies (e.g., as model factories were transferred to them), or more often with foreign suppliers of the new technologies. However, because the technology gap was not very great, the firms found that they could become somewhat self-reliant in a short period of time, rather than depending entirely on continuous assistance from foreign firms.[7]

For some firms—such as Hitachi—nationalism contributed to the firms' desire to rely on their own technological and research resources, whereas for others—e.g., NEC—government policies requiring the "Japanization" of the company as the country moved toward war resulted in the firms' having to rely primarily on their own technological capabilities and that of other domestic enterprises, both affiliates and non-affiliates. Thus, for reasons of both private and public policy, the relative technological self-reliance of Japanese firms in the modern sector—based on and supplemented by periodic imports of new technologies—increased rapidly, and formed a credible base for further technological development.

We have seen how, in the context of this eminently bridgeable technology gap, individual and cooperative efforts involving modern sector domestic firms strengthened the upper end of the national technology base. These efforts began in the prewar period, involving zaibatsu or non-zaibatsu firms (or large firms and government labs, often coordinated by government agencies), and greatly intensified in the postwar period. Moreover, individual and cooperative efforts helped strengthen the "lower" end of the industrial technology spectrum as well.

Regarding the firms' innovative efforts in Japan: it is also important to remember that, in contrast to observed patterns in contemporary developing countries, the processes of modification, adaptation, and then more fundamental transformation of technologies have evolved out of a long history of "tinkering" and experimentation in Japan. Even before the war years cut off technological efforts in Japan from foreign sources of supply, a good deal of modification and adaptation of technologies and products was carried out by both the large-scale and small-scale enterprises. As noted above, even in the modern sector relatively traditional skills were sometimes applied to improve upon or modify imported technologies; this might involve not only "technology blending," but also the partial demechanization of imported technologies to better fit local production and consumption needs and circumstances.[8]

This implies that the firms were not bound by either the intrinsic lack of adaptability of imported technologies, or by either a psychological or "real" need to maintain imported technologies as is. In other words, Japanese firms did not just master a particular production process and stick with that, and then continually import new production processes and ideas each time new models or products were desired. Given the trial-and-error nature of and the lower capital, educational, skill and research requirements for technological development earlier in the century—together with the possibility for in-house and, increasingly, collective efforts (involving both the public and private sectors, together and separately)—conditions were right for the *widespread self-reliant generation of new products and technologies to emerge,* even if it took time to perfect these new attempts. Japanese enterprises could import new technologies periodically, transform them, and build on this base of technological experience accumulated throughout the economy; the public and private sectors could develop more formal scientific and technological institutions over time; and both enterprises and organizations could then move on to the more sophisticated products and technologies associated with the later "technological revolutions," making good use of the country's *increasingly flexible, diverse and relatively well-integrated technological base* embodied in the knowledge, skills, and technological achievements of individuals and groups in both the private and public sectors.

The development of this base was not always smooth: there were many failures and dead-ends. However, the base that gradually emerged went beyond both "know-how" and "know-why" to become creative and innovative in both small and increasingly large ways.

As noted in the preceding chapters, another key factor that aided the Japanese firms' efforts was the willingness of foreign firms earlier in the century to transfer technology and skills, thereby helping to close this technology gap. Earlier in the century, many international firms found it difficult or uneconomical to produce and market their products locally in some of the more distant markets, and were thus somewhat immobile, particularly before their full-scale multinationalization efforts in the

1960s and beyond. This seems to be one factor that contributed to the persistence of traditional tastes and products as well as knowledge and skills in countries such as Japan.[9] Moreover, this sense of distance (together with protectionist policies) meant that locally-made "modern" goods in countries such as Japan did not have to compete immediately with foreign-made goods, or move immediately into highly competitive export markets. Although this degree of protection could have resulted in technological stagnation, several factors—including the perceived economic and political threat from Western countries, the proliferation of domestic firms given the country's prior development and relatively small technology gap, and the requirements of Japan's colonial efforts, as discussed in Chapter 1—all combined to produce the blending of domestic competition and cooperation in prewar and early postwar Japan that laid the basis for continuing technological advance.

Thus, Japanese enterprises, like their counterparts in the early industrialized countries, were able to develop their own partially-independent technological base. However, unlike their Western counterparts, firms in Japan were attempting to do this in a late development context—i.e., a dualistic, largely "semi-traditional," "catch up" context characterized by an institutional and behavioral setting that differed sharply from that of the early industrializers. In this context, technological advance was made possible not only by individual firm efforts and technological purchases, but also, over the years, by increasingly widespread and diverse cooperative efforts involving private enterprises, public enterprises and government agencies, forming technological networks that created an increasingly well-integrated technological base. Individual companies that were strong technologically did not become technological "islands" that prospered with the help of their foreign collaborators. Instead, imported technologies were increasingly transformed and improved upon by both in-house research efforts and initially small-scale (and later large-scale) cooperative efforts, and technology was diffused and upgraded through wide-ranging and diverse types of cooperative ties with other domestic enterprises and institutions.

Cooperative Ties in the Least Industrialized Countries

In contrast to this, the more sophisticated technologies associated with the later (e.g., "second" and "third") technological revolutions, and even the application of these technologies to the "simpler" products of the "first" and "second" revolutions, require of countries now attempting to master these technologies a much more developed scientific and technological (and educational) infrastructure and, across the commodity spectrum, much higher capital, educational, skill and research requirements than was true prior to or earlier in the twentieth century.[10] In addition, although modifications of imported technologies do occur in some cases, the likelihood of more striking transformations at this historical juncture may be less due to (1) the intrinsic lack of adaptability of many of the new imported technologies; (2) the lack of self-confidence on the part of the recipient of the imported technologies to try to transform them, particularly when very sophisticated technologies are involved; (3) the lack of desire to try to transform them, given the relative ease of continuing to depend upon imports; and (4) in some cases, the contractual requirements set by the foreign suppliers of new technologies prohibiting any modifications during the contract period.

Some also suggest that international firms, being much more mobile and globally-oriented than they were earlier in the century, are now much less willing to transfer their technologies outright, especially to firms they perceive as potential competitors. Particularly in high tech industries, they tend to share their technologies only if they receive equally valuable technologies in return. This is a complicated issue, and there is no doubt that in many cases advanced technologies do get transferred. Nonetheless, it appears that international suppliers will often prefer to transfer (often less-than-best practice) technologies on a *piece-by-piece basis*, and either have a hand in their use or otherwise restrict the possible uses of the transferred technologies.

In countries in which the general technological level is nearing the frontier—e.g., in the NICs—this lack of access to best-practice technologies (or, in some cases, even access to standard technologies on anything other than a piece-by-piece arrangement) has spurred the R&D effort. In other cases, however—particularly in the least industrialized countries —these and related factors tend to result in a much greater *continuing* reliance on foreign suppliers of new technologies, with much less of the pattern seen earlier in the century in Japan. As noted above, particularly in the case of the least industrialized countries which face the largest technology gaps, the new technologies may of necessity be restricted to *certain geographical centers and enterprises*, which become more like technological islands (in some ways a modern version of "enclave economies") with strong international connections. This is likely to result in far less diffusion of technologies throughout the economy, delaying or preventing the widespread accumulation of knowledge based on experimenting with and adapting the technology, and thus creating far less of a flexible, diverse, responsive and "indigenous" knowledge and technology base.

Under these circumstances, in the least industrialized countries there appears to be much less scope for widespread technological alliances in the modern sector among domestic enterprises. There is also much less possibility for widespread in-house and cooperative technological efforts across the economy involving modern sector enterprises and other domestic organizations (e.g., government laboratories or public enterprises) bound together by relatively long-term ties.

This has important implications not only for the possibility of cooperation among *modern sector* firms and organizations, it also has important implications for the possibility of forming technological ties *between the modern (usually relatively large) and semi-traditional (usually smaller) enterprises*, and the upgrading of the skills and technologies of the latter (thus contributing as well to the former). First, we need to recognize that in the least industrialized countries the gap between the truly "traditional" technologies and the new imported technologies is so great as to preclude much interaction between the two. To cite an extreme example, the blacksmiths of contemporary developing countries cannot provide the basis for the development of the modern machine tool industry at this point in time, although this was possible in Japan's case earlier in the century.[11] The scope for the "blending" of modern and relatively "traditional" techniques (the equivalent of "Meiji technology"), or even the partial demechanization of technologies appears to be particularly small in the case of current-day science-related technologies.

In the least industrialized countries the relationship between the "modern" and truly "traditional" sector appears to be primarily detrimental to the latter, and not at all symbiotic in Ehrlich's sense. Moreover, in the least industrialized countries even the segment of the small-scale sector that makes use of intermediate technologies and produces nontraditional goods is likely to be represented more by *semi-traditional small and microenterprises* that have little access to capital and modern technologies, and much less by *technologically advancing ("modernizing") small-scale enterprises* (i.e., semi-traditional enterprises in the process of becoming "modern" small-scale enterprises).

This relative lack of a technologically advancing small-scale sector is often referred to as a "missing middle." Back in 1966 Igor Krestovsky noted, "In many developing countries, especially in Africa, there are no small-scale industries whatever, the industrial structure consisting only of large-scale and medium-sized modern industries on the one hand, and of traditional handicrafts and cottage industries on the other."[12] Even in the 1990s analysts still note the fact of a "missing middle" in the industrial structure in the least industrialized countries and the difficulties in creating linkages between what we have referred to as the "modern" and "semi-traditional" sectors.[13] There is certainly evidence of some (although limited) linkages across different types of firms in the *modern* sector of the least industrialized economies, and between modern "formal sector" and tied "informal sector" operations (e.g., home production organized by formal sector firms). However, in contrast with the Japanese case earlier in the century, we find very little of the *systematic and widespread transformation* of semi-traditional firms through direct and indirect affiliations with modern sector firms in these countries. This lack of technological linkages (cooperative ties) *reflects* and in turn *contributes to* the problem of the "missing middle."

This is a serious issue in the least industrialized countries because employment in the manufacturing and associated service sectors is still concentrated largely in the traditional handicraft and cottage industries on the one hand, and in the semi-traditional small and microenterprises on the other (e.g., those engaging in "low wage/low productivity" forms of simple manufacturing and repair services using intermediate technologies such as those based on metalworking or woodworking techniques). Studies in Ghana, one of the more industrialized countries in Africa, indicate that although over the years tenuous linkages have grown between *individual* microenterprises and modern sector firms, by and large there are no regular ties, and one must conclude that in general, modern firms have not helped pull up the level of skills and technologies associated with the microenterprises. Although there is disagreement regarding the extent to which the expansion of and problems associated with the modern sector has resulted in displacement from more traditional occupations and into uncertain and irregular (and sometimes illegal) informal and unorganized sector occupations, there is general agreement that in this context modern firms have little incentive to work closely with, or help pull up technologically, the semi-traditional firms that make up a large part of the informal and unorganized sectors (i.e., there is little in the way of a "symbiotic relationship"). Given the capital, skill, and other requirements of commodities made by the modern sector, and the quality and other requirements demanded by their relatively high income domestic and international markets— together with the ready availability of supplies provided by international collaborators—modern firms will not find it economically attractive or feasible to form long-term cooperative ties with the great majority of small-scale sector firms, apart from the relatively limited number of "modern" (or "modernizing") small-scale enterprises, including those newly created in specific industries. Moreover, public policies in the least industrialized countries tend not to have been very effective to date in addressing these issues and helping to form these linkages.[14]

Thus, in the case of the least industrialized countries, technological ties may tend to develop between *individual* like-sized enterprises, or between *individual* large and small modern sector firms (including subsidiaries of domestic or foreign firms); however, it appears that in contrast with the Japanese case earlier in the century, we are *not* likely to see—at least in the foreseeable future—widespread technological ties across the economy, linking together a large number and wide variety of domestic enterprises, public and private, including modern and modernizing semi-traditional firms, that help to sustain a progressive and relatively even form of industrial development. Instead, in these countries there may be a strong tendency for modern enterprises to become technologically isolated in the sense of being not well-tied to the rest of the economy, and possibly more tied to the economies of other countries.[15]

These tendencies are compounded in regions in which a relative lack of locally-based merchant and early industrial activities, together with colonial policies, held back the development of local entrepreneurial family networks. Whether as a result of their largely agrarian histories or the dictates of the colonial era, the least industrialized countries tend *not* to be characterized by either the informal family networks or the more formal business and industrial houses often found in the NICs and next NICs. (This is not to say that entrepreneurial families do not exist in these countries; however, their scale of operations and range and depth of inter-enterprise ties tend to be much more restricted than would be true of family groupings found in the NICs and next NICs.) Moreover, under these circumstances, the government-industry relationship tends to be much less institutionalized and systematic than would tend to be true of regions with a much longer history of industrial development, and the public sector in this post-colonial context may be either relatively weak or more "outward-oriented" than tends to be true in the more industrialized of the developing countries. For all of these (and other) reasons, it appears that without serious and sustained public policy efforts, patterns of widespread cooperative technological ties are not likely to emerge across these economies in the near future. The modern private sector will not help "pull up" other parts of the economy, and even ties *within* the modern sector will tend to be limited. This could change if the public sector were to play a strong role in (1) helping to bring together modern (and "modernizing") domestic enterprises and organizations, and (2) helping the traditional and semi-traditional units advance to the point of being able to sustain cooperative ties without continual government support. (We will discuss the importance of these policies for late developing countries below.) Without concerted public sector efforts, however, we are likely to see the promotion of cooperative ties only on an individual project-by-project basis, and not in any comprehensive way.

Cooperative Ties in Other
"Early" And "Middle" Latecomers:
The Case of the "NICs" and "Next NICs"

Although the realistic prospects for ongoing cooperative technological ties among domestic enterprises thus appear to be limited—at least at the present time—in the case of the least industrialized countries, they appear to be far greater in the case of the "NICs" and "next NICs." There are certainly significant differences even within these two broad categories: for example, the Asian NICs tend to exhibit patterns of affiliation that are closer to the Japanese experience, whereas the next NICs have certain features in common with the least industrialized economies (and each country example varies enormously according to its own specific historical experiences). However, in general, the prospects for the development of cooperative technological ties appear to be much greater for both the NICs and next NICs than appears to be true for the least industrialized economies.

Both the NICs and next NICs, in contrast with the least industrialized economies, effectively began their attempts at large-scale modern industrial development at an earlier point in time, although later than was true in the Japanese case. Both the NICs and next NICs have come a great distance in terms of merchant, manufacturing and financial activities, and—for better and for worse—have accumulated a great deal of the social and economic infrastructure that is generated in the course of the development of an industrial economy (even though there may be a great deal of unevenness with regard to this socio-economic transformation, particularly in the next NICs).

Regarding the possibility for cooperative technological ties: both the NICs and next NICs possess (albeit to differing degrees) the common features of (1) a relatively large number of technologically advancing enterprises; (2) in most countries, some degree of pre-existing ties among domestic enterprises, often in the form of groups and other formal and informal networks and affiliations; and (3) a history of relatively close government-industry ties, associated in part with the historical tendencies toward industrial dualism and the formation of influential family, community or other political "blocs," and a relatively institutionally developed public sector. Moreover, because of the success of Japanese and other Asian enterprises in terms of technological advance, there is a widely perceived need for the promotion of cooperative institutions and practices involving domestic enterprises and organizations. For example, many of the East and Southeast Asian "deliberation councils"

(institutions that typically coordinate government and industrial interests) have become interested in promoting government-sponsored
research consortia and other cooperative practices in recent years.[16]
Therefore, in both the NICs and next NICs we find strong incentives
favoring cooperative technological ties, together with behavioral and
institutional bases on which to build such efforts; this is true particularly
in the NICs, but also to some extent in the next NICs, as will be explained
below.

Cooperative Technological Ties and the East Asian NICs

The prospects for the further development of cooperative technological ties would appear to be strongest in the East Asian NICs, particularly
in the Republic of Korea and Taiwan. These are the most industrialized
economies and are characterized by relatively strong domestic firms
(both "large" and "small"), inter-enterprise ties in the forms of business
groups and business networks, and a relatively strong public sector and
close government-industry relationship. There are important differences
between the two countries with respect to the specifics of each of these
factors; however, in what follows we will focus on the implications of the
general features they share in common for ongoing cooperative technological ties.

The strength of domestic firms in these two countries stems from a
history of merchant and family-based early industrial activities, as well
as (again, for better or worse) colonial period factory/enterprise and
other institutional developments, land reforms, direct foreign investment
in both the Republic of Korea and Taiwan, and opportunities for new
enterprise growth in the recent high growth years. Industrial enterprises
in South Korea and Taiwan tend not to be overwhelmed by international
firms, and the periodic political and economic shake ups (due to colonial
occupations, successive wars and continuing security concerns) have
worked against economic complacency and rent-seeking behavior.

In both countries the historical precedents and the potential for further
expansion of cooperative ties among domestic enterprises and other
domestic institutions are striking, and have clear-cut parallels with the
Japanese case. In Taiwan the well-known land reform and investments in
rural infrastructure facilitated the growth of modern rural, as well as
urban, small and medium enterprises (these are no longer "traditional"
or even "semi-traditional" units in the sense used above). The small and
medium enterprises, together with the larger public and private sector
undertakings and the business networks (based on family, regional, and
other ties) that extend throughout Taiwan's economy and beyond, provide the basis—both current and potential—for cooperative ties of many

types. As noted in *Business Groups in Taiwan*, the business networks use affiliative ties as a means to enter new industries and enhance their competitive position, among other reasons.[17] Similarly, in the Republic of Korea the large *chaebol* members and other relatively large enterprises have, as in the Japanese case, formed alliances with other group members and affiliates for many different purposes (financial, manufacturing, and other). In recent years they have also developed the basis for cooperative research within the group as the need to do near-frontier and then frontier research becomes more acute.[18]

Government and Group or Network-Sponsored Cooperative Technological Efforts. Regarding inter-enterprise cooperation for research purposes: it is important to recall that in both Taiwan and South Korea, near-frontier and frontier R&D became a concern only in the 1980s, and government-sponsored research projects involving domestic firms have only recently emerged. Prior to this, and to a large extent at the present time, technology has been obtained from international firms; however, increasingly firms have been pushed to master and further develop the imported technologies—particularly in South Korea—rather than rely on the continual import of desired technologies, which may in any case no longer be forthcoming, particularly without some form of technology exchange. In response, government agencies, research institutions and public enterprises in both countries have been playing the roles of central coordinators of important joint research projects in recent years.

In South Korea, for example, although public research institutes maintained poor linkages with private enterprises until at least the mid-1970s, they now appear to play a major role in working with private enterprises in "National R&D Projects" administered by the Ministry of Science and Technology and in "Industrial Base Technology Development Projects" administered by the Ministry of Trade and Industry, as well as in other capacities. One such well-known public research institute is South Korea's ETRI (Electronics and Telecommunications Research Institute), which in recent years has been a coordinator and participant in major research projects. The parallels with Japan's cooperative public enterprise and government-sponsored projects are clear.[19]

South Korea's ETRI-associated projects are often compared with Taiwan's ERSO-related projects, although there are differences.[20] Rather than working closely with a number of private enterprises at the research stage, ERSO (Electronics Research and Service Organization) either develops or imports new technologies and then transfers it to domestic firms, sometimes through spin-off companies; at least this has been the general procedure to this point.[21]

In both countries, concerns about not gaining access to new (particularly frontier) technologies prompted the development of a number of government-sponsored cooperative R&D projects. For example, in both countries cooperative projects were initiated for the development of the 4M and 16M DRAM technologies. In South Korea, this attempt involved a public R&D institute and three of the country's *chaebol*, and Samsung "announced its completion of designing 4M DRAM in 1989 and 16M DRAM in 1990, only a few months after Japan."[22] In Taiwan the Ministry of Economic Affairs was involved in coordinating a "technology developing alliance" ("similar to Sematech") involving the Industrial Research Institute, Taiwan's major IC chip manufacturers, and other domestic enterprises to develop 4M and 16M DRAM chip technologies over a five year period.[23]

Reports have come in on a regular basis in business and trade journals regarding other cooperative research projects in South Korea in recent years. These include such examples as the collaboration involving a public R&D institute and a number of other chaebol for "super-mini-computer" technology, and the collaboration between a public R&D institute and two of the chaebol for optical fiber technology. (In the latter case Corning Glass had refused to transfer the technology to Korean firms, prompting the R&D effort. It is said that the project did not go as expected, but nonetheless is said to have helped the chaebol gain bargaining power in order to acquire foreign technology on favorable terms.) Another example of a South Korean research consortium would be the one set up by companies to do research on liquid crystal displays, based on imported technologies upon which they presumably hope to improve.[24]

It is not clear how much, or what form of, cooperative R&D was actually carried out in these and similar projects.[25] In spite of numerous references to inter-enterprise technological efforts, we do not yet have a detailed picture of either governmental or non-government sponsored inter-enterprise cooperation in South Korea or Taiwan. In addition, more research into modes of technological cooperation—particularly among group and network affiliates *outside* of government-sponsored projects—is needed to clarify our understanding of cooperative technological ties in both the Republic of Korea and Taiwan. However, it is clear that reported cases of inter-and intra-industry cooperative research and, more generally, cooperative technological ties among domestic enterprises and organizations are increasing both in number and scope as requirements for competition change. In both countries the roles of networks and groups, as well as public enterprises and other public institutions (government agencies, research institutes and—to a much lesser degree so far—universities), have facilitated the sharing of information and pooling of skills, resources and ideas, although the specific roles and practices of these institutions differ between the two countries.

Assuming that they continue to prove to be successful, these techno-logical alliances are likely to become more frequent and *long-term* in nature, insofar as problems associated with free riders and opportunistic behavior, and a relative lack of mutual trust, make truly cooperative work more problematic in relatively *short-term* alliances. Moreover, the number of firms and organizations that have the potential for becoming involved in such technological alliances is likely to increase in the coming years as their R&D facilities are strengthened to meet the new demands. Certainly, as the private sector comes to feel the need to put more effort into R&D activities and as the firms' own research capabili-ties and facilities increase, they are likely to put a great deal of pressure on the government for help in the process of technological catch up, par-ticularly when cost, risk, technological and other reasons favor coopera-tive R&D. However, this pressure will only come once dependence on foreign suppliers of ideas and technologies diminishes and domestic firms become equal players technologically.

At the moment, enterprises in both countries continue to depend to a large extent on the continual importation of new ideas and technologies, which has tended to limit the number of domestic firms and organiza-tions involved in cooperative efforts. It is said that in both Taiwan and South Korea smaller firms have often relied on reverse engineering as a means to acquire new technologies, but the larger firms have tended to rely on foreign suppliers of new technologies and ideas. This appears to be true of even the largest firms: although some of the chaebol, for example, do a great deal of their own R&D—both through in-house and cooperative projects involving domestic firms and organizations—others remain highly dependent on international suppliers of new technolo-gies.[26]

All of these enterprises now face the need to develop their own technologies; the question is how to do this most effectively. Under any circumstances, most would argue that some kind of balance and complementarity between locally and internationally generated technol-ogy is needed. As Lall puts it, "The inter-relationship between domestic and imported technologies is thus both a complementary and a competi-tive one. Over time it fluctuates between them, and policies which veer too much either to protection or to free imports of technology can be harmful."[27] If present trends are a good indication, both government and group-sponsored cooperative projects will increase in both of these countries in the future and could play an important role in the creation of new locally-generated technologies. However, as in the Japanese case, large government-sponsored projects are likely to be particularly contro-versial to the extent that economically and politically powerful enter-prises are involved: the South Korean government's ties with the chaebol and the government of Taiwan's responsiveness to influential business networks have provoked widespread opposition. Both large-scale and small-scale projects are likely to increase, but at the same time they will need to be monitored closely because of the potential for the misuse (or undesirable use) of public funds.

Because of the growing importance of locally-based technological development, cooperative technological ties among enterprises and organizations are likely to increase in the future even *without* government involvement. As industrialization advances in a late development context, enterprises on their own tend to create ongoing ties with other enterprises and organizations, both within the country and in some cases extending into new economic "regions." (It has been reported, for example, that in recent years in Hong Kong and Taiwan "the linkage issue has been transformed into one of linkages between domestic companies in the context of dense interfirm networks. These networks now extend to encompass linkages with firms in the People's Republic of China," and evidence suggests that these linkages are being used for purposes of innovation and technological advance, among other uses.[28]) These trends toward an increasing focus on technological and other linkages among domestic firms (along with other means of acquiring and developing new products and technologies) are likely to continue, at least in the case of "large" sector enterprises, and group and network-based enterprises. However, these cooperative ties are much less likely to extend to the large numbers of unaffiliated enterprises in the "small"-scale sector (i.e., outside of a very *limited* number of such firms), for reasons to be discussed below; as a consequence, a different set of policies will be required for this sector.

Cooperative Technological Ties Across "Large" and "Small"-Scale Sectors. We have seen how, in the Japanese case, cooperative technological ties that involve a wide variety of domestic firms and institutions have contributed to the development of a technological base from which other international alliances (e.g., involving technological cooperation or exchanges of technology) can be made. In Japan these ties have extended throughout the economy, and have encompassed firms of widely varying sizes and economic positions. These ties across "large" and "small" enterprises are seen as having had a great deal of significance with respect to the innovation process—specifically, the smaller firms account for a good deal of the technological flexibility and vibrancy of the larger, and the larger can provide substantial technological expertise to the smaller.

In both South Korea and Taiwan, however, technological linkages do not always extend throughout the economy. With respect to South Korea, Kim (1993, p. 382) puts it this way: "Another problem in the

Korean economy is the vital missing link in the presence of related and especially supporting industries. *Chaebols* have largely focused their efforts in end products with heavy dependence on imported parts and machinery. The problem, as Porter (1990) notes, is not the cost of inputs but the effects on the innovation process. Without fluid supports from capable domestic suppliers, Korean firms will remain behind in product and process innovations." Even in Taiwan, which has large sectors of the economy made up of small and medium enterprises, ties with smaller suppliers and subcontractors have been surprisingly lacking.

Thus, although we find evidence of group and network-coordinated technological efforts and government-sponsored cooperative projects in both countries, the one type of cooperative technological ties that we tend *not* to find in these countries is the type that links up larger firms with smaller domestic suppliers and subcontractors—i.e., that which has the effect of not only upgrading the technologies and skills of the suppliers and subcontractors, but also ultimately of providing important sources of new ideas and technologies that help in both product and process innovation.

In order to understand why these linkages across the industrial structure in the domestic economy are weak (particularly relative to the Japanese case), we need to analyze the sources of the "industrial dualism" that exists in these economies (much more obviously so in South Korea), and why stronger and denser linkages across different types of enterprises have not been formed. First, it appears that during the colonial period, given their close relationship to (and, in an important sense, participation in) Japan's economy, the prewar tendencies in both Korea and Taiwan toward industrial dualism (of the "modern" versus smaller-scale "semi-traditional" sort) must be viewed in a broader perspective than would be the case if there had been more autonomous development. In these countries, the semi-traditional units were largely transformed during the colonial period, often through the absorption of labor into new factories and enterprises established at that time.[29]

As noted above, at the present time the small-scale sector can no longer be considered to be even semi-traditional, in contrast with the conditions that continue to exist in the next NICs and in the least industrialized economies. Nonetheless, an industrial divide based on access to markets, capital, technologies and other resources continues to exist in both South Korea and Taiwan, as enterprises with better economic and political connections (and perhaps better prospects to begin with) continue to do much better than those without such ties.[30] Moreover, in a globalized economy in which the more technologically capable firms were created by, or themselves sought out, linkages with foreign firms (often Japanese), the result was that the less technologically advanced units in both South Korea and Taiwan have been generally bypassed as potential suppliers and subcontractors, and now often find themselves in a relatively weak position.[31]

As noted above, this creates potential problems, not only for the segment of the population associated with the smaller, less technologically advanced units, but also potentially for the larger enterprises as well, particularly if they operate without a wide range of capable domestic suppliers. As indicated above, the political consequences of this industrial divide are also considerable: although concerns about increasing economic concentration are much more pronounced in South Korea, in Taiwan as well there is a good deal of concern about "vested interests"—i.e., those enterprises and business groups receiving government favors, including the bulk of R&D support. Consequently, the political fallout from a faltering small-scale sector cannot easily be ignored. The industrial and political divide in these countries is in no sense as dramatic as it tends to be in the least industrialized regions, or even in the next NICs; nonetheless, in a context of increasing wealth accruing to the more successful and well-connected companies and families, concerns are growing rapidly.

Partly in response to these concerns, in recent years public policy in both South Korea and Taiwan has come to focus on problems associated with the industrial dualism that persists in these countries (again, far more so in South Korea). For example, although it has had only limited success thus far, the South Korean government has been trying to upgrade the capabilities of smaller domestic enterprises, both urban and rural, through such programs as the joining of many such enterprises into cooperative groups of small firms and giving them support in their efforts to upgrade their skills and technologies, as well as in other ways trying to promote large-small firm linkages.[32] So far the results have been mixed, and as noted above, the idea of promoting cooperative R&D among smaller firms with very limited research facilities faces inherent difficulties. Nonetheless, serious public policy initiatives—including the promotion of other forms of cooperative technological ties across small-scale enterprises, or in conjunction with more technologically advanced public and private enterprises and organizations—could certainly broaden the technological capabilities of and knowledge base available to the small-scale sector. This is particularly true in the more industrialized countries such as the Republic of Korea and Taiwan, given the level of development of the small-scale sector overall. However, such policies may only come as a result of a sustained political effort involving those most affected. It will be interesting to see how these policies evolve, and with what effect on this "less advanced" sector in the future.

In sum, much has been done in both Taiwan and South Korea in the way of facilitating cooperative technological ties involving private and public enterprises and organizations, at least in the more technologically advanced sectors of the economy. In contrast with the Japanese case, however, cooperative technological ties have not spanned the industrial divide that exists within these countries, and even though the industrial divide that exists is mild relative to those faced by most of the next NICs and the least industrialized countries, it remains a cause of concern. The political and economic consequences of relatively uneven forms of development in both countries are well known, and concerns with economic inequalities and concentrations of wealth and power have exacerbated social tensions, even during these countries' high growth periods; these concerns have brought into question the way in which technology policies (including the promotion of cooperative projects) have been formulated and carried out. The task facing these countries, as in other late developers ("capitalist," "socialist," and other) is not only to attain a stronger domestic technological base, but also to promote more egalitarian forms of industrial development. The promotion of cooperative technological ties across the *entire* range of enterprises can help in this effort.

Cooperative Technological Ties in the Next NICs

As noted above, the next NICs present the "in-between" case, sharing some features with the least industrialized countries and others with the NICs. As in the NICs, factors favoring the development of certain types of technological ties include the presence of the characteristics discussed above (including technologically advancing enterprises, pre-existing inter-enterprise ties, and a relatively strong public sector capable of co-ordinating cooperative efforts). Factors weighing against the construction of such cooperative technological ties exist in all late developing countries, but they are present particularly in the next NICs (and even more so in the least industrialized countries), given their relatively uneven prior paths of development and the later timing of their industrialization efforts. These factors include: (1) the globalization of the economies, which may counter an otherwise primarily domestic orientation among enterprises (i.e., internal and external pressures, in part tied to the technology gap and the internationalization of enterprises, can counter attempts to foster cooperative ties within and throughout the national economy); (2) the relatively personalized, and not yet systematized and well-integrated, nature of enterprises and institutions in these economies, which may also restrict the formation of stable long-term alliances; and (3) the relatively high degree of industrial (as well as social and economic) dualism that prevails in most of these economies, which may make it difficult to foster alliances across the broad spectrum of firms in these countries.

In the following discussion we will examine how these factors that work for and against the creation of cooperative ties play out in the next NICs by first analyzing the prospects for government and group (or network)-sponsored cooperative ties. We will then examine the prospects for the development of cooperative ties across the economy (i.e., across both "large" and "small"-scale sectors).

Government and Group or Network-Sponsored Cooperative Techno-logical Efforts. Regarding *group formations* in the next NICs: as in the case of the East Asian NICs, groups of firms tend to be based on kinship, community (regional/linguistic), and other commonalties, and arise in response to the existing conditions, necessities, and opportunities associated with doing business in late developing countries.[33] Given the merchant, money-lending, land-based and new industrial capital that has accumulated in the hands of domestic families, we find interfirm networks in these countries ranging from "zaibatsu-like" industrial houses in South Asia (composed of relatively large firms and affiliates) to the extended family-based business networks in Southeast Asia, to the dispersed family holdings of the groups and industrial houses of the Philippines, Thailand, Indonesia, Brazil, Mexico and other countries.[34] The scale and nature of these groupings varies tremendously, from country to country and decade to decade. It is notable that the People's Republic of China has also organized in recent years a wide range of industrial groups (including family-based "Mitsubishi-type conglomerates"), given the usefulness of this institution in a late development context.[35] The significance of these groupings should not be underestimated in a late development context.[36]

Although these group formations differ from one another in important ways, they also have much in common, and the inter-enterprise ties between key group or enterprise network members and affiliates in diversified industries in these countries contrast sharply with both the poorly integrated and non-manufacturing nature of family holdings in many of the least industrialized countries on the one hand, and the more individualistic and atomistic behavior of firms in the early developing countries on the other. (Even the typical family firm that existed historically in the U.S. and Britain—whether large or small, and including those in financial groups—operated very differently from their business group counterparts in late developing countries.[37])

Very often the inter-enterprise groupings in the next NICs function in an unstable and unpredictable economic climate, and remain personalized rather than evolving toward more institutionalized and systematic network forms (i.e., in Siu-lun Wong's terminology, they lack "system trust," and may rely more on "personal trust"). However, in more predictable environments with relatively stable legal, financial and political-economic institutions (from the enterprise's point of view), the further extension and evolution of the group structure can take place, as it has in Japan and to a lesser extent in the Republic of Korea and in Taiwan, and inter-organizational "trust" itself can take on a number of new forms.[38]

The groups and networks that prevail in the next NICs tend to be very diversified through their attempts to establish footholds in a wide range of unrelated fields, as new opportunities arise. As in the evolution of groups in Japan and South Korea, there is a tendency to move gradually from a dispersed toward a more integrated structure, with the consolidation of holdings into sets of increasingly related industries as groups begin to specialize in a number of fields in which they have (or hope to have) an advantage. This increases the technological and manufacturing logic tying companies together, and lays the basis for more systematic cooperative efforts among firms in complementary and, occasionally, even dispersed industries. As the group structure evolves, the key members of each set of industries are thus in a good position to become central coordinators of cooperative efforts.

It should be kept in mind that successful technological cooperation involving group members is likely to come only after the enterprises have learned to work together for other purposes. Groups arise for a wide variety of reasons in a late development context—for example, to "grab up" investment opportunities throughout the emerging industrial economy in highly dispersed fields (each facing relatively shallow markets); to provide supplies for other group enterprises; to provide financial support and services for other group enterprises; to give family members managerial positions; and for political and other reasons. The fact that group members may not currently be engaged in joint research does not in any way preclude this from developing in the future.

Nonetheless, in many of the next NICs the group formations tend to be still at a relatively *early* stage of development, and for now they provide only preliminary arenas for cooperative technological efforts. In view of this, comparisons are often made with Japan's prewar zaibatsu rather than with postwar keiretsu or other group formations. The industrial houses in the next NICs, like the prewar zaibatsu, are much less likely to have a professional management at the top and are much more dependent on the qualities of particular family members. They also tend to be in flux with regard to strategies, industries, and modes of operation, and are much less institutionalized in their practices than would be the case with "older" (i.e., more "mature" or developed) enterprise groupings.[39]

For these and other reasons, there are many potential barriers to the possibility of key group enterprises or institutions acting as central coordinators of cooperative projects involving group or network members. For example, there is a tendency for the family-based groups to fragment over time as succeeding generations fall into territorial and other disputes.[40] Splits within the group may allow subsets of the family empire to pursue their individual strengths, but they are likely to reduce the possibility for cooperation across industries. Moreover, even if the group remains diversified and united, this does not guarantee that they will be concerned about technological advance (e.g., they may remain stagnant oligopolies behind what are essentially protected markets, in a context that some have likened to "monopoly capitalism").[41]

Even the "opening up of the economy" may not necessarily result in group members making an effort to work together to master, transform and ultimately improve upon imported technologies. Given the technology gap (reflecting the general expertise of domestic firms vis-à-vis the international standard), the relative mobility of international firms, and the requirements for international competition, the pressures and incentives to rely on the continuing importation of foreign technologies and ideas may be even stronger than in the case of the East Asian NICs.

Many point out that the tendency at the present time to import repeatedly (rather than generate) new ideas and technologies discourages the development of other promising approaches, and can undermine the development of adaptive and transformative skills within the domestic economy.[42] Thus we can see that in some cases the scope for cooperative technological ties among domestic firms can be significantly restricted if firms do indeed come to depend more on foreign suppliers of ideas and production processes, rather than attempting to master (e.g., through imports, or reverse engineering) and then substantially modify technologies through their own efforts. The Japanese case illustrated the need for a tolerance for less than state-of-the-art technologies as local capabilities were strengthened over time; this tolerance was coupled with strong incentives to widen the knowledge and technology base and gain experience in carrying out adaptations and innovations. The practice of importing "again and again" may undercut this process.

As noted above with respect to the East Asian NICs, it is also true that as firms grow and become more powerful economically they develop incentives to expand their research facilities and conduct their own in-house and cooperative research. They are also likely to try to negotiate better terms for the transfer of technology from international firms, rather than remaining junior partners (or, in some of the next NICs and least industrialized economies, partners in name only—i.e., essentially "fronts" for international subsidiaries).

In this way, we can see the group formations in the next NICs as offering a great deal of *potential* for the development of cooperative technological ties as one means to widen the local technology base. However, this potential will remain unused if conditions do not push group or network members to work together, but rather allow them to either deemphasize technological advance or rely solely on others for new ideas and technologies, without much further modification.

The government-industry relationship and public policy initiatives are important in determining the conditions that will influence the technological efforts of public and private enterprises, including family-based groups and enterprise networks. Government policy can help to mediate the relationship between domestic and international firms, and coordinate ties among domestic enterprises and institutions.

In principle, the public sector of at least the more developed latecomers should be able to, among other things: (1) act as a buffer between the local level of technological achievement and the international standard, protecting domestic firms from the full force of international competition until they have caught up sufficiently (without allowing stagnant monopolies or oligopolies to form); (2) provide a system of government labs and research support for public and private enterprises; (3) be able to set up effective government agencies that could coordinate projects involving both "large" and "small" enterprises; (4) provide public enterprises and/or organizations that could work either separately from or in close conjunction with the private sector and the "third sector" (NGOs/non-profit organizations); and (5) provide a stable economic environment conducive to the development of long-term cooperative ties. Certainly Japan, with its relatively early timing of industrialization (and the relatively manageable technology gap it faced), together with its degree of development and thus economic autonomy, was able to provide these institutions and practices and facilitate the development of a wide range of cooperative ties among public and private enterprises and organizations. The explanation for this is not simply cultural (i.e., a "cooperative culture")—for example, there was often historically a great deal of antagonism between many of these institutions—but given certain policies and historical conditions, cooperative ties could emerge.[43]

Many of these opportunities for and challenges facing efforts to develop cooperative ties can be seen in the case of India, one of the larger of the next NICs. As has been true in Japan earlier in the century, the People's Republic of China prior to (and to some extent following) the recent reforms, and to varying degrees in South Korea and Taiwan in recent years, India has followed a policy of attempting to build up domestic expertise in scientific and technological fields with the goals of avoiding technological dependence on foreign countries and firms and strengthening the domestic industrial economy (including domestic public and private enterprises). The achievements as a result of these policies have been considerable.[44]

However, in contrast to Japan and the Asian NICs, India did not follow the pattern of importing technologies and then requiring and facilitating their further transformation by domestic enterprises and research institutions. Instead, technology imports were restricted, and very uneven results came out of efforts at purely "indigenous" innovation, with both notable successes and failures.[45] Moreover, the bulk of R&D activities were carried out in public laboratories and institutions, and a common complaint was that their research was not responsive to the needs of industry, and to private enterprises in particular. (It is useful to recall that this was a common complaint of Japanese industry as well, at least until the high growth years.)

Nonetheless, as industry progressed and the economy began to be liberalized, R&D moved into a wider range of government-sponsored research institutions whose goals included the development of new technologies for use by both private and public sector enterprises. (Typically, research results have been made available to enterprises through licensing.) By the late 1980s India seemed to be on the verge of an early form of "East Asian-style" government-industry cooperation for technological advance, particularly in fields such as electronics as embodied in the C-DOT, C-DAC and other projects.[46] Public sector funding of R&D (and, to a much smaller extent, private sector funding) remained the dominant pattern, and planning documents began to contain references to cooperative research and cooperative research associations.[47] Moreover, individual cases of cooperative research involving private and public enterprises or organizations began to emerge.[48]

In 1991 that changed completely. The liberalization of the Indian economy had been proceeding for some time, but with the implementation of structural adjustment policies beginning in 1991 relative technological self-reliance was no longer considered a feasible option (or even a desirable goal, according to some policy analysts). In the ensuing years private enterprises as well as public enterprises and research institution have rushed to sign contracts with foreign suppliers of technology (e.g., private enterprises from the largest to the relatively small-scale have entered into contracts with Japanese, U.S., European, South Korean, and other suppliers, and C-DOT now works with Motorola, among others). Some argue that these policy changes have had a deleterious effect on the accumulation of skills and linkages tied to indigenous research and development efforts, even if certain *individual* cases of local R&D have become more efficient.[49] Certainly, as noted above, it appears that at least for some time, most enterprises are deemphasizing their own R&D

efforts in favor of relying on foreign suppliers for ideas and technologies. Moreover, it appears that instead of using their own individual or collective means to transform and upgrade the imported technologies, most find it more economical to simply import "again and again" the production processes associated with each new model and product.[50]

Nonetheless, this is likely to change as the private and public enterprises that do well in the present economic climate begin to feel the need to engage in more of their own research, both in-house and, potentially, cooperative. Already there are calls in India for a return to greater indigenous R&D efforts, including the use of R&D consortia.[51] Some have even called for the creation of MITI-like organizations.[52] In addition, some firms have justified their recent (non-technological) tie-ups with other Indian firms as resulting from the perception that they are not always given equal treatment by international collaborators.[53] Even among some of the Indian industrial houses, which to date have not been highly concerned with R&D, it appears that in recent years whatever research is being done is being made available to group members, and there is renewed interest in group-based affiliations as the process of industrialization proceeds.[54] Thus, the prospects for the development of government and group-sponsored cooperative technological ties in India, as in other next NICs, are mixed, with evidence of contradictory trends at the present time. However, as industrialization proceeds and the need for locally-generated innovations increases (either as exchangeable technology or as solutions to local problems), the possibilities for various types of cooperative efforts open up. The groups and business networks are in the process of adapting to new economic requirements, and are exploring new ways of working together. Moreover, the East Asian examples of technological advance have opened up entirely new perspectives regarding public policies and institutional "norms," including such issues as the role of the public enterprises, different types of industrial policies, and cooperative versus singular (individual) efforts at technological advance.[55]

It will be interesting to see the extent to which cooperative ties for the development of "indigenous" technologies will become a focus of government and group-sponsored initiatives in the future, as industrialization proceeds and technological requirements increase in the next NICs. As in the NICs, the large-scale government-sponsored projects are likely to be controversial, and to the extent that the "East Asian model" is interpreted as promoting a "government-[big] business" relationship for the "good of the country," there is likely to be widespread opposition which would include opposition to projects involving the politically influential enterprises.[56] In contrast, relatively small-scale cooperative projects involving completely unaffiliated small enterprises (i.e., those that are not closely tied to the economically powerful and politically influential enterprises) are likely to be regarded differently, as will be discussed below.

Cooperative Technological Ties Across "Large" and "Small"-Scale Sectors. In principle, cooperative technological ties need to be extended throughout a wide range of enterprises, public and private, helping to diffuse new ideas and technologies and upgrade the general level of skills and expertise in order to avoid a highly dualistic economic and social structure, and allow a good relationship encompassing a diverse range of firms and affiliated suppliers—i.e., helping to provide the diverse and flexible technological base that will be responsive to the needs of all segments of the economy, and helping to transform skills as necessary to adapt to a changing environment. The promotion of co-operative ties between large and less technologically advanced small firms, or among small firms and other organizations, are seen as two ways to help move toward this goal.

Regarding "large" (including incipient "large" modern sector firms) and "small" firm ties: the Japanese case indicated that systematic ties between the large-scale and less technologically advanced small-scale sectors of various types can help diffuse technology, generate employ-ment opportunities, and eventually raise skill (and ultimately wage) levels throughout the economy. The ties between the sectors may involve formal ties (as formal affiliates or subcontractors), or more informal ties, but large and small enterprises—both public and private—that work together in a relatively long-term relationship are in principle much more likely to share technology and ideas with one another and evolve a more egalitarian cooperative relationship over time than those that engage only in short-term periodic transactions.

As discussed above, in the earlier late developers (e.g., Japan and the East Asian NICs) the semi-traditional industrial sector has been largely modernized, and ties involving relatively large and relatively small enterprises (or "groups" of small enterprises) have been recognized as socially as well as economically beneficial, and public as well as private sector policies have acted to foster these types of ongoing cooperative technological ties. On the other extreme, in the least industrialized countries, ties between modern large-scale enterprises and the semi-traditional small workshops/enterprises, or ties among the latter in association with government agencies and organizations, have been recognized as desirable, but as difficult to achieve.

In the next NICs, we find a much more complicated picture. Modern small-scale firms (of domestic or foreign origin) exist alongside an "older" small- and very small-scale sector characterized by much lower levels of technology, as well as very low wage subcontracting units attempting to get by from contract to contract, rural small-scale enterprises, handicraft-based cottage industries, and everything in between.

This complex industrial structure is not the industrial dualism of the more *advanced industrial economies* (with a modern "large" firm sector on the one hand and a less advanced "small" firm sector on the other, using "large" and "small" more in the sense of potential for growth and access to resources than referring strictly to size). It is also distinct from the industrial dualism of the *least industrialized countries*, with the modern sector on one extreme and the traditional and semi-traditional small and microenterprises on the other and a largely "missing middle" in between (that has not as yet filled in with "modernizing" small enterprises).

In contrast, in the *next NICs* the industrial structure is sometimes referred to as "multistructured" rather than "dualistic," given the multitude of levels that extend from the traditional handicraft and cottage industries through the semi-traditional small and microenterprises (that blend in with the traditional and "modernizing" units), through the different layers of "modernizing" small and microenterprises, which then begin to blend in with the modern sector enterprises. In the next NICs there is still a "missing middle," but not in the more extreme form found in the least industrialized countries.

Regarding technological cooperation across these different layers: it is clear that the prospects for technological cooperation between large and small enterprises are relatively high in the case of modern small enterprises, and would be much more problematic in the case of cottage industries, but what of the levels in between—i.e., the enterprises possessing a relatively low level of technology, but which desire to and are in need of the upgrading of their skills and capabilities? Certainly, the "modernizing" enterprises may be able to develop ties with other enterprises, and under the right conditions could benefit from such governmental policies as those promoting subcontracting arrangements, or requiring international firms to use local suppliers and subcontractors (i.e., through local content and other regulations). However, "subcontracting exchanges" and incentives are notoriously difficult to make work in the way desired, and international firms often get around local content laws where they exist, if economic incentives are strong enough.[57]

In the Japanese case, we have argued that large firms and other institutions may have had highly exploitative ties with the small-scale sector in the prewar period, but the technology gap was not insurmountable, markets were protected, and large firms had to depend on the smaller firms, particularly in the 1930s and 1940s. Ideas and technologies were thus transferred to the small-scale sector and by the postwar period the small firms' capabilities had risen to the point that ties between large firms and small unaffiliated enterprises, and parent firms and several layers of subcontractors, sub-subcontractors, and so on, could knit together in large networks the knowledge and skill of firms in different sectors of the economy, facilitating in some cases more egalitarian relationships between the two sectors.

However, this type of relationship may not be a realistic possibility for the great majority of small and microenterprises in the next NICs—at least without *concerted government, private sector, and increasingly third (NGO/non-profit) sector efforts.* Given their low levels of technological proficiency, small-scale suppliers of producer and consumer goods and services may not be able to develop more than a tenuous relationship with larger enterprises, one that involves very little in the way of long-term commitments and transfers of technology. Moreover, suppliers of low quality consumer or final goods often find themselves at the mercy of merchants, brokers, and other middlemen who have an irregular, short-term and often exploitative relationship to them; under these circumstances, there is little opportunity to obtain information about changing markets and new technologies, or upgrade skills. Without ongoing cooperative ties of a healthier nature, many of these units may run into great difficulties in adapting to a changing economic environment.

Taking India again as a concrete example, we find that the prospects for the creation of technological alliances between the large and small-scale sectors, facilitating technological diffusion and cooperation, are high with regard to industries that include small entrepreneurial firms already possessing a relatively high level of technology and expertise— e.g., software firms working together with other enterprises in the computer industry, as well as relatively specialized subcontractors (some of these, in fact, may be considered incipient "large" firms in the sense used here—i.e., they may have far more access to resources and far more potential for growth than other small-scale enterprises). However, in India this "modern" segment of small-scale enterprises is numerically and geographically restricted, and in the less advanced (often semi-traditional) segment there appears to be relatively little scope for large-small cooperative technological ties that would involve long-term commitments and significant attempts to upgrade the small units' capabilities. The relationship is much more tenuous, often involving irregular contacts.

Particularly in the "low wage/low productivity" end of the spectrum—which represents the vast majority of small and very small enterprises in India—large firms are typically not helpful to the smaller units, and the small units' owners generally have neither the means to substantially upgrade their skills and technologies themselves, nor have they the ability to specialize as part of commodity chains and become more efficient in their lines of production, given the tenuous nature of their ties to larger enterprises, merchants, brokers, and other middlemen.[58] Exceptional cases and segments of industries can be distinguished, but for the majority of manufacturing enterprises in the unorganized sector (which represents the majority of employment in manufacturing, as well as services and agriculture, in both the next NICs and in the least industrialized countries), regular and healthy ties to larger enterprises and organizations are difficult to find—these ties certainly do not come as easily to present day India as they did to Japan earlier in the century.

Some analysts, such as C.T. Kurien, are of the view that in economies such as India's large-scale firms often just handle the marketing of products made by these smaller units under highly exploitative (unhealthy and poorly paid) working conditions, and have little incentive to help them raise their level of expertise.[59] Others use small firms only in periods of exceptional demand, or in the context of the seasonal fluctuation of demand, or when cost-cutting at the sacrifice of quality makes their services attractive.[60] For more demanding markets, the larger firms prefer to automate or do the work in-house, in the view of Kurien and other analysts. Even public sector enterprises may maintain ties to the small-scale sector in ways that are highly controversial. These unequal and exploitative ties are not always present, but in the next NICs they are frequently a part of the industrial environment.[61]

At the moment, we can only speculate about the future of large and small firm technological cooperation, particularly where such unequal inter-enterprise ties continue to exist in large numbers. There are calls, transcending ideological boundaries, for increased government support for training programs, legal protection, and other policies targeting different types of small and microenterprises that will help improve the circumstances and upgrade their capabilities, taking the specific circumstances of each into account.

In order to promote a strong small-scale sector, some analysts in India in the past have looked to the Japanese example for ideas regarding the fostering of an institutional and legal structure that will help generate a dynamic small-scale sector.[62] Others look to the more recent programs in both Japan and South Korea designed to promote cooperative technological ties among large numbers of small firms in order to upgrade their skills and technologies, and gain other types of information (e.g., regarding rapidly changing market conditions and opportunities).

However, the small-scale enterprises of Japan and even South Korea are quite advanced technologically and institutionally relative to the majority of small and microenterprises in the next NICs and the least industrialized countries. Thus, the recent programs initiated within Japan and South Korea may not be entirely applicable to those in the "low wage/low productivity" segment of the industrial spectrum.

Some analysts prefer not to look to Japan and South Korea at all for examples to follow, and prefer to study such examples as that of the People's Republic of China in recent decades in order to begin thinking about policies that could help foster closer and more mutually beneficial between the large- and small-scale sectors, and among small enterprises, in other latecomer countries.[63] The ties between large and small enterprises in the People's Republic have been no doubt more egalitarian in nature, and in many ways are indeed more applicable to contemporary developing countries. Still, in spite of the vast historical and institutional differences between the two countries, it is interesting that at least the intentions of Chinese policies in recent decades have some intriguing parallels to the earlier Japanese case in the sense of recognizing the need to promote inter-enterprise ties in order to build up a strong domestic economy, and then acting to try to meet that need by promoting a wide range of technological linkages among enterprises and organizations across the economy (including "large-large," "large-small," "small-small," and other forms of cooperative ties).

As late developing countries facing technological gaps and dualistic economies (China much more so than Japan), both countries have at different periods in their histories made a priority of promoting a strong socioeconomic infrastructure and the indigenous development of new technologies as well as the advancement of certain "traditional" areas of knowledge and expertise. The People's Republic of China, during the post-revolutionary decades and even during the post-reform period, has tried to create an environment in which systematic ties between rural and urban enterprises and between large and small enterprises/ production units facilitated the diffusion and upgrading of technologies (among other goals) with the intention of strengthening the economy and society overall, rather than focusing narrowly on the urban and large-scale sector. Moreover, the respect accorded local knowledge and skills that allowed for China's version of "Meiji technology," and the promotion of widespread small-scale technological improvements across the economy, have interesting parallels with the Japanese case.

Although some critics regard these policies in China, which to some extent bypassed market forces, as inefficient and wasteful, it can also be argued that these very policies have helped establish the foundation for the dynamism of recent years and laid the basis for a strong technological catch up process. Moreover, the explicit promotion of a "cooperative culture" within and between enterprises would appear to give a strong basis for the continuing expansion of ongoing cooperative ties across a wide range of enterprises.[64] These ties also appear to be critically important as one means to help counteract the increasing economic and industrial dualism of recent years, as seen in the growing contrasts in the People's Republic between the extremes of the very large modern sector enterprises on the one hand and the very marginal but proliferating informal sector workshops and service units on the other, along with the different layers in between.

Efforts to encourage cooperative technological ties have included the reorganization of large numbers of small enterprises in a particular industry into "industrial groups."[65] Although these groups are different from the larger, more diversified industrial groups that have been established in the People's Republic of China in recent years, the purpose in both cases has been to increase the efficiency and technological capabilities of the participating enterprises.

Other government-sponsored programs in China to promote ongoing technological ties among small enterprises also often involve long-term ties with public research institutions, larger enterprises, and other organizations. For example, in the collection of articles edited by Bhalla (1991), a number of different approaches to the question of how to organize or otherwise aid the unorganized manufacturing sector are discussed.[66] The authors remind us of the importance of these projects, given that small and medium enterprises constitute over 98% of the total number of industrial enterprises in China.[67]

As seen in these and other examples of cooperative efforts in recent years and over the past decades, China's public sector industrial extension services to the small and microenterprises (e.g., through the SPARKS and other programs) figure prominently in attempts to help the small-scale sector upgrade its skills and technologies and adapt itself to changing markets.[68] This approach may work in countries where public sector institutions are relatively effective in reaching this heterogeneous sector. Such programs are also likely to have more success with some industries and regions than others (e.g., industries that have an intrinsic need for a technological division of labor, industries in which the degree of competition does not preclude the successful entrance of initially less advanced enterprises, and regions that are close to urban areas or are along major transportation routes).

We should keep in mind that in the People's Republic of China all of these cooperative ventures are evolving in response to relative successes and failures, and overall policy changes. For example, as part of efforts at the upgradation of the technological capabilities of smaller enterprises, in recent years subcontracting relationships have also been reorganized in order to better utilize imported technologies: what forms subcontracting relationships will take in the future is difficult to predict. Moreover, although it is not clear what types of policies are emerging to deal with very small-scale units in the country's growing informal economy, in general, public policy in recent years has favored the formation of ongoing linkages among enterprises and organizations and the formation of cooperative technological ties. The process has certainly been more complex and uneven than in the earlier Japanese case, given China's particular timing of industrial transformation, the vast nature of the economy, and the diversity of the population (representing very different paths and levels of regional industrial development). Nonetheless, the consistent domestic focus of China's "socialism" and Japan's "cooperative capitalism" has had the effect of helping to integrate their respective economies technologically in a way that contrasts with the more externally-linked late developing countries, which are often characterized by the lack of well-established technological and other connections between domestic enterprises and institutions outside of relatively restricted groupings.

Many may argue that *both* the Japanese and Chinese cases are of little relevance to contemporary developing countries. Certainly, very few other latecomers have gone through the same type of economic reorganization experienced during the post-revolutionary years in China, very few have the large and attractive domestic market that strengthens China's hand in dealing with foreign firms, and needless to say, very few have the still largely centralized political and economic structure that characterizes post-reform China. Nonetheless, both the Japanese and Chinese cases in their own ways, as well as the experiences of South Korea, Taiwan, and other countries, indicate that a wide range of cooperative technological ties across the economy are possible and can be fostered through the involvement of private, public and "third sector" organizations. None of these are blueprints to be followed, but rather indicate a small sample of the attempts that have been made to develop cooperative technological ties as a way to promote more even forms of development and avoid sharp industrial divides.

In many late developing countries cooperative technological ties are evolving in response to the extension of market forces into previously non-market spheres, with all the destabilizing forces and new requirements and opportunities that this represents. Within these changing conditions, cooperative ties may emerge—and can be promoted—among different types of enterprises and institutions, depending upon the particular circumstances of each country. For example, the emergence of cooperatives and non-governmental organizations (NGOs), particularly in the next NICs since the 1980s, has created new possibilities for the promotion of cooperative technological ties across small-scale and microenterprises and organizations in the so-called "people's sector" in these countries (i.e., individuals, family workshops and enterprises either tenuously tied to, or not tied to institutions in the "organized" sector).[69] Here, ongoing cooperative ties among the very small-scale units or cooperatives and other organizations—including ties to research institutions, marketing associations, universities, NGOs, and other organizations—could help to pool technologies, ideas, knowledge, skills and resources, and help to ensure the growth of enterprises that would not be able to progress, or in some cases even survive, on their own, particularly when faced with a changing economy.

As noted in Alter and Hage's book, *Organizations Working Together* (1993)—which cites Japanese cooperative efforts, among others, as models on which to build—ongoing long-term ties between organizations in the non-profit sector can facilitate important projects involving the coordination of knowledge from a wide range of fields. The authors' specific concern in this book is with projects involving relatively small decentralized organizations providing services to the public in advanced industrial countries; however, the idea of ongoing cooperative ties (as opposed, for example, to short-term consultancies) involving micro-enterprises, craft and other cooperatives, and other types of enterprises and organizations in developing countries can be equally important to the "low wage/low productivity" segments of the urban and rural populations. The cooperative ties and cooperative projects in these critical segments of the developing economies would obviously be quite different from those that are designed to aid larger private and public sector enterprises in their attempts to advance technologically, but similar principles would underlie such efforts—i.e., the need to pool resources and information in order to upgrade and redirect skills and technologies in a changing economic environment. These small units do face the need to develop new products and processes and solve challenging technical problems, in the context of the rapidly changing economies and societies within which these units are embedded.

Again, we can neither assume that at the present historical juncture the "organized" private sector alone will be able to help these small-scale enterprises to upgrade and redirect their skills and technologies (keeping in mind that the latter represents by far the greatest number of people employed in manufacturing); we also cannot assume that short-term injections of aid, consultants, or R&D help will be sufficient to help the microenterprises redirect themselves, either. *Ongoing cooperative relationships*—with public sector, non-profit sector, and in some cases private sector organizations—may be critical for this to succeed in a changing, and highly dualistic or multistructured, economic context.[70]

There has been some discussion in recent years of the possibility for small handicraft or artisanal units cooperating with one another and blending advanced technologies with more traditional technologies in order to survive and grow in the changing national and international economy. In this context, studies of the "blending of technologies" involving the application of advanced technologies to clusters or groups of small relatively "traditional" enterprises in Japan and Italy have received much attention in recent years. In these cases, groups of small companies have decided to share information with each other and do cooperative research and development, and not at the government's request.[71]

How applicable these ideas are to the small and microenterprises of contemporary developing countries, as opposed to the industrially advanced and highly skilled artisanal firms that continue to flourish in Japan, Italy, and other relatively industrialized contexts, is not at all clear.[72] Even comparisons between the majority of microenterprises in developing countries and the small-scale artisanal enterprises set up by European immigrants as well as local entrepreneurs in Latin American urban centers appear to be misleading, to the extent that such enterprises are also industrially advanced and entrepreneurial in character.[73] However, under the right circumstances—particularly when ongoing ties with universities, research institutions, NGOs, governmental organizations (e.g., marketing associations), and other enterprises provide support—there may be some scope for a "blending of technologies," and as the small and microenterprises evolve the Japanese, Italian and other cases will become more relevant. All of these modes of cooperative undertakings need to be explored, and adapted to the particular circumstances of each of the late developing economies.

Conclusions

In this chapter we have examined the implications of industrial dualism, inter-enterprise groupings, and the government-industry relationship in different types of late developing economies with regard to the possibilities for the emergence of cooperative technological ties. We noted that such ties were more likely to develop under conditions of relatively mild (as opposed to extreme) forms of industrial dualism; in the presence of family and other inter-enterprise groups and networks (and therefore possibly a history of cooperation for other purposes, including marketing, financial and other services); and in the presence of government organizations, public enterprises, and other institutions that can act as "central coordinators" of cooperative efforts. Even under less favorable conditions, it was argued that certain types of cooperative ties could be fostered through governmental and non-governmental initiatives in a late development context—e.g., those involving public enterprises and organizations, cooperatives, NGOs, and private enterprises—as the need and opportunities for such ties increase over time.

The emergence of cooperative technological ties can be seen as one possible response to the requirements of competition at this historical juncture, particularly in fields in which a wide range of skills and resources must be combined in a short period of time, and particularly in a rapidly changing economic context that requires flexibility and a great deal of information in order to adapt to the changes. Cooperative technological ties and research efforts may form part of larger economy-wide (and primarily domestically-oriented) practices that have been referred to as manifestations of both "cooperative capitalism" and "market socialism." They may also develop in somewhat different forms in more outward-looking ("globalized") economies.

In this study we have emphasized the wide range of forms that cooperative technological efforts can take in a late development context, as well as the potential benefits of cooperative technological ties. Such ties may prove to be very useful as a way to pool, diffuse, and generate new ideas, but the ultimate goals to which these ideas are directed will be decided by each particular country within the context of the dynamics of its own particular path of development.

We have also tried to emphasize that some forms of cooperative research—particularly large-scale, government-sponsored projects—could, in a late development context, involve a significant misuse of public funds, with much less beneficial consequences. For developing countries as well as the advanced industrial countries, extreme caution must be used before trying to "borrow" institutions, practices and policies, taking into account each region's particular political and economic conditions. The use of cooperative technological ties to establish more egalitarian conditions may help a country steer away from the volatile social and political conditions associated with highly uneven industrial transformation in a late development context; poorly chosen policies regarding cooperative ties could do just the opposite.

For much of the late developing world, important concerns include trying to break free from problems created by industrial dualism, collusion, and domination by powerful families, all the while avoiding the prospect of over-dependence on imported technologies and ideas that were developed for entirely different purposes in entirely different social and economic contexts. The promotion of conditions favoring collusive government-industry or interfirm relationships (e.g., through the adoption of an extreme interpretation of the "East Asian" model of development) that ends up perpetuating these trends and further dividing the population is obviously not the answer.

However, in a late development context, the answer also does not appear to lie in the promotion of a model of impersonal and individualistic competition, with the resulting intra-and inter-organizational conflicts bred of setting individuals and organizations against each other with a "winner takes all" solution, and very little mutual support (i.e., one interpretation of the "Western" model of development). When contrasted with these extremes, the idea of *cooperative* ties, and organizations across the economy working together in a coordinated way, pooling resources, creating a more flexible and diverse knowledge base, and thereby helping to strengthen large segments of the economy both technologically and economically, may have a good deal of appeal. (The Native American image of the strength of branches linked together, and the weakness of branches lying parallel to one another, is relevant: both the *less* as well as the *more* technologically "advanced" need the knowledge that can be gained through such linkages, and in a rapidly changing late development context a lack of the strength and flexibility that can be gained through a supportive environment can have profound consequences.)

If designed in a practical way and initiated in a socially desirable context, these cooperative practices could be particularly useful. Activists and policy makers in developing countries need to be aware of the considerable benefits—as well as the potential dangers—associated with these practices, and examine carefully the particular circumstances of each case before helping to institute policies that promote or discourage cooperative ties. *Ongoing* and *flexible* inter-organizational ties based on trust and mutual support—as opposed to rigid, or more narrowly self-striving and individualistic approaches—have worked in many arenas. Cooperative ties that are carefully designed to broaden the *technological possibilities and knowledge base* can be equally viable and socially beneficial, under the right conditions.

Notes

1. However, as will be discussed below, much more detailed studies of these projects are needed to assess how "cooperative" they actually were.

2. Kim (1991), p. 278.

3. In no two studies will there be exact agreement regarding which countries should be considered to be "NICs" (or "NIEs") and which should be considered to be "next NICs." Obviously, the distinction is not clear-cut and the categories are fluid. In a general sense, the distinction indicates that there is a difference between industrializing countries both in terms of the timing of their development efforts and the degree of industrialization achieved. On the one end of the spectrum, South Korea and Taiwan are often referred to as "newly industrialized economies," and on the other end Nigeria has occasionally been referred to as a

"next NIC," although recent economic trends have resulted in serious questions about Nigeria's future path of industrialization. In between fall most of the larger economies of Latin America, South and Southeast Asia, and the People's Republic of China, among others. Singapore and Hong Kong are usually referred to as "NICs," but as city-state economies they are usually viewed as analytically distinct cases.

4. For more regarding explicit comparisons between *prewar* Japan and contemporary developing countries, see Nafziger (1995). Nafziger takes up such issues as the role of the government in the economy, technology gaps, industrial dualism, and other important topics, and compares conditions found in different periods in Japan's history prior to World War II (Meiji, Taisho, and early Showa periods) to conditions typically found in developing countries in recent decades. Cf. also Ohkawa and Ranis (1985), Francks (1992), and other sources for general comparisons between Japan's course of development and that of contemporary developing countries.

5. Ogura (1967), p. 679. The relatively low capital, technological and research requirements associated with the imported technologies of the time allowed the transformation of both the *processes* tied to the production of "traditional" products and the products themselves. These conditions further allowed the proliferation of small-scale units or enterprises supplying new versions of "traditional" goods and services, eventually doing so (in many cases) in association with the large-scale modern sector.

6. On the latter cf., for example, Susantha Goonatilake, *Aborted Discovery: Science and Creativity in the Third World* (1984), and Abdur Rahman, *Intellectual Colonisation: Science and Technology in West-East Relations* (1983).

7. Again, there were two important aspects of the technology gap: one involving the semi-traditional sector vis-à-vis the modern sector, and one involving the modern sector vis-à-vis the international standard. For Japan earlier in the century, in neither aspect was the gap so great that it made it exceedingly difficult for domestic firms to catch up and compete.

8. As Odagiri and Goto (1993, p. 81) note, "Indigenous technology was important not only on its own, particularly in traditional industries, but also in providing the ability to select among the technologies available in developed countries, and in adapting and assimilating them to fit to domestic conditions. This fact was most notable in the textile industry, the second largest manufacturing industry at the time (next to food processing) and the largest exporting industry before World War II." They also give another example, drawn from the iron and steel industry of the late nineteenth century, to illustrate the importance of indigenous skills and knowledge in adapting and improving upon imported technologies in order to fit local conditions and meet local needs.

9. Fruin (1992) discusses how, in spite of heavy pressure from "better quality, sometimes cheaper, more varied Western imports" in some industries, rural enterprises survived in the late 19th century by focusing on "simple, straightforward goods" for urban and rural markets that they understood well (pp. 107-108). He adds, "Needless to say, given the distance from Western markets, relatively low standards of living, and limited growth opportunities in the

Japanese market at this time, Western firms were reluctant to invest in developing shipping storage, transportation, and sales facilities" (pp. 112-113), and relied on Japanese enterprises instead.

10. Cf. Bhagavan (1990) for one analysis of successive technological revolutions and their impact on the developing world. Bhagavan distinguishes the technologies associated with the "first technological revolution," based in steam power and other relatively early technologies developed during the 1760-1860 period, from the more complex technologies—including electric power—of the "second revolution" that originated during the 1860-1960 period, and again from the new ("third revolution") technologies that emerged after 1960. He argues that the first revolution used primarily the skills of individual engineers, mechanics, and master craftsmen, who employed craft and industrial experience as their source of skills. In contrast, the second revolution is seen as employing industrial engineers, scientists, and emerging R&D departments, with technical personnel increasingly possessing research degrees and research experience in the physical and engineering sciences (steel, railroad equipment, autos, chemicals, electrical equipment and synthetic textiles are cited as representative industries of this period). Finally, the third revolution is viewed in terms of scientists and engineers in professional R&D departments and institutions, increasingly drawing their skills from advanced degree programs in electronics, computer science and information processing, and other science-related fields (as technology becomes increasingly tied to scientific knowledge, rather than primarily to trial-and-error techniques). No matter how many "revolutions" are identified, most analysts agree that capital, research and other requirements have tended to increase over the successive technological "revolutions."

11. Watanabe (1983) discusses how blacksmiths in Japan provided the technological base for the modern metal manufacturing and engineering industries, and how the former goldsmiths, silversmiths and gunsmiths contributed to the development of the armaments industry, in his excellent historical chapter (Chapter 2, "Inter-Sectoral Linkages in Japanese Industries: A Historical Perspective"). In contrast, for accounts of the difficulties facing "traditional" blacksmiths in some of the least industrialized countries, cf. Muller (1984) regarding Tanzania, Suliman (1980, cited in Watanabe, 1983) regarding the Sudan, and other studies that indicate how far the gap is now between the traditional skills and the requirements of modern industry. As a consequence, a large segment of "traditional" and semi-traditional units have been threatened by the expansion of the modern sector. For example, in discussing the relationship in sub-Saharan Africa between the development of large-scale industry on the one hand, and rural small-scale and cottage industries on the other, Samuel Wangwe argues that "the relationship between them has been more competitive than complementary, with large-scale industry developing at the expense of, rather than in support of, rural industries" (cf. Wangwe, 1991, pp. 280-291 for a more detailed discussion of this issue).

12. Krestovsky (1966), pp. 4-5.

13. As Steel and Webster note, "Some observers argue that there is a `missing middle' in the size distribution in African countries which must be filled for

industrial development to proceed" (Steel and Webster, 1991, p. 1, referring to studies by Kilby, 1988, among others). They also point out that the "bulk of manufacturing employment in most African countries" is found in small firms, particularly in the microenterprises.

In countries such as India the "missing middle" has also been a subject of concern (cf., for example, National Council of Applied Economic Research, 1993, p. 286, for a statement of the problem). However, it will be argued below that in the NICs, and especially in the next NICs, the industrial structure tends to be more complex and is not as highly polarized as is often the case in the least industrialized countries.

14. Steel and Webster (1991) note than in the wake of structural adjustment policies in Ghana, microenterprises in particular have been hurt since they "have not mastered the new environment" and "seem unable to change products in the face of mounting competition." This has been compounded by public sector cutbacks, the lack of alternatives to irregular self-employment, and the weak purchasing power of the lower income population which "constrains the prospects for individual microenterprises. Although some microenterprises will succeed and grow, most are likely to continue hand-to-mouth as increases in demand are quickly competed away" (p. x).

It is also interesting to note Steel and Webster's discovery that almost all of the small firms in their Ghana study knew nothing about the institutional services that exist, in part, to serve them (and vice versa—the institutional services did not know much about them). Although this may in large part reflect the problems faced by public institutions in countries such as Ghana (particularly under conditions of structural adjustment), it also reflects the difficulties in reaching a very heterogeneous and dispersed population, and it further indicates the need for "organizing the unorganized sector" in order to ensure that it can effectively confront and deal with the demands of a changing economy. The fact that some of the "modern" (and "modernizing") small enterprises in their study did succeed in creating formal and informal linkages with large firms or government institutions indicates that if enterprises can be helped to make it into this "middle" ground, cooperative technological ties are more likely to develop and they are more likely to be able to survive in the unstable environment of a rapidly changing economy.

15. To some, this appears to be an outgrowth of the earlier colonial relationship, although in a distinctly post-colonial form. Cf., for example, Adebayo Adedeji (1981), Chapter 1.

16. Regarding examples of "deliberation councils" —e.g., Japan's MITI, South Korea's Export Promotion Council, and the Malaysian Business Council—see Chapter 4 of the World Bank's *The East Asian Miracle: Economic Growth and Public Policy* (1993), among other sources.

17. See China Credit Information Service (1983/1984), pp. 3-4. We should note that some have objected to the use of the term "business group" in Taiwan's case, given that the groups' boundaries are not as clear-cut as in the cases of South Korea's chaebol or Japan's business and industrial groups. (Cf. Hamilton, 1991, p. 19, for a short discussion regarding the publication *Business Groups in Taiwan;* see

also Numazaki in the same volume.) Siu-lun Wong (1991) argues that the relatively unclear boundaries of Taiwan's business networks has to do in part with what he calls a lack of "system trust." He defines "system trust" in terms of a stable legal, public policy and government-industry relationship, without which enterprises find it difficult to cooperate closely with other enterprises and organizations outside of a small circle of well-known affiliates. Wang suggests that in Taiwan ties among firms (e.g., in the form of business networks) are based primarily on family ties and "personal trust" (or occasionally on native place, birth year, or other criteria), but they tend to be unstable—particularly at the margins of the extended family—and cannot extend much beyond close blood (or other) relationships because of the lack of an environment conducive to ties among a wide range of firms and individuals. Here, he suggests, personal trust *compensates for* rather than complements system trust. (Others have noted that the historical distinction between "mainlanders" in the government and "native" Taiwanese business families may have contributed to the relative lack of support for the latter—e.g., in contrast to the very close government-chaebol relationship seen in South Korea in recent decades.)

Nonetheless, it is clear from the Japanese and Korean cases that even with an increase in "system trust," "personal trust" remains important, and business network ties continue to be advantageous for both political and economic reasons. Their boundaries may become more formal under such conditions, but the element of flexibility (i.e., the possibility of changing membership rolls or working with enterprises outside of group/network boundaries) becomes more important as well as economic development progresses. (Regarding the idea of "personal trust" in Taiwan's business networks, see also Kao Cheng-shu's article in the Hamilton volume.)

18. In South Korea we find that in recent years large numbers of cooperating firms from the same group have regularly worked together in order to enter new industries and adopt new technologies. They do this by circulating engineers and other technical experts around within the group—i.e., from company to company—as is necessary to meet their technological needs. For example, according to Amsden, "(A) new subsidiary would most likely be established by a task force typically formed at the group level and comprising qualified managers, engineers, and even supervisors from existing companies within the group. In the case of Hyundai, for example, managers from its construction arm were transferred to its shipbuilding arm to aid in project management. Later, engineers from its shipbuilding arm, who had a knowledge of anticorrosion, were loaned to its automobile affiliate where a new paint operation was coming on stream. Such transfers increased the capability to diversify and were facilitated by a central "brain" and a uniform group culture. Within a very short time, therefore, the business groups in South Korea were multiproduct yet still under family management, with salaried managers in command at the industry level and a capability to enter new industries quickly." (Amsden, 1989, p. 128.)

19. For example, NTT-sponsored projects that involved NTT "family" members have clear parallels with some of the ETRI projects. With respect to ETRI's TDX (digital switches) project, Evans (1992, p. 12) notes that "while ETRI

is the lead organization in design and development, the major *chaebol* have also been involved in the process from the beginning." ETRI researchers typically are joined in the R&D process by researchers from some of the major South Korean private firms in the industry (e.g., 600 engineers from four private firms joined 200 ETRI researchers on the TDX-10 project).

20. Evans points out that "Taiwan's ERSO...operates in a manner similar to ETRI even though Taiwan's very different patterns of industrial organization changes the character of its private sector ties...Both South Korea and Taiwan draw on the model of Japan's Ministry of International Trade and Industry (MITI) during its golden age in the 1950s and 1960s [i.e., the postwar catch up period]." (Evans, 1992, p. 13.) Evans discusses the role played by government organizations as "handmaidens" of private industry in many of the more industrialized developing countries, complementing rather than supplanting the private sector. Although the Indian case discussed in this article has changed enormously since the article was written, Evans' analyses of the roles played by South Korea's ETRI and Taiwan's ERSO are generally consistent with other studies of the two organizations.

21. For a discussion of these procedures see, for example, Hou and Gee (1993), pp. 397-9. Ting (1987) noted that by the 1980s ERSO was already acquiring technology abroad and conducting its own R&D in semiconductors and computer software. It also took on such projects as jointly developing (with Hewlett-Packard and the large Taiwan business group, Formosa Plastics) a "completely computerized and automated circuit-board plant" (p. 150). Since the mid-1980s, ERSO and other research organizations appear to have expanded their R&D and other cooperative projects in a number of different fields of importance to Taiwan's enterprises as they move up the technology "ladder." Regarding ERSO and its role in the 1980s, see also Henderson (1989). For more on ETRI, the Korean Institute of Electronics Technology (KIET) and other electronics-related research institutes, cf. Bloom (1992), among other sources.

22. For details, see Kim (1993), p. 377 and elsewhere.

23. For details see, for example, Hou and Gee (1993), pp. 399-400. A more recent variant on this theme involved the Taiwan government contributing plant and equipment (from an earlier semiconductor research project) to a joint venture of domestic chip makers. The government's share was 30% ("Taiwan Chip Maker Vanguard is Aiming for the Big Leagues," *Asian Wall Street Journal*, October 18, 1994, p. 9). The participating enterprises included Taiwan Semiconductor Manufacturing Corporation, U.S.I. Far East Corporation (a petrochemical manufacturer), China Development Corporation (an investment bank), Orient Semiconductor Electronics Ltd. (a manufacturer of printed-circuit boards), and the Far Eastern Textile Group.

24. In 1993 they received 5 billion won (about $6 million) from the government, but were hoping for another $250 million in government support over a four year period ("From Korea, a Challenge to Japan," *New York Times*, May 12, 1994).

25. For example, regarding the development of "industrial research cooperatives" in South Korea, Kim (1993) notes that the Technology Development

Promotion Act of 1977 was designed to facilitate these joint R&D undertakings, but it was only when subsidies were offered that enterprises decided to participate in the program, with eleven cooperatives established by 1982 and forty-six by mid-1989 (the forty-six cooperatives were comprised of 986 firms, of which 756 were small and medium-sized firms). Kim comments, "Most existing cooperatives, however, are in name only with little substance...they neither have adequate R&D facilities nor full-time researchers to take advantage of subsidies to R&D cooperatives" (p. 375).

This is understandable, given that the majority of participants in this government-sponsored case were small and medium enterprises which have little in the way of R&D facilities and presumably have had little experience with cooperative research efforts (as will be discussed below). Nonetheless, Kim's assessment is a good indication that we would need to look carefully into all of these projects in order to estimate how much cooperative research was actually carried out.

26. In South Korea (as opposed to Thailand, for example) the importation of technology has been, at least in principle, allowed with the understanding that it will be rapidly assimilated and mastered; however, the propensity to master and then transform the new technologies will differ according to the firm, industry, and market toward which the new commodities are directed. (Regarding a case in which the South Korean government decided not to try to prevent a "continuing dependence" on imported technology, see "Samsung Wins Permission to Make Cars," *Financial Times*, December 8, 1994: "But in an apparent attempt to mollify Hyundai, the government decided yesterday to allow it to import [minivan] technology...from Mitsubishi. It had threatened earlier to block the technology transfer as part of an effort to promote technological independence for the Korean car industry.") For a general account regarding South Korean attempts at developing technological self-reliance, see Mukerjee (1986), among other sources.

27. Cf. Lall (1982) and his more recent writings, regarding this idea of complementarity and balance.

28. From Henderson (1994), p 276. Ting cites additional studies—e.g., Redding and Tam (1985)—that support the contention that flexible business networks in Hong Kong (and Taiwan) aid in the development of "indigenous technology." Cf. Ting (1987) on this and related points.

29. Cf. Ho (1978, and more recent writings) on the decline of the labor force in "traditional" occupations and the concurrent rise in factory-based occupations in Taiwan.

30. The political benefits of forming industrial groups (e.g., chaebol in South Korea) are well recognized. The same is true to a large extent in the case of Taiwan's business networks. For a very interesting discussion of political ties and business networks (*guanxiqiye*, or "related enterprises") in Taiwan, see Numazaki (1991), along with other articles in the same volume. Numazaki gives several examples to illustrate his argument that not only business networks, but also *cross-group* networks, are used to gain access to the political elite and often serve as an "important channel of communication and cooperation between the state

and business and between different *guanxiqiye*." He concludes (on p. 90) that "capital links among leading enterprises are so intertwined that they are woven into the large web of interfirm relations. In light of this, I have a hypothesis that Taiwan's *guanxiqiye* is less a `business group' than a relatively dense cluster of corporations in the much larger network of entrepreneurs that is the social foundation of what Hamilton (1989) calls Taiwan's `*guanxi* capitalism'."

31. Regarding South Korea, the process by which Japanese colonial possessions were sold off cheaply to private individuals, the tie-ups with foreign firms, and the government promotion of large enterprises and relative neglect of the small (in urban and, even more so, in rural areas) is a well-known part of the country's post-colonial history. In Taiwan, the post-colonial evolution of the industrial structure took a very different course, but here as well—given the demands of and alternatives available to the more technologically advanced (and well-connected) firms—the less advanced enterprises have not been "pulled up" and they now face a very uncertain future, particularly given the strength of the NT dollar and new competition from developing countries. Cf. Lau (1990), among other sources, regarding these changes and the government's response in the form of a more explicit industrial policy.

32. The programs established by the Republic of Korea to help upgrade the technologies of small and medium enterprises—including the formation of research cooperatives to stimulate joint R&D—are discussed in Lee (1991) and Kim (1993), among other sources.

33. The South Indian case of the Nattukottai Chettiars is a good example of groups that formed in response to these requirements. At first, the Chettiars (historically moneylenders) did not want to adopt the group form, but found it difficult to work in the Indian context without it. Cf. Ito (1966) regarding this case. On a related note, a very interesting article by Roy (1994) discusses the difference between the "commodity" and "service" castes in India, both of which made early industrial products. The products of commodity castes were of better quality and in the pre-colonial period were sold in local markets, whereas the products of the "service" castes were for local use. Roy describes how the former often benefited from the new opportunities provided by the colonial economy, whereas the latter often could not survive the destructive forces of the colonial period. Moreover, the author discusses how the former were able to survive and prosper on the basis of (family and other) *business networks*, from which the latter were excluded; "service" caste families were not able to form their own networks, upgrade their products, or compete, under these conditions.

34. For information on the "industrial house" form as it appears in many developing countries in recent decades, cf. Amjad (1982), China Credit Information Service (1983-present), Chou (1988), Cordero (1977a and b), Gereffi (1993), Ghosh (1973, 1974a, 1974b), Hattori (1984), Ito (1966, 1975, 1978, 1983, 1984), Kucchal (1984), Leff (1976, 1978, 1979a, 1979b), Koppel and Peterson (1975), Siddharthan (1987), Strachan (1976), White (1974), and articles in Okochi and Yasuoka (1984), among other sources in English, Japanese, Korean, Spanish, and other languages. (The articles by Cordero, Gereffi, Leff, Strachan, and other

sources in English, and the studies in Spanish and Portuguese on "groups" in Mexico, Brazil and other countries in Latin America provide interesting comparisons with the Asian examples that have been the focus of this study.)

35. Regarding "the Mitsubishi-type conglomerates that China now hopes will establish the country commercially in the world market," and the differences between current attempts in the PRC to build large family-based business groups and the "freewheeling conglomerates" that emerged in China in the early 1980s, cf. "Hit by Setbacks, Past Titons of China, Inc. Grow Cautious," *The Asian Wall Street Journal*, June 23-24, 1995. According to another report on new industrial groups in the People's Republic, "Market reform in China is producing an expanding corps of fast-growing conglomerates which will be in the forefront of foreign trade initiatives and industrial restructuring...The assessment—conducted by the Development Research Centre under the government's State Council, the State Statistics Bureau, the Management World, and Beijing Magazine—found China's largest companies recorded higher growth and efficiency in 1993 and were evolving into industrial groups that will set the pace for reforming the loss-ridden state sector..." Of the top 500 industrial groups, most were centered in the coastal provinces, and were often found in the metallurgical and industrial transport machinery sectors ("Fast Growth for Chinese Groups," *Financial Times*, September 17, 1994).

36. As Swaminathan (1992, p. 204) puts it, regarding industrial houses in India, "In the context of this study of the growth and functioning of the TVS group we would like to submit the following: Given the reality of industrial activity in the country [i.e., India], that it is dominated and directed by business groups/houses, and given the fact that the resources, talent and personnel at the disposal of the government are limited, industrial policy, specifically that relating to and encouraging domestic R&D should be formed taking the business house/group as the basic unit." The importance of industrial houses overall has not diminished in the post-liberalization era, although they are still undergoing changes in response to the new economic conditions.

37. As noted above, the literature on business groups and networks in Latin America and Asia is growing, and some analysts make contemporary and historical comparisons with enterprise development in the "West" (i.e., the early industrializing countries). For example, Hamilton (1991) presents interesting general comparisons between the development of Chinese family firms and the development of commercial organizations/enterprises in Europe.

38. For more on the idea of "trust" (in various forms) as it has developed in Japan's postwar economic environment, see Sako (1992).

39. The looser *business networks* in the next NICs may also be judged to be less "developed" than those found in a more industrialized context such as Taiwan's, but this needs to be established by closer comparisons with business networks, which as yet have not been studied to the same extent as the more formal *industrial house* form of inter-enterprise groupings.

40. Under certain conditions intermediaries may put pressure on important industrial houses to avoid splits. In India, for example, a senior official of a financial institution ("FI") noted, "Wherever a split is taking place among industrial

groups we want to ensure that there is a proper responsibility centre. Otherwise, if we take up an exposure in a group based on our relationship with one of the family members and the management control ends up with someone else we might have problems." ("End Feuds, FIs Tell Corporates," *The Hindu*, Business Line, p. 1, March 18, 1995.)

41. Leff (1979b) notes that the groups that are characteristic of many late developing countries are a reflection of a path of economic development that is radically different from that experienced by the early industrializers. He writes, "In these conditions, private capitalism is often viewed unfavorably in the less-developed countries. The capitalism which is condemned is not the competitive capitalism of nineteenth century England, with which the less-developed countries have little domestic experience—but rather their own version of 'monopoly capitalism.' Moreover, the disillusion is especially great because industrialization was expected to *reduce* the concentration of economic power. Earlier, a small number of large land-owning families held dominant economic power; the only change which appears to have resulted from industrialization is that economic power is now concentrated in the hands of a relatively small number of Groups." As Leff indicates, the use of the phrase "monopoly capitalism" in late developing countries (this would include Japan as well) is very different from that which Baran and Sweezy had in mind when they wrote their well-known book of this title. We should note that the phrase "state monopoly capitalism" has also tended to be popular in many late developing countries, including Japan, given the relatively large role of the government in the economy and its close ties to the largest firms; it may be less applicable to a "post-liberalization" type of economy, but the latter remains very far from the nineteenth century image of competitive capitalism that has continued into the ideology associated with "modern" (neoclassically based) economics.

42. For example, in her study of the research efforts of India's TVS group (one of the country's business groups) in the auto parts industry, Swaminathan (1992) noted that the group found it more economical to "import again and again" new technologies rather than invest in in-house (or cooperative) research. Moreover, she pointed out that the R&D activity of the group was conducted strictly "within the parameters specified by their foreign collaborators"—i.e., during the contract period the foreign suppliers apparently did not allow much in the way of changes to the technologies, discouraging efforts to master and adapt or improve upon the technologies.

Similarly, P. Mohanan Pillai and J. Srinivasan (1992, p. 158), in their analysis of the Indian machine tool industry in the period of gradual liberalization, cite an UNCTAD study that pointed out that "by and large, Indian firms have preferred licensing agreements with foreign firms almost every time a new product was added in the product structure. Where foreign technology is resorted to, scant attention is given to building up domestic design capability. This study shows that there have been few serious attempts at adapting imported technology to domestic factor proportions and, consequently, the cost reductions produced by technical changes in the direction of capital-saving innovations have not taken place. The implicit link between the efficiency of machine tools and technical change and innovation through domestic R&D was thus lost. The point to emphasize is that continuing low efficiency is not due to the `old age' of the machine stock or to lack of modernization, as the advocates of liberalization would argue, but is also a question of how efficiently the industry is organized to transform the new technology into a nucleus for technological change in the entire economy."

43. For analysts in developing countries that perceive their circumstances to be too different from those prevailing in Japan and other East Asian countries due to "cultural" differences, it is worth recalling that "culture" as well as politics and economics can change very rapidly, albeit in a complex evolutionary way. It may be useful to note that many European visitors to Japan in the early twentieth century found the inhabitants of the Japanese islands to be lazy, dirty, and habitually late, among other features that are direct opposites of current stereotypes. (This is based on a number of early twentieth century writings by Europeans containing their impressions of Japan and the Japanese, collected by Professor Beverly Nelson; personal communication.) In this regard, Roberts quotes a 1927 issue of the *Japan Gazette*, which stated that Japan would never become a rich country because "the advantages conferred by nature, with the exception of the climate, and the love of indolence and pleasure of the people themselves forbid it. The Japanese are a happy race, and being content with little are not likely to achieve much." (Roberts, 1973, p. 116.) No matter how biased these particular accounts may be, it is impossible to deny that what appear to be important sociological or "cultural" characteristics of a country today may not have been common at all at an earlier point in time. Moreover, analysts in developing countries should note that neither the government-industry nor inter-firm relationships in prewar Japan took the "efficient" forms that they appear to have attained (at least to the casual eye) in recent years. (It may also be useful to recall that Japan's prewar political scandals have interesting parallels in many developing countries today.) "Efficiency," "cooperative attitudes," and "altogether original" ways of innovating are learned behaviors, rather than enduring cultural traits.

44. For an interesting discussion of India's earlier experience with technology policies, see Lall (1984, 1987), among other sources.

45. Joseph (1992) discusses the problems inherent in this approach with respect to the electronics industry.

46. Cf., for example, G.B. Meemamsi (1993).

47. Rahman's description of these cooperative research associations was as follows: "(The) government meets fifty per cent of the expenditure where industry comes forward to establish cooperative research associations. These cover the areas of textiles including man-made fibres, cement, rubber, paint, plywood, jute, tea, electricals, and automobiles. In some cases, government taxed the industry and receipts were used to fund research for the industry, e.g., cement" (1990, p. 15; see also Rahman, 1984). Bagchi (1987, p. 22) noted, "The government's function as a co-ordinator is seen clearly...when it takes an initiative in setting up research organizations which are run on a cooperative

basis by firms in a particular industry (many such organizations exist in India and South Korea)."

48. In the field of supercomputers, for example, the private sector firm Wipro worked with both the National Aeronautical Laboratory (in Bangalore) and the Bhabha Atomic Research Centre (in Bombay) on separate projects. (Cf., for example, "Byte by Byte: C-DAC Catapults India into the Super League of Supercomputers," *Sunday*, October 2-8, 1994.)

49. An interesting study by Mani (1995, pp. 100-101) argues that the "repetitive import of foreign technology, in areas in which technology import and domestic R&D are substitutes rather than complements, can have very deleterious consequences for the domestic development of skills (or the process of building up of indigenous capability)." The study examines two cases drawn from the experience of the Indian telecommunications industry: (1) the C-DOT case and (2) earlier attempts at the development of an Electronic Switching System (ESS). Mani describes how the achievements of local researchers and industry were overlooked by the government, and multinationals were invited in. "Demoralized and insulted, the highly motivated team has started disintegrating... The two cases drive home the point that, in the Indian telecom switching equipment industry, the concept of local skill development has never been seriously thought through. Continued dependence on foreign sources has naturally become the order of the day in the industry" (pp. 120-1).

Joseph, in the same volume, echoes Mani's concern. His empirical analysis suggests that "firms with higher local R&D effort tend to have a higher employment generating capacity. But the available evidence shows a general decline in the R&D intensity of firms in the eighties. Moreover, most of the firms resort to foreign collaborations as a substitute for and not to complement their local technology generating efforts. This, in turn, leads to an increased dependence on foreign technology and has a dampening effect on the employment generating capability of the industry. On the whole, it appears that while liberalization of the kind that India follows today may lead to higher output growth in the short run, it will be at the cost of long-term sustained growth and the employment generating capacity of the industry." (Joseph, 1995, p. 142.)

50. The propensity to import technology, particularly since 1991, is also shown in the reluctance of Indian companies to use indigenous technologies produced by Indian government R&D laboratories, even though the labs' technology sales *abroad* increased fourfold between 1991-92 and 1993-94 ("Indigenous Technology—Science of Selling," *India Today*, October 31, 1994, p. 154).

51. As Dr. G.K. Deb, the director of the Electronics Research and Development Centre, Calcutta, argues, "In the post-economic liberalisation era when many of the information technology areas are opened to participation by private companies and multinational corporations, it will be very wise to accept the consortia approach by our R&D organisations in order to make sure that our IT industry does not become solely and wholly a manufacturing venture, but also becomes one engaging itself in R&D." ("R&D at Cross-roads," *Telematics India*, May 1995, p. 70.) Similarly, Rohit Bansal notes, "There are worries, perhaps for the first

time, that Indian industry would find access to international technology become more difficult in times to come. It is feared, for example, that Indian firms are already entering tie-ups merely as assemblers and fabricators, without wresting any role whatsoever in the design and conceptual process. Similar exclusion is coming up in the area of `dual use technologies' where developed nations are barring technology exports to India of any designs and processes that have `sensitive' applications...The message, broadly, seemed reminiscent of `national self dependence' in the Nehruvian model...Besides strengthening venture capital institutions to fund indigenous projects, a major concern of experts was to kick-off `industry consortia in India for generic research at the pre-competitive stage'." ("Industry Insecure Over Tech Inflows," *The Times of India*, May 15, 1995.)

52. As noted by C.N.R. Rao (1990), "A judicious choice of technology, product mix and of futuristic Research, Design and Development has to be made in all sectors of our industry. For this purpose, technology forecasting, assessment and information is essential. It is hoped that the Technology Information, Forecasting and Assessment Council (TIFAC) established recently will provide the leadership in this direction. If pursued and directed properly, the Indian TIFAC could, in principle, become the equivalent of the Japanese MITI. It is, therefore, essential that we commission in-depth studies on technologies in the various sectors." ("Science and Technology Planning: Issues and Priorities," *Indian Journal of Social Science*, Vol. 3, No. 3, July-Sept. 1990, p. 342.)

53. Regarding tie-ups among domestic enterprises in India, Robin Abreu noted (in reaction to a few recent non-technological alliances), "Last month, two of the country's largest consumer durables companies, Videocon and BPL, gave the foundering swadeshi movement a new meaning. They formed a strategic alliance to fight foreign brands such as Akai, Sony and Goldstar, entering the market in the wake of liberalisation. Obviously inspired in part by their own Japanese collaborators—Matsushita and Sanyo—who compete with international brands in markets across the world, it is, nevertheless, an unusual alliance. They have been fierce competitors so far, and overcoming the resulting distrust must count as quite an achievement. On one or more counts, this kind of marriage may not remain unusual anymore as Indian companies join hands among themselves to fight foreign brands and use their larger size to take the battle to overseas markets." Regarding a separate alliance with a domestic enterprise, Mukesh Gupta (Vice-Chairman of Lloyds Steel, an Indian enterprise) is quoted as saying "We did not tie up with a foreign company because foreign companies take all the malai (cream) and Indian companies get all the chhachh (leftovers)." (In "Domestic Tie-Ups: Together They Stand," *India Today*, February 28, 1995.)

54. In response to a set of questions pertaining to cooperative R&D prepared as part of this study, a reply from DCM Shriram Industries, Ltd. noted, "Almost all large Indian industrial groups have their own Research and Development bases from where group members/affiliates get the required technology." Ranbaxy and Escorts were named as examples of "some of the many groups which have their own R&D bases catering to all group members/affiliates' needs." (Response dated June 14, 1995.)

Some groups have historically worked more closely together, coordinating their members' activities, whereas others have not. For example, of the two predominant industrial houses in India, one—the Tata group—has clearly tried to work as a single entity through its holding company, Tata Sons, whereas the second—the Birla group—has not tried so actively in the past to work in a closely coordinated manner. As J.R.D. Tata, Chairman of Tata Sons, described his group's strategy, "All the heads of the Tata companies say it is not only a question of pride in the group's high reputation but they find there is a synergy, an advantage, in staying together." (*India Today*, February 28, 1990, pp. 117-120.)

55. For example, it is interesting that, in contrast to "Western" policies promoting the rapid opening of economies in the developing world, the Japanese government has been promoting a much more cautious and gradual approach to liberalization, and even neoclassically-trained Japanese economists often reject or greatly qualify the principles of free trade and open economies, particularly for developing countries, based on Japan's own historical experience. Moreover, several recent accounts discuss MITI's spreading of Japanese industrial policy experience to developing countries as an alternative to free market orthodoxy. As one analyst noted, "In the Japanese view, developing countries should treat the free-market advice of Western economists with caution. The ex-communist economies of Eastern Europe, for example, need not rush to privatise state firms. And governments should seek to promote development through clever intervention in the economy. In November MITI's institute invited Polish, Indonesian and Nigerian academics to Tokyo to discuss the usefulness of industrial policy. This is a lesson America would be unlikely to teach, for it likes to pretend that it has no industrial policy...China is Japan's most eager pupil." ("The New Nationalists," *The Economist*, January 14, 1995, pp. 19-21.) This alternative perspective easily extends into questions of institutional arrangements—e.g., cooperative versus more individualistic approaches in a wide range of settings.

56. For example, Amit Mitra, Secretary-General of the influential FICCI (Federation of Indian Chambers of Commerce and Industry), seems to interpret the "East Asian model" in this way. He argues, "All of these fresh developments suggest that India is moving slowly towards the East Asian model that has come to be called the QIO State—where close government and business cooperation converts the State into a 'quasi-internal organisation.' Often, informal but binding ties develop between key representatives of the state and the private sector serving a common goal. These informal ties soon give way to institutional arrangements reinforcing the continuity of the synergy." (Cf. Mitra's article, "India, Incorporated: an Interesting Interface is Slowly Emerging Between Politicians, Civil Servants and Business Leaders," *The Hindustan Times*, May 14, 1995.) In other words, from his point of view the emergence of an "India, Inc." would be a positive development. However, this is not likely to be a very popular view if it is seen as extending even further the potential for influence-peddling, corruption, and the concentration of wealth and economic power.

57. Regarding the difficulties in establishing linkages in a globalized and liberalized economy, cf. Watanabe (1983), Chapter 5 ("Technical Co-operation between Large and Small Firms in the Filipino Automobile Industry"), among other examples.

58. Nirmala Banerjee (1990) discusses the differences between the "craftsmen and artisans" of the microenterprises in developing countries with dualistic or multistructured economies, and the English craftsmen and artisans of the early Industrial Revolution. She points out even skilled artisans in countries such as India know their job by imitation only, and "with all his ingenuity and desperation, he is usually totally dependent on others for designing work and a change in the patterns of orders can make him totally redundant" (p. 218). To illustrate the contrast, she quotes Landes (1969) regarding the English artisans of the Industrial Revolution: "Even more striking is the theoretical knowledge of these men. They were not, on the whole, the unlettered tinkerers of historical mythology" and had access to a great deal of current practical information and theoretical insights, including regarding technologies and changing markets. Banerjee notes (on p. 218), "The artisan of Calcutta has no such source because no such literature is published in a language that he can understand at a cost he can afford. Therefore, though living in one of the world's major cities, he gets no advantage from the growing stock of academic expertise or practical experiments elsewhere. The few government efforts at providing such knowledge or information are so far removed that they rarely reach the artisan. Given that the industrial technology today is much more sophisticated than during the British industrial revolution, Calcutta's artisans have little change of keeping up with it, from their isolated position."

Of course, the circumstances Banerjee describes extend far beyond Calcutta into much of the unorganized sector. (To gain a sense of the growing numbers of workers in India that earn their livelihoods outside of the organized sector, an article in *The Economist*, January 21, 1995, p. 19, pointed out that "the share of the labour force in the `organised' private sector fell from 3.3% to 2.8% between 1981 and 1991, a curious phenomenon in a developing country.") See also Institute of Economic Growth (1995), among other sources, regarding these issues. These studies indicate the growing importance of the unorganized sector, and the significance of its ties (or lack thereof) to the organized sector.

59. Cf. Kurien (1992, 1994) and other writings by this author.

60. Banerjee illustrates how these ties work in the electric fan industry in Calcutta, where small workshops survive (barely) by producing substandard work for larger firms (e.g., watering down paint in a way that will not be apparent until after the goods are sold). As Banerjee puts it, "this relationship is dominated not so much by motives of mutual profitability but of blatant exploitation of the small by the large to an extent which makes it difficult to understand the behaviour of the small in terms of standard concepts (such as, profitability or cost minimisation)." (Banerjee, 1988, p. 184.) She describes how, since the 1960s, larger producers have "started to farm out work on several intermediate stages of production to various small units," often using the small units to lower costs, avoid labour organisations, and meet fluctuations in demand (in some cases, the small units are "buffers" that supplement the larger firm's production, and always face sudden cut-offs in demand). They are in a particularly weak position if brokers (middleman) are involved in the relationship. The small units, she points out, can only survive by *not* doing the work

properly, and by using family labor as much as possible. If the small unit "owner" hires additional workers, he "utilises women whenever possible in unskilled operations and pays them relatively low rates" (p. 195). If there is no work for these small units from any buyer, the workers must leave their tools idle and take to such occupations as buying and selling scrap, running errands, and doing other temporary services (p. 194).

61. A provocative article by P.M. Mathews (1992) expresses concern about the subordination of small-scale units in the form of women's organizations—cooperatives, organizations sponsored by caste and religious groups, and others—to both state corporations and private corporations. Taking the example of KELTRON, a public sector enterprise in Kerala, Mathews argues that the conditions of employment may be good from the employer's point of view, but not for the women and cooperatives involved.

62. Cf. Vepa (1988) for one such example.

63. See, for example, Saith (1987) regarding his analysis of small firm-oriented policies in the People's Republic of China, Japan, and elsewhere.

64. See Tung (1982), among other sources, for a discussion of this "cooperative culture" in the industrial sector in the People's Republic of China prior to and particularly after market reforms were undertaken. Tung contrasts this both with the behavior of U.S. enterprises and with the prevailing attitudes in China at the beginning of the century; she thus argues that a "cooperative culture" can be fostered, under the right conditions, and is not a "given" for a particular society at all times and under all conditions (e.g., as a product of "Confucianism").

65. Regarding the process of joining small enterprises into larger "industrial groups," and the importance of other forms of ongoing cooperative technological ties, Cai Liyi (1991, p. 229) points out, "Under market socialism where competition is likely to grow, many enterprises believe they cannot compete alone. Rather, they seek collaboration with the relevant enterprises, departments, research centers, colleges, and universities for the mutual benefit of all the parties. As a result, joint enterprises and large industrial groups are mushrooming. By relying on advanced technology and effective managerial techniques these entities can improve their labor productivity, lower unit costs of production, and, through rational use of resources, can raise social and economic benefits." He continues (on p. 229) with specific examples of the reorganization of small units into "industrial groups": "By way of illustration, owing to competition, several hundred electric fan factories merged into six giant groups, which have as their nuclei factories that produce such reputable brands as the `Chrysanthemum' and the `Great Wall.' In the city of Guangzhou, 56 industrial groups were established by amalgamating 443 small firms. An example is the electronic group in Shenzen that consists of over 150 electronic enterprises and electronic services companies. A common characteristic of these groups is that they all have a nucleus that is either a noted factory or a famous brand name or a large firm. Furthermore, all of them have included in their membership institutes of research, colleges and universities, and small and medium enterprises. This form of cooperation takes advantage of economies of large scale, a wide range of enterprises' functions, amelioration of their structure, an improved rate of exploitation of resources, an

increased return on capital investment, and better varieties of their products. At the same time, it will lead to a greater capacity for capital accumulation, market expansion and response to market fluctuations."

66. Again with respect to the Chinese example, Wu Tianzu discusses cases of technological cooperation among small and large enterprises in the PRC (e.g., a small shoe-making unit set up by twenty-eight farmers and the large Shanghai Transport and Export Company for Recreational and Sports Goods), and cooperation between small enterprises and research institutions (e.g., Zhejiang Fan Motor Factory with Shanghai Jiaotang University); Guan Ze-wen et al. discuss the Chinese government's programs to upgrade rural township enterprises technologically; and, as noted above, Cai Liyi (in the same volume) discusses joint research projects involving (1) cooperation among enterprises, and (2) cooperation between enterprises/units and research institutions. The virtues of these studies include their discussion of not only the significant achievements, but also the problems faced in carrying through successful cooperative projects, including the need to form long-term cooperative ties.

67. Other accounts give examples of "combined groups," which are set up on the local level to develop new technologies needed by the industries in the area. Potential participants include such organizations as research institutions, factories and enterprises, trading corporations, and local high schools. For an example of one such combined group, see Bagchi (1987), p. 103.

68. Regarding the relationship in earlier years between larger assembly factories in urban areas and smaller parts manufactures in rural areas (and other large-small and urban-rural linkages), see also Sigurdson (1983).

69. Cf. R. Jhabvala, "Employment in the Peoples' Sector: Practical Experiences from SEWA, India," Self Employed Women's Association, Bhadra, Ahmedabad, 1995.

70. Although this study has been concerned primarily with industrial units and enterprises, the principles extend to rural small-scale agricultural enterprises as well: the existence of a supportive network of organizations working together on a long-term basis can make the difference between agricultural enterprises (including cooperatives) doing well, or not being able to compete.

71. Besides the extensive literature concerning the idea of "flexible specialization" and networks of small firms in advanced industrial countries, cf. also Bergman et al. (1991) for specific examples of networks among small-scale enterprises—as well as involving large and small enterprises—in advanced industrial contexts.

72. Even in Taiwan, in spite of the prevalence of business networks, public enterprises and other coordinating (and cooperating) institutions, there is apparently not much evidence—at least so far—of the Italian industrial district phenomenon in which enterprises specialize in order to obtain collective efficiency: the phenomenon of "flexible specialization," as carried out by *allied small and medium-sized enterprises*, does not seem applicable to enterprises that are still in the process of technological catch-up, but rather appears to emerge under conditions of relatively "advanced" (and well-established in an industrial context) artisanal and industrial production. In this regard see, for example,

Lauridsen (1995) for an interesting interpretation of conditions facing small and medium enterprises in South Korea and Taiwan. For a more extensive discussion of specific cases of "technology blending" in the developing world, see Bhalla and James (1988) and Colombo and Oshima (1989), among other sources.

73. Peattie (1982) gives one such example, from Colombia.

Appendix

This appendix includes translations of the two questionnaires administered in Japan. In addition to these questions, response sheets were provided to the persons interviewed in order to facilitate their responses.

The *first questionnaire* was intended to discern general trends with respect to changes in the organization and behavior of selected firms as they attempted to innovate more effectively in new fields. (It was supplemented by response sheets for questions 1, 3, 5 and 6 in Section I.) The first part of this questionnaire (Section I) focused on general questions regarding new product strategy, product innovation, and organizational change. Section II then examined specific cases of new product innovation and the ways in which innovative efforts were carried out. The *second questionnaire* focused exclusively on patterns of cooperation. For this questionnaire a large number of specific cases of inter-enterprise cooperation were examined in detail; these were later reexamined through follow-up interviews with others knowledgeable about the cases. (Response sheets for Questionnaire 2 are shown on pages 207–210.)

Questionnaire # 1:
Questionnaire on Innovation and Organizational Change

One important factor in determining the rate of economic growth is investment in the development and production of totally new products and related technologies ("totally new" in the sense of creating new markets and needs, rather than being simple improvements on existing products). In this regard, I am particularly interested in the reasons that and means by which large firms make this type of development effort, and in the extent to which they can continually generate major new products and industries. I would like to evaluate whether there has been a movement within large firms toward organizational changes that allow a more steady stream of significant new product innovations, including the emergence of long-term corporate planning departments, larger R&D staffs, greater expenditure on R&D, and increasingly systematic interfirm cooperation (or interdivisional ties, in the case of highly diversified firms) as a means by which firms generate new technology and move into new fields.

Therefore, I would very much appreciate your views on the following questions. Please answer on as general or specific a level as your time permits, but I hope that you will be able to accompany your answers with as many examples and as much quantitative information (even if in rough percentages) as possible. Please note that questions 1, 3, 4 and 5 in section I are particularly important.

Again, my sincere thanks for your help in this.

I. General questions regarding the development of and entrance into new industries

A. New product strategy

1. Regarding your company's policy emphasis on finding and developing new products (again, "new" in the sense of serving new needs, rather than simply improving or differentiating existing products or extending existing markets):

    How important is this effort to your company, relative to improving its existing product lines, increasing its market share, undertaking rationalization, or other product strategies? Has there been a change in this policy over the past years—i.e., is this emphasis increasing or decreasing relative to the past?

2. By what general criteria (risk, capital requirements, potential competition in new markets, relation to existing products, etc.) does your firm select the specific type of new product investment? Do these new products tend to be closely related to your technological base? Does your company attempt to diversify its range of products and technologies *specifically* in order to be able to move easily into new industries and create new types of products? Or is your long-term strategy more to concentrate on a relatively specialized range of industries (using a relatively narrow technological product base) and introduce new products within the framework of those industries?

B. Specific product innovations

3. What are some of the most important new product areas your firm is developing? Please include "technological frontier" and "complex" or "systems"-type products, if applicable (even if still in the planning stage). [N.B.: "complex" here implies products that involve the integration of knowledge from several different fields.]

    a. How in each of these cases has your firm gained access to these new products and technologies? (Own R&D, etc.)

    b. Have these efforts resulted in the setting up of new divisions within your company, of new affiliated firms, or in other types of organizational changes?

    c. Do these products involve cooperation with other firms in order to develop these new products or technologies? If so, what is the relation of these firms to your own company (independent producers, customers, or affiliated firms)?

    d. In the case of cooperation with other producers (independent or affiliated), are they from industries that are the same as or different from your own?

4. Regarding cooperation with other companies for the development and production of joint products or relatively large-scale projects:

    a. Does your company usually cooperate with the same companies over time, or with different companies at different times? Do these cases of cooperation generally follow along lines of group affiliation, and is there a trend in this regard? (Please give examples and data, if possible.) Who generally initiates these efforts in the group case?

    b. Do these cases of cooperation generally result in the formation of *kogaisha*, new divisions within one of the companies involved, or other types of joint organization? Do you maintain long-term joint R&D staffs with any other companies (if so, how many, with approximately how many people involved)?

    c. What are the main benefits of interfirm cooperation? (Access to technology, insuring markets, etc.—please give examples, and indicate relative importance of each, if possible.)

    d. What are the main disadvantages of interfirm cooperation? Please give examples, and note any changes over time, if possible.

C. Organizational changes

5. How does your firm insure to itself a steady stream of new products?

    a. Do you have a long-term planning or market development staff to guide the company's long-term production or diversification efforts, and if so, is it growing in number of personnel and importance? (Please give approximate figures, if possible.)

    b. Is there a trend in your company toward increased expenditures on R&D for major new product innovations, and a larger, more diversified R&D staff in order to continually produce new products? Please give information on (approximate) average yearly R&D expenditure as a percentage of total sales, and on the number of R&D personnel, indicating the trend, if possible.

    c. To what extent does this "new product" R&D involve basic research, and to what extent is it applied? (Please estimate the relative percentages and indicate the trend over time.)

    d. Does your firm work with university scientists or engineers, or with independent researchers (individuals or institutions) in order to develop products or technology? Is there a trend in this regard?

6. How does your company generally learn about new potential fields? (Own planning staff, R&D staff, customers, university affiliates, industry meetings, consultants [individuals, affiliated research institutes, other research institutes], trading companies, etc.—please give examples, and indicate the relative importance of each source, if possible). Does your company actively seek information on potential new products unrelated to your present product lines?

II. *Specific questions regarding the case of [office automation]*[*]

1. Why did your company choose to enter the field of office automation? How does your entrance into this field fit into your long-term market development or diversification plan? Do these products compete with, act as complements to, or have no connection to your main product lines? What advantages and disadvantages did your company see itself as having in this effort, and to what extent were you confident of being able to find a market for these products?

2. By what means has your company gained access to this new technology (own R&D, joint R&D, purchases of innovations, etc.—please give quantitative information, if possible). Has this effort involved setting up new divisions within your company, or establishing new subsidiaries (*kogaisha*)?

3. Does your company cooperate, or plan to cooperate, with other firms in the production and development of office automation equipment? If so, why did you decide to make this cooperative effort (technological reasons, risk sharing, capital requirements, customer request, etc.)? How important is the other firms' role, why were those particular firms chosen, have you worked with them in the past, and will you continue to work with them in the future on this and other projects? Are they customers, producers in the same industry, or producers in different industries? (Please indicate in each case.) To what extent is your interindustry cooperation interdivisional, rather than interfirm?

4. What type of R&D is necessary for the development of office automation equipment? To what extent is basic research involved, and to what extent applied? (Please give relative percentages.) Approximately what percentage of total R&D is "interindustry" R&D (combining knowledge from different fields), and under what organizational framework (e.g., interdivisional or interfirm joint R&D labs) is this carried out? (Please give examples and quantitative data, if possible.)

5. How did you learn about this field? Who proposed and who decided on the entry into this field (market planning staff, R&D staff, etc.)? Do you plan further diversification into other fields as a outgrowth of this effort?

---

[*] Other cases discussed in similar way.

Questionnaire # 2:
Questionnaire on Joint R&D

I. This part of my research is concerned with the possibility of the systematic development of new products and technology, especially via interfirm (or interdivisional) cooperation in the sense of joint research and development (R&D). This issue is especially interesting in the case of Japan, where it played a historically significant role in the emergence of many industries and continues to play an important role in product development. Therefore, I would very much appreciate your views on the following questions. The questionnaire begins with an attempt to understand the sources of technology in the computers and telecommunications field, then examines specific cases of joint research and development.

Again, thank you for your help in this.

A. I would appreciate your comments on the following cases of joint R&D, and any additional examples you might be able to cite. Please note on the attached sheets:

1. The reason(s) for cooperation: what advantages does interfirm cooperation have over R&D done entirely within the firm (i.e., why was it not all done within one company)? Does this involve combining *different* technologies, or achieving economies of scale by combining *similar* technologies (joining of capital, sharing of risk)?
2. Did this involve some basic research, or was it strictly applied research (development of new products based on existing know-how)?
3. Why were these particular companies chosen?
4. How was this project initiated?
5. How was this project first conceived?
6. How was it carried out?
7. What was the outcome of this cooperation?
8. What difficulties were experienced in this type of joint R&D?
9. Was government support necessary, and if so, what type?

B. Please note, to the best of your knowledge, how the main bodies of technological knowledge in the following subfields of computers and telecommunications (and related fields) were obtained. If more than one method was used, please give examples of each type and note at what stage each type was important. (E.g., please mark (A) if obtained when first attempted to enter field, or (B) if obtained later on when further developments were occurring in the field.) Please use the attached sheets for responses.

II. In addition to information on the above questions, I would appreciate any written material that could be made available to me on the following topics. I am interested in material covering the entire postwar period, but especially in the Showa 40s and 50s (1965–present). Please note that the starred (*) topics are particularly important.

*1. Diversification (development of new product fields) as reflected in new divisions, new subsidiaries (*kogaisha*), affiliated companies (*kanren gaisha*), joint ventures, etc.

*2. R&D expenditures (and personnel figures, if available): postwar trends (especially Showa 40s, 50s)
   a. overall
   b. basic vs. applied
   c. "special projects" vs. "ordinary R&D"
   d. central (or general) research institutes vs. other research institutes, broken down by field

*3. Cooperation with university scientists and engineers: postwar trends (number affiliated with firms, overall value of contracts, etc.)

4. Government, NTT or other support in the field of computers and telecommunications: postwar trend (type of support)

5. Ratio of external (imported or purchased) to own technology, by decade

6. Annual reports for the postwar period (every 5–10 years, and by year for the Showa 40s and 50s, if available)

7. List of major innovations in the postwar period.

Thank you again for your time and cooperation.

Short Description of Case of Cooperation

A1. Reasons for cooperation:
    a. Advantages over development entirely within the firm
       Access to new technology ___
       Capital, risk sharing ___
       Shortening of development time ___
       Too far from main field to undertake alone ___
       Too large a project to undertake alone ___
       Other (please explain) ___
    b. Different technologies, or economies of scale?

  2. Type of research involved:
     Basic research only ___
     Both basic and applied ___
     Applied research only ___

  3. Reasons why these companies chosen
     Their technology ___
     Their sales network ___
     Group connections ___
     Other (please explain) ___

  4. How was this project initiated?
     Own company ___
     Cooperating company ___
     Government agency ___
     Group research or planning organization ___
     Other (please explain) ___

  5. How was this project first conceived?
     Customer request ___
     General development in field ___
     Specific scientific breakthroughs ___
     Other (please explain) ___

  6. How was it carried out?
     New division established ___
     New company established ___
     No change in organization ___
     Other (please explain) ___

  7. What was the outcome of this cooperation?
     Continuing as a joint effort ___
     Continuing within the company (which?) ___
     Discontinued ___
     Other (please explain) ___

  8. What difficulties were experienced in this joint R&D?

  9. Was government, NTT, or other support necessary, and if so, what type?

B. Please note, to the best of your knowledge, how the main bodies of technological knowledge in the following subfields of computers and telecommunications (and related fields) were obtained. If more than one method was used, please give examples of each type and note at what stage each type was important. (E.g., please mark (A) if obtained when first attempted to enter field, or (B) if obtained later on when further developments were occurring in the field.) Please use the space provided below, or attach a separate sheet if more convenient.

Subfield (or related field)	Purchase of technology [names of cooperating companies]	Development within own firm [new division, subsidiary?]	Joint R&D [names of cooperating organizations]
Computers			
Early relay, tube, para-metron			
Transistor			
Current, all sizes			
Terminal and peripheral equipment			
Pattern recognition system			
Software development			
Others			
Electronic Devices			
Vacuum tubes			
Transistor			
IC			

Subfield (or related field)	Purchase of technology [names of cooperating companies]	Development within own firm [new division, subsidiary?]	Joint R&D [names of cooperating organizations]
LSI			
VLSI			
Electronic tubes, lasers, etc.			
Others			
Communications Equipment			
Switching (crossbar, electronic, etc.)			
Transmission (analog, digital)			
Microwave			
Data communication			
Facsimile			
Optical communication			
Terminals			
Satellite communication			
Others			
Office Automation			
Copiers			

Subfield (or related field)	Purchase of technology [names of cooperating companies]	Development within own firm [new division, subsidiary?]	Joint R&D [names of cooperating organizations]
Word processors			
Micrographic systems			
OCRs			
Office computers			
Voice control typewriter			
Others			
Home Information Systems			
Medical Equipment			
Transportation Systems (high speed trains, monorails, etc.)			

References

Adedeji, Adebayo. 1981. "General Background to Indigenization: The Economic Dependence of Africa," in Adebayo Adedeji, ed., *Indigenization of African Economies*. London: Hutchinson University Library for Africa.

Alter, Catherine and Jerald Hage. 1993. *Organizations Working Together*. Newbury Park, CA: Sage Publications.

Amjad, Rashid. 1974. *Industrial Concentration and Economic Power in Pakistan*. Lahore: South Asian Institute.

_____ . 1982. *Private Industrial Investment in Pakistan, 1960-1970*. Cambridge: Cambridge University Press.

Amsden, Alice H. 1989. *Asia's Next Giant: South Korea and Late Industrialization*. New York: Oxford University Press.

_____ . 1991. "The Diffusion of Development: The Late-Industrializing Model and Greater East Asia." *American Economic Review*, Vol. 81, No. 2, May 1991.

Amsden, Alice H. and Takashi Hikino. 1993. "Borrowing Technology or Innovating: An Exploration of Two Paths to Industrial Development," in Ross Thomson, ed., *Learning and Technological Change*. New York: St. Martin's Press.

Anchordoguy, Marie. 1988. "Mastering the Market: Japanese Government Targeting of the Computer Industry." *International Organization*, Vol. 42, No. 3, Summer 1988.

Averitt, Robert T. 1968. *The Dual Economy: The Dynamics of American Industry Structure*. New York: W.W. Norton.

Baark, Erik and Jon Sigurdson. 1981. *India-China Comparative Research: Technology and Science for Development*. London: Curzon Press, Ltd.

Bagchi, A. K. 1987. *Public Intervention and Industrial Restructuring in China, India and Republic of Korea*. New Delhi: ILO/Asian Employment Programme (ARTEP).

_____ , ed. 1995. *New Technology and the Workers' Response: Microelectronics, Labour and Society*. New Delhi: Sage Publications.

Banerjee, Nirmala. 1988. "Small and Large Units: Symbiosis or Matsyanyaya?", in K.B. Suri, ed., *Small Scale Enterprise in Industrial Development: The Indian Experience*. New Delhi: Sage Publications.

_____ . 1990. "Making a Living in Calcutta: Employment in the Informal Sector," in Jean Racine, ed., *Calcutta 1981: The City, Its Crisis and the Debate on Urban Planning and Development*. New Delhi: Concept Publishing Company.

Bergman, E.M., G. Maier and F. Todtling, eds. 1991. *Regions Reconsidered: Economic Networks, Innovation, and Local Development in Industrialized Countries*. London: Mansell Publishing Ltd.

Bhagavan, M.R. 1990. *The Technological Transformation of the Third World*. London: Zed Books.

Bhalla, A.S., ed. 1991. *Small and Medium Enterprises: Technology Policies and Options*. London: Intermediate Technology Publications.

Bhalla, A.S. and D. James, eds. 1988. *New Technologies and Development— Experiences in 'Technology Blending.'* Boulder, CO: Lynne Rienner Publishers.

Bloom, M. 1992. *Technological Change in the Korean Electronics Industry*. Paris: OECD Development Centre.

Bozeman, Barry, Michael Crow and Albert Link, eds. 1984. *Strategic Management of Industrial R&D*. Lexington, MA: Lexington Books.

Broadbridge, Seymour. 1966. *Industrial Dualism in Japan: A Problem of Economic Growth and Structural Change*. London: Frank Cass.

Buckley, Peter J., ed. 1994. *Cooperative Forms of Transnational Corporation Activity*. (The United Nations Library on Transnational Corporations: Volume 13.) London and New York: Routledge.

Cai Liyi. 1991. "Cooperation Between Research and Educational Institutions and Small Enterprises in China," in A.S. Bhalla, ed., *Small and Medium Enterprises: Technology Policies and Options*. London: Intermediate Technology Publications.

China Credit Information Service, Ltd. 1983. *Business Groups in Taiwan 1983/84*. Taipei: CCIS. (Published yearly.)

Chou, T.-C. 1988. "The Evolution of Market Structure in Taiwan." *Revista Internationale di Scienze Economiche e Commerciali*, Vol. XXXV, No. 2.

Chukwujekwu, Sam. 1991. "Development of Design and Manufacturing Capabilities in a Small Nigerian Company," in A.S. Bhalla, ed., *Small and Medium Enterprises: Technology Policies and Options*. London: Intermediate Technology Publications.

Clark, Kim B., Robert H. Hayes, and Christopher Lorenz, eds. 1985. *The Uneasy Alliance*. Boston: Harvard Business School Press.

Clark, Kim B., Robert H. Hayes, and Steven C. Wheelwright. 1988. *Dynamic Manufacturing: Creating the Learning Organization*. New York: The Free Press.

Colombo, U. and K. Oshima. 1989. *Technology Blending—An Appropriate Response to Development*. London: Cassel-Tycooly.

Cooper, Charles, ed. 1973. *Science, Technology and Development: The Political Economy of Technical Advance in Underdeveloped Countries*. London: Frank Cass.

Cordero, Salvador. 1977. "Concentracion industrial y poder economico en Mexico." *Cuadernos del CES*, 18, Centro de Estudios Sociologicos, El Colegio de Mexico.

Cordero, Salvador and Rafael Santin. 1977. "Los Grupos Industriales: Una Nueva Organizacion Economica en Mexico." *Cuadernos del CES*, 23, Centro de Estudios Sociologicos, El Colegio de Mexico.

Coulson, Andrew. 1982. *Tanzania: A Political Economy*. Oxford: Clarendon Press.

Cowhey, Peter F. and Jonathan D. Aronson. 1993. *Managing the World Economy: The Consequences of Corporate Alliances*. New York: Council on Foreign Relations.

Cusumano, Michael A. 1985. *The Japanese Automobile Industry*. Cambridge, MA: Harvard University Press.

Dahlman, Carl J. and Fernando Valadares Fonseca. 1987. "From Technological Dependence to Technological Development: The Case of Usiminas Steelplant in Brazil," in Jorge M. Katz, ed., *Technology Generation in Latin American Manufacturing Industries*. London: Macmillian.

Dawson, Jonathan. 1988. "Small-Scale Industrial Development in Ghana: A Case Study of Kumasi." London: Overseas Development Administration, ESCOR.

Dimancescu, Dan and James Botkin. 1986. *The New Alliance: America's R&D Consortia*. Cambridge, MA: Ballinger Publishing Co.

Doane, Donna L. 1993. "The Significance of Timing and the Degree of Economic Backwardness in Theories of Late Development." *Social Concept* Summer Conference, Burlington, VT, August 1993.

Dodwell Marketing Consultants. 1980. *Industrial Groupings in Japan*. Tokyo: Dodwell Marketing Consultants. (1980 and other years.)

Dore, Ronald. 1971. *The Late Development Effect*. Brighton, England: Institute of Development Studies, University of Sussex.

_____ . 1983. *A Case Study of Technology Forecasting in Japan: The Next Generation Business Technologies Development Programme*. London: The Technical Change Center, October 1983.

Eads, George and Richard Nelson. 1986. "Japanese High Technology Policy: What Lessons for the United States?", in Hugh Patrick, ed., *Japan's High Technology Industries*. Seattle: University of Washington Press.

Ehrlich, Eva. 1984. *Japan: A Case of Catching-Up*. Akademiai Kiado, Budapest (translated by Gyorgy Hajdy).

Evans, Peter B. 1992. "Indian Informatics in the 1980s: The Changing Character of State Involvement." *World Development*, Vol. 20, No.1.

Evenson, Robert E. and Gustav Ranis. 1990. *Science and Technology: Lessons for Development Policy*. Boulder, CO: Westview Press.

Farber, D. and P. Baran. 1977. "The Convergence of Computing and Telecommunications Systems." *Science*, Vol. 195, No. 4283, March 18, 1977.

Ferguson, Charles. 1990. "Computers and the Coming of the U.S. Keiretsu." *Harvard Business Review*, July-August 1990.

Francks, Penelope. 1992. *Japanese Economic Development: Theory and Practice*. London: Routledge.

Fransman, Martin. 1990. *The Market and Beyond: Cooperation and Competition in Information Technology Development in the Japanese System*. Cambridge: Cambridge University Press.

Freeman, C., J. Clark and L. Soete. 1982. *Unemployment and Technical Innovation: A Study of Long Waves and Economic Development*. London: Frances Pinter.

Friedman, David. 1988. *The Misunderstood Miracle: Industrial Development and Political Change in Japan*. Ithaca, NY: Cornell University Press.

Fruin, W. Mark. 1992. *The Japanese Enterprise System: Competitive Strategies and Cooperative Structures*. Oxford: Clarendon Press.

Fusfield, Herbert I. and Carmela S. Haklisch. 1982. *Trends in Collective Industrial Research*. New York: NYU Graduate School of Business Administration, September 1982.

Futatsugi, Yusaku. 1973. "The Measurement of Interfirm Relationships." *Japanese Economic Studies*, Vol. II, No. 1, Fall 1973.

_____. 1976. *Gendai Nihon no Kigyo Shudan*. Tokyo: Toyo Keizai.

_____. 1986. *Japanese Enterprise Groups*. Kobe: The School of Business Administration, Kobe University.

Gereffi, Gary. 1993 [1990]. "Big Business and the State: Latin America and East Asia Compared," in Mitchell A. Seligson and John T. Passe-Smith, eds., *Development and Underdevelopment: The Political Economy of Inequality*. Boulder, CO: Lynne Rienner Publishers. (Also in G. Gereffi, *Manufacturing Miracles: Paths to Industrialization in Latin America and East Asia*. Princeton: Princeton University Press.)

Gerlach, Michael L. 1992a. *Alliance Capitalism: The Social Organization of Japanese Business*. Berkeley: University of California Press.

_____. 1992b. "Economic Organization and Innovation in Japan." Revised manuscript, Russell Sage Foundation, May 1992.

Gerschenkron, Alexander. 1962. *Economic Backwardness in Historical Perspective*. Cambridge, MA: Harvard University Press.

Ghosh, Arun, K.K. Subrahmanian, Mridul Eapen, and Haseeb A. Drabu, eds. 1992. *Indian Industrialization: Structure and Policy Issues*. Delhi: Oxford University Press.

Ghosh, Arabinda. 1973. "Industrial Concentration by the Managing Agency System in India, 1948-1968." *Economic and Political Weekly*, June 9, 1973.

_____. 1974a. "Japanese Zaibatsu and Indian Industrial Houses: An International Comparison." *The American Journal of Economics and Sociology*, July 1974.

_____. 1974b. "Role of Large Industrial Houses in Indian Industries." *The Indian Economic Journal*, April-June 1974.

Goontilake, Susuntha. 1984. *Aborted Discovery: Science and Creativity in the Third World*. London: Zed Books.

Goto, Akira. 1982. "Business Groups in a Market Economy." *European Economic Review*, Vol. XIX, No. 1.

Goto, Akira and Ryuhei Wakasugi. 1988. "Technology Policy," in Ryutaro Komiya, Masahiro Okuno, and Kotaro Suzumura, eds., *Industrial Policy of Japan*. New York: Academic Press.

Goyal, S.K. et al. 1984. *Studies in National Development: Small-Scale Sector and Big Business*. New Delhi: Corporate Studies Group, IIPA.

Granovetter, Mark S. 1973. "The Strength of Weak Ties." *American Journal of Sociology*, 78.

Gregory, Gene. 1982. "The Japanese Propensity for Innovation: Electronics." Institute of Comparative Culture, Business Series. Bulletin No. 86. Tokyo: Sophia University.

_____. 1985. *Japanese Electronics Technology: Enterprise and Innovation*. Tokyo: The Japan Times, Ltd.

Gresser, Julian. 1980. *High Technology and Japanese Industrial Policy: A Strategy for U.S. Policymakers*. U.S. Subcommittee on Trade. Washington, D.C.: U.S. Government Printing Office.

Guan Ze-wen, Ge Zi-quan, Cai Qi-Xiang, Huang Ju-xun, Wei Jian-fei, Chen Zu-huang, Le Xin-shui, and Liang Zuo-jie. 1991. "Technological Transformation of Small and Medium Enterprises in China," in A.S. Bhalla, ed., *Small and Medium Enterprises: Technology Policies and Options*. London: Intermediate Technology Publications.

Gupta, Devendra B. and Bishwanath Goldar. 1995. "Subcontracting in Indian Industry: A Study of Small-Large Industry Linkages." Delhi: Institute of Economic Growth.

Hadley, Eleanor. 1970. *Antitrust in Japan*. Princeton, NJ: Princeton University Press.

Hamilton, Gary G. 1991. "The Organizational Foundations of Western and Chinese Commerce: A Historical and Comparative Analysis," in Gary Hamilton, ed., *Business Networks and Economic Development in East and Southeast Asia*. Hong Kong: Centre of Asian Studies, University of Hong Kong.

Hamilton, Gary G., William Zeile, and Kim Wan-Jin. 1989. "The Network Structures of East Asian Economies," in Steward Clegg and Gordon Redding, eds., *Capitalism in Contrasting Cultures*. Berlin: deGruyter.

Hattori, T. 1984. "The Relationship between Zaibatsu and Family Structure: The Korean Case," in A. Okochi and S. Yasuoka, eds., *Family Business in the Era of Industrial Growth: Its Ownership and Management*. Tokyo: University of Tokyo Press.

Henderson, Jeffrey. 1989. *The Globalisation of High Technology Production: Society, Space and Semiconductors in the Restructuring of the Modern World*. London: Routledge.

_____. 1994. "Electronics Industries and the Developing World: Uneven Contributions and Uncertain Prospects," in Leslie Sklair, ed., *Capitalism and Development*. London: Routledge.

Hewlett, Sylvia Ann and Richard S. Weinert, eds. 1982. *Brazil and Mexico: Patterns in Late Development*. Philadelphia: Institute for the Study of Human Issues.

Hikino, Takashi and Alice H. Amsden. 1991. "Staying Behind, Stumbling Back, Sneaking Up, Soaring Ahead: Late Industrialization in Historical Perspective." Conference Paper, New York University, April 23-24, 1991.

HI-OVIS Visual Information System Development Association. (Undated.) "Optical Visual Information System Hi-OVIS." Tokyo: Visual Information System Development Association (VISDA)-MITI Judicial Foundation.

Ho, Samuel P.S. 1978. *Economic Development of Taiwan 1860-1970*. New Haven: Yale University Press.

Hou Chi-Ming and San Gee. 1993. "National Systems Supporting Technical Advance in Industry: The Case of Taiwan," in Richard R. Nelson, ed., *National Innovation Systems: A Comparative Analysis*. New York: Oxford University Press.

Imai, Ken-ichi. 1980. "Japan's Industrial Organization and its Vertical Structure." Hitotsubashi University, August 1980.

_____ . 1987. "Network Industrial Organization in Japan." Hitotsubashi University, June 1987.

_____ . 1990. "Japan's Business Groups and Keiretsu in Relation to the Structural Impediments Initiative." Hitotsubashi University, March 1990.

Imai, Ken-ichi and Hiroyuki Itami. 1984. "Interpenetration of Organization and Market: Japan's Firm and Market in Comparison with the U.S." *International Journal of Industrial Organization*, Vol. II, No. 4.

Imai, Ken-ichi and Ryutaro Komiya. 1994. "Characteristics of the Japanese Firm," in Kenichi Imai and Ryutaro Komiya, eds., *Business Enterprise in Japan: Views of Leading Japanese Economists*. Cambridge, MA: MIT Press.

Imai, Ken-ichi, Ikujiro Nonaka, and Hirotaka Takeuchi. 1985. "Managing the New Product Development Process: How Japanese Companies Learn and Unlearn," in Kim B. Clark, Robert H. Hayes, and Christopher Lorenze, eds., *The Uneasy Alliance: Managing the Productivity-Technology Dilemma*. Boston, MA: Harvard Business School.

Institute of Economic Growth (S.N. Mishra, Bishwanath Goldar et al.). 1995. *India's Industrial Policy*. Delhi: IEG, January 1995.

Ito, Shoji. 1966. "A Note on the 'Business Combine' in India." *The Developing Economies*, Vol. IV, No. 3, September 1966.

_____ . 1975. "Studies in Indian Zaibatsu: Roles of Inter-Corporate Investment." *Journal of Intercultural Studies* (Osaka), No. 2.

_____ . 1978. "On the Basic Nature of the Investment Company in India." *The Developing Economies*, Vol. XVI, No. 3, September 1978.

_____ . 1984. "Ownership and Management of Indian Zaibatsu," in Akio Okochi and Shigeaki Yasuoka, eds., *Family Business in the Era of Industrial Growth: Its Ownership and Management*. Tokyo: University of Tokyo Press.

_____ , ed. 1983. *Hatten-tojokoku no Zaibatsu*. Tokyo: Institute of Developing Economies.

Japan Company Handbook (Kaisha Shikiho). Tokyo: Oriental Economist (Toyo Keizai). (Published semiannually.)

Japan Economic Institute. 1981. "Government-Funded Industrial R&D in Japan." Report No. 42, November 6, 1981. Washington, D.C.: JEI.

Jhabvala, Renana. 1995a. "Employment in the People's Sector." Self Employed Women's Association, Bhadra, Ahmedabad.

_____ . 1995b. "Textiles in the People's Sector: Impact of Global Trading Practices on Women in the Unorganized Textile Sector in India." Self Employed Women's Association, Bhadra, Ahmedabad.

Johnson, Chalmers. 1986. "MITI, MPT, and the Telecom Wars: How Japan Makes Policy for High Technology." Colloquium paper: Center for Japanese Studies, UC Berkeley, September 10, 1986.

Joseph, K.J. 1992. "The Growth Performance of the Electronics Industry in India and South Korea: A Comparative Analysis," in Arun Ghosh, K.K. Subrahmanian, Mridul Eapen, and Haseeb A. Drabu, eds., *Indian Industrialization: Structure and Policy Issues*. Delhi: Oxford University Press.

_____. 1995. "Output Growth, Technology Behavior and Employment: Indian Electronics Industry Under Liberalization," in A.K. Bagchi, ed., *New Technology and the Workers' Response: Microelectronics, Labour and Society*. New Delhi: Sage Publications.

Kagaku Gijutsu Hakusho (White Paper on Science and Technology). Tokyo: Foreign Press Center. (Published yearly.)

Kagaku Gijutsu Yoran (Indicators of Science and Technology). Tokyo: Okurasho Insatsukyoku. (Published yearly.)

Kao, Cheng-shu. 1991. "'Personal Trust' in the Large Businesses in Taiwan: A Traditional Foundation for Contemporary Economic Activities," in Gary Hamilton, *Business Networks and Economic Development in East and Southeast Asia*. Hong Kong: Centre of Asian Studies, University of Hong Kong.

Kato, Hiroshi and Kazuo Noda, eds. 1980a. *Nippon Denki (Series: Nihon no Kigyo)*. Tokyo: Soyosha.

_____. 1980b. *Toshiba (Series: Nihon no Kigyo)*. Tokyo: Soyosha.

Keizai Chosa Kyokai. 1971-1990. *Keiretsu no Kenkyu: Kigyo Teikei. (Kigyo Teikei no Bunseki; Kigyo Teikei no Doko.)* Tokyo: Keizai Chosa Kyokai.

_____. 1960-1974. *Nenpo Keiretsu no Kenkyu*. Tokyo: Keizai Chosa Kyokai.

Kilby, Peter. 1988. "Breaking the Entrepreneurial Bottleneck in Late-Developing Countries: Is There a Useful Role for Government?" *Journal of Development Planning*, 18.

Kim, Eun Mee. 1991. "The Industrial Organization and Growth of the Korean Chaebol: Integrating Development and Organizational Theories," in Gary Hamilton, ed., *Business Networks and Economic Development in East and Southeast Asia*. Hong Kong: Centre of Asian Studies, University of Hong Kong.

Kim, Linsu. 1993. "National System of Industrial Innovation: Dynamics of Capacity Building in Korea," in Richard R. Nelson, ed., *National Innovation Systems: A Comparative Analysis*. New York: Oxford University Press.

Kiyonari, Tadao and Hideichiro Nakamura. 1977. "Establishment of the Big Business System." *Japan Economic Studies*, Fall 1977.

Kobayashi, Koji. 1978. "The Japanese Computer Industry: Its Roots and Development." Third U.S.-Japan Computer Conference, San Francisco, CA, October 1978. Tokyo: NEC.

Kobayashi, Yoshiro. 1977-78. "Kigyo Shudan no Bunseki." *Keizai Hyoron*, XXVI, XXVII, August 1977 to June 1978.

Kodama, Fumio. 1986. "Technological Diversification of Japanese Industry." *Science*, Vol. 233, July 18, 1986.

_____. 1991. *Analyzing Japanese High Technologies: The Techno-Paradigm Shift*. London and New York: Pinter Publishers.

Komiya, Ryutaro, Masahiro Okuno and Kotaro Suzumura, eds. 1988. *Industrial Policy of Japan*. San Diego, CA: Academic Press, Inc.

Kongstad, P. 1980. "Kenya: Industrial Growth or Industrial Development," in J.F. Rweyemamu, ed., *Industrialization and Income Distribution in Africa*. Dakar: CODESRIA Book Series.

Koppel, Bruce and Richard E. Peterson. 1975. "Industrial Entrepreneurship in India: A Reevaluation." *The Developing Economies*, Vol. XIII, No. 3, Sept. 1975.

Kosei Torihiki Iinkai Jimukyoku, ed. 1984. "Minkan Kigyo ni Okeru Kenkyu
Kaihatsu Katsudo no Jittai to Kyoso Seisakujo no Mondai" (The Realities of
Research and Development Activities in Private Firms and Problems from the
Perspective of Competitor Policy). Report dated September 28, 1984.
Krestovsky, Igor. 1966. "Role of Small-Scale Industries in Developing Countries."
Small-Scale Industries in Africa and India: An Africa Quarterly Supplement,
July-September 1966.
Kucchal, S.C. 1984. The Industrial Economy of India. Allahabad: Chaitanya
Publishing House.
Kurien, C.T. 1992. The Economy: An Interpretive Introduction. New Delhi and
Newbury Park, CA: Sage Publications.
_____. 1994. "Indian Economic Reforms in the Context of Emerging Global
Economy," in Uma Kapila, ed., Recent Developments in Indian Economy: Part III,
The Ongoing Economic Reforms. Delhi: Academic Foundation.
Lall, Sanjaya. 1982. "Technological Learning in the Third World: Some
Implications of Technological Exports," in Frances Stewart and Jeffrey James,
eds., The Economics of New Technology in Developing Countries. Boulder, CO:
Westview Press.
_____. 1984. "India's Technological Capacity: Effects of Trade, Industrial,
Science and Technology Policies," in Martin Fransman and Kenneth King,
eds., Technological Capacity in the Third World. New York: St. Martin's Press.
_____. 1987. Learning to Industrialize: The Acquisition of Technological Capability by
India. London: Macmillian.
Landes, D.S. 1969. The Unbound Prometheus: Technological Change and Industrial
Development in Western Europe from 1750 to the Present. Cambridge: Cambridge
University Press.
Lau, Lawrence J., ed. 1990. Models of Development: A Comparative Study of Economic
Growth in South Korea and Taiwan. San Francisco, CA: ICS Press.
Lauridsen, Laurids S. 1995. "New Technologies, Flexibilization and Changing
Capital-Labour Relations: The East Asian NICs, with Special Reference to
Taiwan and South Korea," in A.K. Bagchi, ed., New Technology and the Workers'
Response: Microelectronics, Labour and Society. New Delhi: Sage Publications.
Lee, Kyung Tae. 1991. "Technical and Managerial Extension Services for Korean
Small and Medium Enterprises," in A.S. Bhalla, ed., Small and Medium
Enterprises: Technology Policies and Options. London: Intermediate Technology
Publications.
Leff, Nathaniel. 1976. "Capital Markets in the Less-Developed Countries: The
Group Principle," in Ronald I. McKinnon, ed., Money and Finance in Economic
Growth and Development. New York: M. Dekker.
_____. 1978. "Industrial Organization and Entrepreneurship in Developing
Countries: The Economic Groups." Economic Development and Cultural Change,
Vol. XXVI, No. 4, July 1978.
_____. 1979a. "Entrepreneurship and Economic Development: The Problem
Revisited." Journal of Economic Literature, Vol. XVII, No.1, March 1979.
_____. 1979b. "'Monopoly Capitalism' and Public Policy in Developing
Countries." Kyklos, Vol. XXXII, No. 4.

Link, Albert N. and Laura L. Bauer. 1989. *Cooperative Research in U.S. Manufacturing*. Lexington, MA: Lexington Books.

Little, Ian M.D., Dipak Mazumdar and John M. Page, Jr. 1987. *Small Manufacturing Enterprises: A Comparative Analysis of India and Other Economies*. NY: Oxford University Press (for the World Bank).

Lockwood, William W. 1954. *The Economic Development of Japan: Growth and Structural Change, 1868-1938*. Princeton, NJ: Princeton University Press.

Magaziner, Ira C. and Thomas M. Hout. 1970. *Japanese Industrial Policy*. Berkeley, CA: Institute of International Studies, University of California.

Malerba, Franco. 1983. "Technological Change, Market Structure and Government Policy: The Evolution of the European Semiconductor Industry." Ph.D. dissertation, Department of Economics, Yale University.

Mani, Sunil. 1995. "Technology Import and Skill Development in a Microelectronics-Based Industry: The Case of India's Electronic Switching Systems," in A.K. Bagchi, ed., *New Technology and the Workers' Response: Microelectronics, Labour and Society*. New Delhi: Sage Publications.

Mansfield, Edwin. 1988. "Industrial R&D in Japan and the United States: A Comparative Study." *American Economic Review Proceedings*. 78:223-228.

Masuda, Yuji. 1977. "Emerging Core Firms in the Japanese Economy," in *Engineering Industries of Japan*, No. 14. (The Economic Research Institute, Japan Society for the Promotion of Machine Industry.)

Mathew, P.M. 1992 [1986]. "Women's Industrial Employment in India," in Berch Bergeroglu, ed., *Class, State and Development in India*. New Delhi: Sage Publications. (Originally appeared in the *Bulletin of Concerned Asian Scholars*, Vol. 18, No. 3, 1986.)

Matthews, Ron. 1986. "Technological Dynamism in India and Japan," in Erik Baark and Andrew Jamison, eds., *Technological Development in China, India, and Japan: Cross-Cultural Perspectives*. New York: St. Martin's Press.

Meemamsi, G.B. 1993. *The C-DOT Story: Quest, Inquest, Conquest*. New Delhi: Kedar Publications.

Ministry of International Trade and Industry (MITI). 1975. *Background Information: National Research and Development Programs*. Tokyo: MITI, February 1975.

———. 1981. *Japan's Industrial Policy*. Tokyo: MITI, June 1981.

Mir, Javed H. and Donna L. Doane. 1995. "Socio-Ecological Determinants of Land Degradation and Rural Poverty in Northeast Thailand." *Environmental Conservation*, Vol. 22, No. 1, Spring 1995.

Mitsui and Co., Ltd. (Undated.) "The Mitsui Story: Three Centuries of Japanese Business." Tokyo: Mitsui and Co., Ltd. (First published monthly as a supplement to *Mitsui Trade News*.)

Miyashita, Kenichi and David W. Russell. 1994. *Keiretsu: Inside the Hidden Japanese Conglomerates*. New York: McGraw-Hill.

Miyazaki, Yoshikazu.1966. *Sengo Nihon no Keizai Kiko*. Tokyo: Shinhyoronsha.

———. 1973. "The Japanese-Type Structure of Big Business." *Japanese Economic Studies*, Vol. II, No. 1, Fall 1973.

_____. 1976a. "Big Corporations and Business Groups in Postwar Japan." *The Developing Economies*, Vol. XIV, No. 4, December 1976.

_____. 1976b. *Sengo Nihon no Kigyo Shudan (1960-1970)*. Tokyo: Nihon Keizai Shimbunsha.

Morikawa, Hidemasa. 1992. *Zaibatsu*. Tokyo: University of Tokyo Press.

Mowery, David C. 1988. *International Collaborative Ventures in U.S. Manufacturing*. Cambridge, MA: Ballinger.

Mowery, David C. and Nathan Rosenberg. 1985. "The Japanese Commercial Aircraft Industry Since 1945: Government Policy, Technical Development, and Industrial Structure." An Occasional Paper of the Northeast Asia-United States Forum on International Policy, Stanford University, April 1985.

_____. 1994. "International Collaboration in R&D," in John Cantwell, ed., *Transnational Corporations and Innovatory Activities*. (The United Nations Library on Transnational Corporations: Volume 17.) London and New York: Routledge.

Mukerjee, Dilip. 1986. *Lessons from Korea's Industrial Experience*. Kuala Lumpur: Institute of Strategic and International Studies.

Muller, Jens. 1978. "Promotion of Manufactures of Rural Implements in the United Republic of Tanzania," in UNIDO, *Industrialization and Rural Development*. New York: United Nations.

_____. 1984. "Facilitating an Indigenous Social Organization of Production in Tanzania," in Martin Fransman and Kenneth King, eds., *Technological Capability in the Third World*. New York: St. Martin's Press.

Nadar, N. Thanulingom. 1985. *Small Scale Industry Interrelationship with Large Scale Industry*. Coimbatore (India): Rainbow Publishers.

Nafziger, E. Wayne. 1995. *Learning from the Japanese*. Armonk, NY: M.E. Sharpe.

Nakamura, Takafusa. 1966. "The Modern Industries and the Traditional Industries." *The Developing Economies*, Vol. IV, No. 4, December 1966.

_____. 1981. *The Postwar Japanese Economy*. Tokyo: University of Tokyo Press.

Nakatani, Iwao. 1984. "The Role of Intermarket Groups in Japan," in Masahiko Aoki, ed., *The Economic Analysis of the Japanese Firm*. Amsterdam: North Holland.

National Council of Applied Economic Research (NCAER) and Friedrich Naumann-Stiftung (FNS). 1993. "Structure and Promotion of Small-Scale Industries in India: Lessons for Future Development." New Delhi: NCAER and FNS, December 1993.

Nebashi, Masato. 1980. "Four-Year Joint Project by Five Rival Computer Manufacturers." Tokyo: VLSI Technology Research Association.

_____. 1981. "VLSI Technology Research Association." Tokyo: VLSI Technology Research Association, March 1981.

NEC. 1972. *Nippon Denki Kabushiki Kaisha 70-nenshi*. Tokyo: NEC.

_____. 1980. *Nippon Denki Saikin 10-nenshi*. Tokyo: NEC.

Nelson, Richard R. 1987. "Innovation and Economic Development: Theoretical Retrospect and Prospect," in Jorge M. Katz, ed., *Technology Generation in Latin American Manufacturing Industries*. London: Macmillian.

_____, ed. 1993. *National Innovation Systems: A Comparative Analysis*. New York: Oxford University Press.

Nihon Keizai Shimbunsha. 1980. *Fukugo Sentan Sangyo.* Tokyo: Nihon Keizai Shimbunsha.

Nikko Research Center. 1980. *Japanese Industries: New Technologies and Potential Growth Areas of the 1980s.* Tokyo: Nikko Research Center, October 1980.

Nippon Telegraph and Telephone Public Corporation. (Undated.) "Electrical Communications Laboratories." Tokyo: NTT.

Nishiguchi, Toshihiro. 1994. *Strategic Industrial Sourcing: The Japanese Advantage.* New York: Oxford University Press.

Niwa, Fujio and Hiroshi Goto. 1993. "Japanese Collaborative R&D—An Analysis of the Present Structures in Order to Determine Future Trends," in Hajimi Eto, ed., *R&D Strategies in Japan: The National, Regional and Corporate Approach.* Amsterdam: Elsevier Science Publishers.

Numazaki, Ichiro. 1991. "The Role of Personal Networks in the Making of Taiwan's *Guanxiqiye* (Related Enterprises)," in Gary Hamilton, ed., *Business Networks and Economic Development in East and Southeast Asia.* Hong Kong: Centre of Asian Studies, University of Hong Kong.

Odagiri, Hiroyuki and Akira Goto. 1993. "The Japanese System of Innovation: Past, Present, and Future," in Richard R. Nelson, ed., *National Innovation Systems: A Comparative Analysis.* New York: Oxford University Press.

OECD. 1972. *The Industrial Policy of Japan.* Paris: OECD.

_____. 1978. *Policies for the Stimulation of Industrial Innovation,* Volume II-1. Paris: OECD.

Ogura, Takekazu. 1967. *Agricultural Development in Modern Japan.* Tokyo: Fuji Publishing Company.

Ohkawa, Kazushi and Gustav Ranis with Larry Meissner, eds. 1985. *Japan and the Developing Countries: A Comparative Analysis.* New York: Basil Blackwell.

Okamoto, Yasuo. 1979. *Hitachi to Matsushita.* Tokyo: Chuo Koronsha.

Okimoto, Daniel I. 1989. *Between MITI and the Market: Japanese Industrial Policy for High Technology.* Stanford: Stanford University Press.

Okimoto, Daniel I., T. Sugano and F. Weinstein, eds. 1984. *Competitive Edge: The Semiconductor Industry in the U.S. and Japan.* Stanford: Stanford University Press.

Okochi, Akio and Shigeaki Yasuoka. 1984. *Family Business in the Era of Industrial Growth: Its Ownership and Management.* Tokyo: University of Tokyo Press.

Okumura, Hiroshi. 1983. *Shin Nihon no Roku Dai-Kigyo Shudan.* Tokyo: Daiyamondosha.

_____. 1991. "Intercorporate Relations in Japan," in Gary Hamilton, ed., *Business Networks and Economic Development in East and Southeast Asia.* Hong Kong: Centre of Asian Studies, University of Hong Kong.

Orru, Marco. 1991. "Practical and Theoretical Aspects of Japanese Business Networks," in Gary Hamilton, ed., *Business Networks and Economic Development in East and Southeast Asia.* Hong Kong: Centre of Asian Studies, University of Hong Kong.

Ozawa, Terutomo. 1980. "Government Control Over Technology Acquisition and Firms' Entry into New Sectors: The Experience of Japan's Synthetic-fibre Industry." *Cambridge Journal of Economics,* Vol. IV, No. 2, June 1980.

Pacific Basin Reports. 1972. *1972 Handbook of Japanese Financial/Industrial Combines*. San Francisco: Pacific Basin Reports.

Parthasarathi, A. 1979. "India's Efforts to Build on Autonomous Capacity in Science and Technology for Development." *Development Dialogue*, pp. 46-49.

Patrick, Hugh. 1986. "Japanese High Technology Industrial Policy in Comparative Context," in Hugh Patrick, ed., *Japan's High Technology Industries: Lessons and Limitations of Industrial Policy*. Seattle: University of Washington Press.

Patrick, Hugh and Thomas P. Rohlen. 1987. "Small-Scale Family Enterprises," in Kozo Yamamura and Yasukichi Yasuba, eds., *The Political Economy of Japan, Volume I: The Domestic Transformation*. Stanford, CA: Stanford University Press.

Peattie, Lisa R. 1982. "What is to be Done with the 'Informal Sector'? A Case Study of Shoe Manufacturers in Columbia," in Helen I. Safa, ed., *Towards a Political Economy of Urbanization in Third World Countries*. Delhi: Oxford University Press.

Peck, Merton J. 1983. "Governmental Coordination of R&D in the Japanese Electronic Industry." Department of Economics, Yale University, March 1983.

Peck, Merton J. and Akira Goto. 1981. "Technology and American Growth: The Case of Japan." *Research Policy*, Vol. X, No. 3.

Peck, Merton J. and Shuji Tamura. 1976. "Technology," in Hugh Patrick and Henry Rosovsky, eds., *Asia's New Giant*. Washington, D.C.: Brookings Institution.

Pillai, P. Mohanan and J. Srinivasan. 1992. "The Age and Productivity of Machine Tools in India," in Arun Ghosh, K.K. Subrahmanian, Mridul Eapen, and Haseeb A. Drabu, eds., *Indian Industrialization: Structure and Policy Issues*. Delhi: Oxford University Press.

Piramal, Gita and Margaret Herdeck. 1986. *India's Industrialists* (Volume I). Washington, D.C.: Three Continents Press.

Porter, M.E. 1990. *The Competitive Advantage of Nations*. New York: The Free Press.

Pugel, Thomas, Yui Kimura, and Robert G. Hawkings. 1984. "Semiconductors and Computers: Emerging International Competitive Battlegrounds," in R. W. Moxon, T.W. Roehl, and J.F. Truitt, eds., *International Business Strategies in the Asia-Pacific Region*, Volume 2. Greenwich, CT: JAI Press.

Radtke, Schrade F. and Adolph L. Ponikvar. 1984. *Cooperative Research and Development*. New York: American Management Associations.

Rahman, Abdur. 1983. *Intellectual Colonisation: Science and Technology in West-East Relations*. Delhi: Vikas Publishing House.

_____ . 1984. *Science and Technology In India*. New Delhi: National Institute of Science, Technology and Development Studies.

_____ , ed. 1990. *Science and Technology in India, Pakistan, Bangladesh and Sri Lanka*. Essex, UK: Longman.

Rao, C.N.R. 1990. "Science and Technology Planning: Issues and Priorities." *Indian Journal of Social Science*, Vol. 3, No. 3, July-September 1990.

Redding, Gordon and Simon Tam. 1985. "Networks and Molecular Organizations: An Exploratory View of Chinese Firms in Hong Kong," in

Proceedings of the Academy of International Business, South-East Asia Regional Meeting, Hong Kong, July 1985.

Rice, Richard. 1982. "Origins of Private Research and Development in Japan: The Hitachi Case." Department of History, University of Tennessee/Chattanooga.

Roberts, John G. 1973 [1989]. *Mitsui: Three Centuries of Japanese Business.* New York: Weatherhill.

Roehl, Thomas. 1987. "Stormy Open Marriages Are Better: Evidence from U.S., Japanese and French Cooperative Ventures in Commercial Aircraft." *Columbia Journal of World Business,* Summer 1987.

_____. 1988. "Japanese Industrial Groupings: A Strategic Response to Rapid Industrial Growth." University of Washington, Seattle, WA, March 1988.

Rokuhara, Akira, ed. 1985. *Kenkyu Kaihatsu to Dokusen Kinshi Seisaku* (R&D and Anti-Monopoly Policy). Tokyo: Gyosei.

Rotwein, Eugene. 1976. "Economic Concentration and Monopoly in Japan—A Second View." *Journal of Asian Studies,* Vol. 36, No. 1, November 1976.

Roy, Tirthankar. 1994. "Foreign Trade and the Artisans in Colonial India: A Study of Leather." *The Indian Economic and Social History Review,* Vol. 31, No. 4.

Saith, Ashwani. 1987. "Contrasting Experiences in Rural Industrialization: Are the East Asian Successes Transferable?", in Rizwanul Islam, ed., *Rural Industrialisation and Employment in Asia.* New Delhi: ILO/ARTEP (Asian Employment Programme).

Sakakibara, Kiyonori. 1983. "From Imitation to Innovation: The Very Large Scale Integrated (VLSI) Semiconductor Project in Japan." Sloan Working Paper, MIT, October 1983.

Sako, Mari. 1992. *Prices, Quality and Trust: Inter-firm Relations in Britain and Japan.* Cambridge: Cambridge University Press.

Samuels, Richard J. 1987. "Research Collaboration in Japan." WP 87-02, Massachusetts Institute of Technology-Japan Science and Technology Program, Cambridge, MA.

Sandberg, Lars G. 1982. "Ignorance, Poverty and Economic Backwardness in the Early Stages of European Industrialization: Variations on Alexander Gerschenkron's Grand Theme." *Journal of European Economic History,* Vol. 11, No. 3, Winter 1982.

Sato, Ryuzo. 1986. "Japan's Challenge to Technological Competition and Its Limitations," in Thomas A. Pugel and Robert G. Hawkins, eds., *Fragile Interdependence: Economic Issues in U.S.-Japanese Trade and Investment.* Lexington: Lexington Books.

Saxonhouse, Gary. 1979. "Industrial Restructuring in Japan." *Journal of Japanese Studies,* Vol. V, No. 5, Summer 1979.

_____. 1981. "Japanese High Technology, Government Policy, and Evolving Comparative Advantage in Goods and Services." Department of Economics, University of Michigan.

Scherer, Frederic M. 1984. *Innovation and Growth: Schumpeterian Perspectives.* Cambridge MA: MIT Press.

_____. 1992. "Schumpeter and Plausible Capitalism." *Journal of Economic Literature,* Vol. XXX, No. 3, September 1992.

Scherer, Frederic M. and David Ross. 1990. *Industrial Market Structure and Economic Performance*. Third Edition. Boston: Houghton-Mifflin.

Semiconductor Industry Association. 1983. *The Effect of Government Targeting on World Semiconductor Competition: A Case Study of Japanese Industrial Strategy and Its Costs for America*. Cupertino, CA: SIA.

Shibagaki, Kazuo. 1966. "The Early History of the Zaibatsu." *The Developing Economies*, Vol. IV, No. 4, December 1966.

_____. 1973. "The Logic of Japanese Imperialism." *Annals of the Institute of Social Science* (University of Tokyo), No. 14.

_____. 1984. "Zaibatsu: Their Development, Strategy and Prospect." Berlin: Verlag Ute Schiller, Occasional Papers No. 48.

Siddharthan, N.S. 1981. *Conglomerates and Multinationals in India: A Study of Investment and Profit*. Delhi: Institute of Economic Growth.

Sigurdson, Jon. 1974. *The Role of Small Scale and Rural Industry and Its Interaction with Agriculture and Large Scale Industry in China*. The Economic Research Institute at the Stockholm School of Economics.

_____. 1983. "The Changing Pattern on Inter-Sectoral Relationships in the Rural Machinery Industry in China," in Susumu Watanabe, ed., *Technology, Marketing and Industrialisation: Linkages Between Large and Small Enterprises*. Delhi: ILO.

Smitka, Michael J. 1991. *Competitive Ties: Subcontracting in the Japanese Automotive Industry*. New York: Columbia University Press.

Steel, William F. and Leila M. Webster. 1991. *Small Enterprises Under Adjustment in Ghana*. Washington, D.C.: World Bank Technical Paper No. 138.

Steers, Richard M., Yoo Keun Shin and Gerardo R. Ungson. 1989. *The Chaebol: Korea's New Industrial Light*. New York: Harper and Row.

Stewart, Frances. "Arguments for the Generation of Technology by LDCs." *The Annals*, 458.

Strachan, Harry W. 1976. *Family and Other Business Groups in Economic Development: The Case of Nicaragua*. New York: Praeger Publishers.

Suliman, Ali Ahmed. 1980. "Some Technological Issues of Informal Sector Industries in Khartoum." World Employment Programme Research Working Paper WEP 2-22/WP6Z. Geneva: ILO, July 1980.

Suzuki, Masabumi. 1986. "Comparative Study of the American and Japanese Policies Concerning Cooperative R&D." WP 86-00, MIT-Japan Science and Technology Program, Cambridge, MA.

Swaminathan, Padmini. 1992. "Liberalization, Market Concentration and Growth: A Study of the TVS Group of Companies," in Arun Ghosh, K.K. Subrahmanian, Mridul Eapen, and Haseeb A. Drabu, eds., *Indian Industrialization: Structure and Policy Issues*. Delhi: Oxford University Press.

Taira, Koji. 1970. *Economic Development and the Labor Market in Japan*. New York: Columbia University Press.

Teranishi, Juro, Akira Goto, and Kazuo Serizawa. 1975. "Shihon Shijo To Kogyo Group." *Keizai Hyoron*, XXIV, November 1975.

Ting, Wenlee. 1987. "East Asia: Pathways to Success," in Aaron Segal, ed.,

Learning by Doing: Science and Technology in the Developing World. Boulder: Westview Press.

Toshiba Corporation. 1979. "Electronics Changes the Office." Toshiba Office Automation Fair, November 1979.

Toyo Keizai. *Kigyo Keiretsu Soran*. Tokyo: Toyo Keizai.

Tsuru, Shigeto. 1977. *The Mainsprings of Japanese Growth: A Turning Point?* Paris: The Atlantic Institute for International Affairs, February 1977.

Tung, Rosalie L. 1982. *Chinese Industrial Society After Mao*. Lexington, MA: Lexington Books.

Turner, Louis. 1987. *Industrial Collaboration With Japan*. London: Routledge and Kegan Paul.

Tyabji, Nasir. 1989. *The Small Industries Policy in India*. Calcutta: Oxford University Press.

Uekusa, Masu. 1987. "Industrial Organization: The 1970s to the Present," in Kozo Yamamura and Yasukichi Yasuba, eds., *The Political Economy of Japan*, Vol. 1. Stanford, CA: Stanford University Press.

Uno, Kimio. 1984. "Recent Trends in R&D and Patents—A Quantitative Appraisal," in Hajimi Eto and Konomu Matsui, eds., *R&D Management Systems in Japanese Industry*. Amsterdam: North Holland.

U.S. Congress. 1983. "Research and Development Joint Ventures" (hearing), July 12, 1983.

_____ . 1984. "Japanese Technological Advances and Possible United States Responses Using Research Joint Ventures" (report), October 1984.

_____ . 1987. "Cooperation in Industrial Research and Technology Development" (hearing), July 15, 1987.

_____ . 1990a. "Joint Ventures in the Semiconductor Industry" (hearing), March 29, 1990.

_____ (Congressional Budget Office). 1990b. "Using R&D Consortia for Commercial Innovation: SEMATECH, X-ray Lithography, and High Resolution Systems," July 1990.

_____ . 1991a. "Semiconductors: The Role of Consortia" (hearing), July 23, 1991.

_____ . 1991b. "Japan's Keiretsu System" (hearing), October 16, 1991.

U.S. Department of Commerce. 1983. "The New Climate for Joint Research." Conference Proceedings, May 13, 1983.

U.S. General Accounting Office. 1982a. *Industrial Policy: Case Studies in the Japanese Experience*. Washington, D.C.: GAO, October 20, 1982.

_____ . 1982b. *Industrial Policy: Japan's Flexible Approach*. Washington, D.C.: GAO, June 23, 1982.

Uyeda, Teijiro and Tosuke Inokuchi. 1936. *Small-Scale Industries of Japan: The Electric Lamp Industry*. Tokyo: Japanese Council, Institute of Pacific Relations.

Vepa, Ram K. 1988. *Modern Small Industry in India*. New Delhi: Sage Publications.

Vonortas, Nicholas S. 1991. *Cooperative Research in R&D-Intensive Industries*. Aldershot: Averbury.

Wakasugi, Ryuhei and Akira Goto. 1985. "Kyodo Kenkyu Kaihatsu to Gijutsu Kakushin" (Joint R&D and Technological Innovation), in Yasuo Okamoto and

Takaaki Wakasugi, eds., *Gijutsu Kakushin to Kigyo Kodo*. Tokyo: Tokyo University Press.

Wangwe, Samuel. 1991. "The Contribution of Industry to Solving the Food Problem in Africa," in Jean Dreze and Amartya Sen, *The Political Economy of Hunger, Volume 3: Endemic Hunger*. Oxford: Clarendon Press.

Watanabe, Susumu. 1983. "Introduction," "Inter-Sectoral Linkages in Japanese Industries: A Historical Perspective," and "Technical Co-operation between Large and Small Firms in the Filipino Automobile Industry" (Chapters 1, 2, and 5, respectively), in Susumu Watanabe, ed., *Technology, Marketing and Industrialisaton: Linkages Between Large and Small Enterprises*. Delhi: ILO.

Wheeler, Jimmy W., Merit E. Janow, and Thomas Pepper. 1982. *Japanese Industrial Development Policies in the 1980s: Implications for U.S. Trade and Investment*. New York: Hudson Institute, October 1982.

White, Lawrence J. 1974. *Industrial Concentration and Economic Power in Pakistan*. Princeton: Princeton University Press.

Wong, Siu-lun. 1991. "Chinese Entrepreneurs and Business Trust," in Gary Hamilton, ed., *Business Networks and Economic Development in East and Southeast Asia*. Hong Kong: Centre of Asian Studies, University of Hong Kong.

World Bank. 1993. *The East Asian Miracle: Economic Growth and Public Policy*. New York: Oxford University Press.

Wray, William D. 1989. *Managing Industrial Enterprise: Cases from Japan's Prewar Experience*. Cambridge, MA: Council on East Asian Studies, Harvard University.

Wu Tianzu. 1991. "Technological Transformation of Small Enterprises in Zhejiang Province, China," in A.S. Bhalla, ed., *Small and Medium Enterprises: Technology Policies and Options*. London: Intermediate Technology Publications.

Yamamura, Kozo. 1964. "Zaibatsu, Prewar and Zaibatsu, Postwar." *Journal of Asian Studies*, Vol. XXIII, No. 4, August 1964.

————. 1986. "Joint Research and Antitrust: Japanese vs. American Strategies," in Hugh Patrick, ed., *Japan's High Technology Industries*. Seattle: University of Washington Press.

Yamanaka, Tokutaro and Yoshio Kobayashi. 1957. *The History and Structure of Japan's Small and Medium Industries—With Two Specific Surveys*. Tokyo: The Science Council of Japan, Division of Economics and Commerce, Economics Series No. 15, March 1957.

Yasuoka, Shigeaki. 1984. "Introduction," in Akio Okochi and Shigeaki Yasuoka, eds., *Family Business in the Era of Industrial Growth: Its Ownership and Management*. Tokyo: University of Tokyo Press.